DATABASE MANAGER
IN
MICROSOFT® BASIC

No. 1567
$18.95

DATABASE MANAGER IN MICROSOFT® BASIC

BY GREG GREENE

TAB TAB BOOKS Inc.
BLUE RIDGE SUMMIT, PA. 17214

FIRST EDITION

SECOND PRINTING

Printed in the United States of America

Reproduction or publication of the content in any manner, without express permission of the publisher, is prohibited. No liability is assumed with respect to the use of the information herein.

Copyright © 1983 by TAB BOOKS Inc.

Library of Congress Cataloging in Publication Data

Greene, Greg.
Database manager in microsoft basic.

Includes index.
1. Data base management. 2. Basic (Computer program language) I. Title.
QA76.9.D3G726 1983 001.64 83-4877
ISBN 0-8306-0167-8
ISBN 0-8306-0567-3 (pbk.)

Contents

Introduction — viii

1 The Equipment — 1
The Computer System—Languages

2 Introduction to the Database Manager System — 5
Databases—Features of the Database Manager System—Data Organization—Groundwork for the Input Routines

3 Data Input Routines — 16

4 Essential Subroutines — 21
Subroutines for Special Function Keys, Error Traps, and the Menu—Subroutines for Screen and Input Control—The Menu

5 The Database Parameter File — 30
Setting Up the Database Parameter File—Establishing the Basis for Mathematical Capabilities

6 Dealing with the Data File — 40
Subroutines to Execute the Mathematical Operations—The Menu for Using the Data File

7 Changing the Data File — 48
Routines to Change the Data—Deleting Data

8	**Accessing the Data**	58
	Retrieving Information—Subdividing Files	

9	**Reporting the Data**	68

10	**Sorting and Other Final Touches**	77
	Reviewing the Parameters—Sorting Routines—Housekeeping Subroutines—Converting the Program for Your Machine	

11	**Additional Ways to Use the Data Files**	86
	Mailing Labels—Form Letters—Simple Graphs	

Appendix A	**The Database Manager Program Listing**	96

Appendix B	**Flowcharts of the Database Manager Program**	111

Appendix C	**User's Manual for the Database Manager Program**	150
	Definitions—Program Features—Using the Program	

Appendix D	**A TRS-80 Input Routine**	160

Appendix E	**An Alternate Packing Process**	162

Index		165

This book is dedicated to my mother, who taught me that nothing is impossible to achieve if you are willing to do your best, and my father, who showed me how.

Introduction

The age of the microcomputer is upon us. Many people have rushed out and bought a computer expecting that it would be a useful tool. Too often they have found that, while the machines themselves are capable of great things, the software or programs that enable them to function do not work. After purchasing their computers, they find that the knowledge required to program the machines is not as easy to acquire as they would like.

Like many of you, I bought my computer with the idea of using it for a number of tasks. "Sure," I told my wife, "It will keep track of all kinds of things, like recipes, Christmas card mailing lists, and the like." The trouble was that, although the machine could indeed do all those things, it would require a program for each separate task!

In order to bring some order to this seemingly never-ending process of writing innumerable programs for similar applications, I wrote the programs contained in this book. With these programs and others that you will be able to develop from them, you will be able to have your computer keep track of all those things that you want it to. You can use the programs if your computer system runs a disk-based version of Microsoft BASIC. This includes the Heath/Zenith line or any other machine that runs CP/M. The Radio Shack TRS-80 Models I and III both use versions of Microsoft BASIC, as do the Apple and many others. The programs are written in Version 5.1 of Microsoft BASIC, and were developed on a Heath H-8 using dual disk drives (100K per drive), and an H-19 terminal. Examples of the changes required to make the programs run on the TRS-80 and other machines are included.

If you have a microcomputer system that uses a form of Microsoft BASIC and includes a disk drive, and are interested in getting greater performance from it now, this book is for you. Even if you are just interested in seeing how a disk-based database for a microcomputer system can be implemented, this book is for you. The programs are presented in both source code and flowcharts so that you will be able to follow the development process. Thus, if the source is not directly compatible with your system, you can make the adjustments required.

Chapter 1

The Equipment

This chapter takes a look at what a typical computer system is, how it is organized, and how it performs. The systems that are covered are those computer systems that have one or more disk drives. Disk drives are devices that are used by the computer for long-term storage of information. If your system does not have a disk drive attached to it, and if you are not planning to add one to it, you will not be able to use the programs and examples in this book.

THE COMPUTER SYSTEM

Figure 1-1 is a diagram of a typical microcomputer system, showing the major parts. In it the console is connected to a monitor, a printer, and a set of disk drives.

Computers are very, very dumb machines. They can do nothing without being told what to do, when to do it, what information to use, the information, and where to store it. They are also very, very fast machines. This is their advantage. Once they are instructed how to accomplish a specific task, they will do so in an incredibly short space of time. It is this speed of operation that results in their widespread use.

The computers that are widely used by the general public are computers that essentially do one of two things. Either they perform a dedicated task such as playing the nth variation of space villains or they store and process information. It is the machines in the latter category that we are interested in.

Information storage and processing is a task that computers can do well, if they are given the correct routines to work with. In the type of computer system that we will be dealing with, the processing of information takes place within the computer in the area called RAM. RAM can store both a program and data. (A *program* is a set of instructions that the computer will follow; *data* is the information it will use when it performs these tasks.) Different programs can use and manipulate the same data. Simply put, the program acts on the

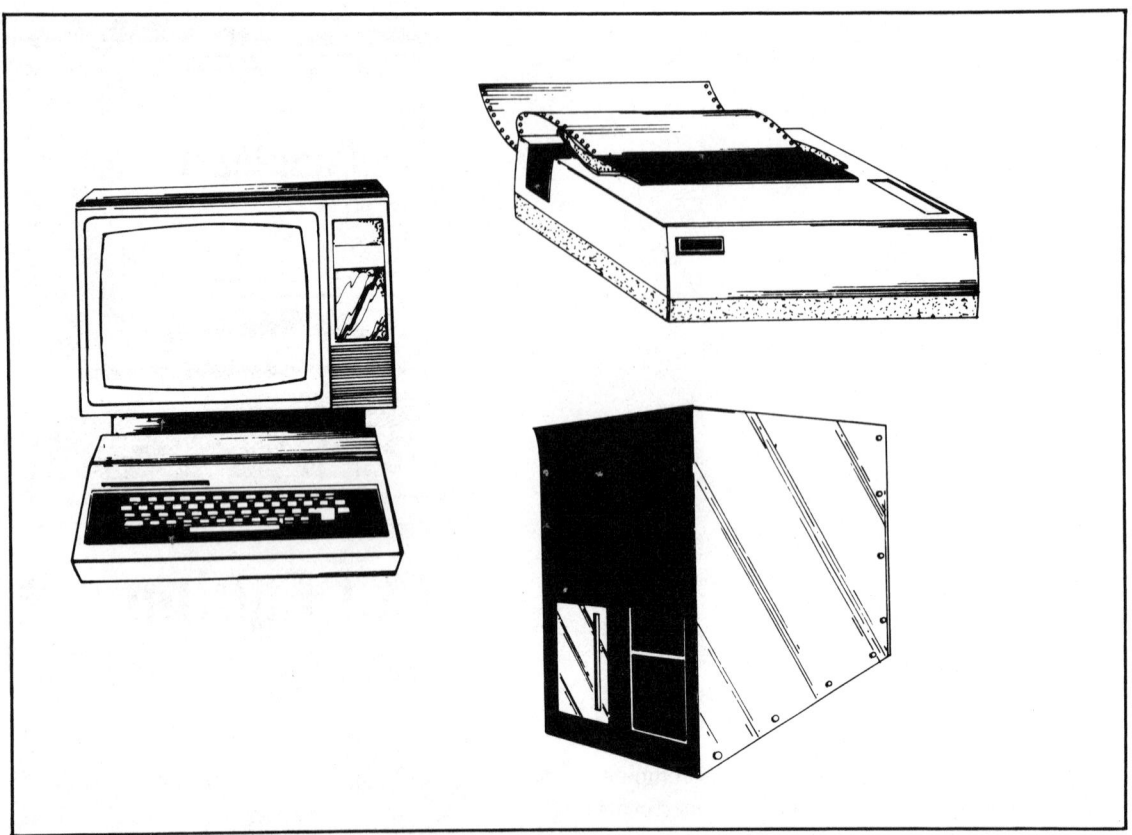

Fig. 1-1. A typical computer system.

data and may change it; the data is acted on by one or more programs but will never change the program. It is important to have this idea clear in your mind.

The data that the program works with is stored in one of two places in our system. Either it is on the disk, or it is in the computer's memory. If it is in the computer's memory, it can be changed and looked at very quickly; if it is on the disk then it cannot be changed or looked at quickly. Why then, you might ask, would anyone want the data on the disk, and not in memory? There are two reasons. First, the data in memory will be lost when the power is shut off. Second, the total amount of data we can keep in memory is limited. When the data is stored in memory, the limit is in the order of 64 thousand characters of information or less. These characters are usually referred to as *bytes*. A byte reflects the amount of memory required to store one character of information, and a *character* is typically a letter of the alphabet or a number.

Some machines, especially the newer ones that are coming out, can store a greater number of bytes in their memories, up to and even beyond 1 million bytes. These machines are not, as of the writing of this book, in great use. For the purposes of this book, we will concern ourselves with the computer system that has a limit of 64K of memory. (One K is one thousand bytes.)

Unfortunately not all 64K of memory is available for data storage. Some space is needed for the programs we will be using, and the computer needs some more space for the various routines that are required to get information to and from the terminal screen, printer, and disk drives and for other internal requirements. In point of fact, there is really about 30K of usable memory space, and this will have to hold both the programs and the data. The disk drive, however, can hold a great deal more information. How much depends on your system. If you only have one disk drive, and it must hold some routines required by the system, you could, as in the case of a TRS-80 owner, be limited to about 30-40K per disk. If you have a system, like Heath or Zenith, that uses larger capacity drives, you can have up to 750K per disk. In any case, disk drives hold one great advantage over the 64K of memory in the machine: you can use as many of them as you need (or can afford). By using this method of multiple disks you can utilize your microcomputer for the storage and retrieval of information in a practical way.

Data and programs are stored on disks by a set of programs called an operating system. Sometimes the operating system is supplied by the manufacturer, and sometimes it is an extra that you must buy. If you have a Radio Shack TRS 80 computer, an Apple, or a PET the operating system that you have is one that is tailored to your particular system and is incompatible with most other systems. If you are using the operating system called CP/M, you have one that allows compatibility with any other system that uses CP/M, no matter what the make or model. If you are planning to use the data only on your own machine, all this is of little or no importance. If you are planning to use the information on different systems, it is of immense importance.

The actual writing of information to the disk and reading from it is done in terms of a unit of measurement called a *sector*. A sector is often 256 bytes long, although this varies according to the hardware you are using. Some systems using BASIC allow you to read in more or even less than one sector at a time. This will allow you to use every bit of space on the disk. Other systems, like Radio Shack, force you to read and write in single-sector units only. This may waste some space on the disk.

Look at the special diagram shown in Fig. 1-2. This is called a *memory map*. A memory map is a

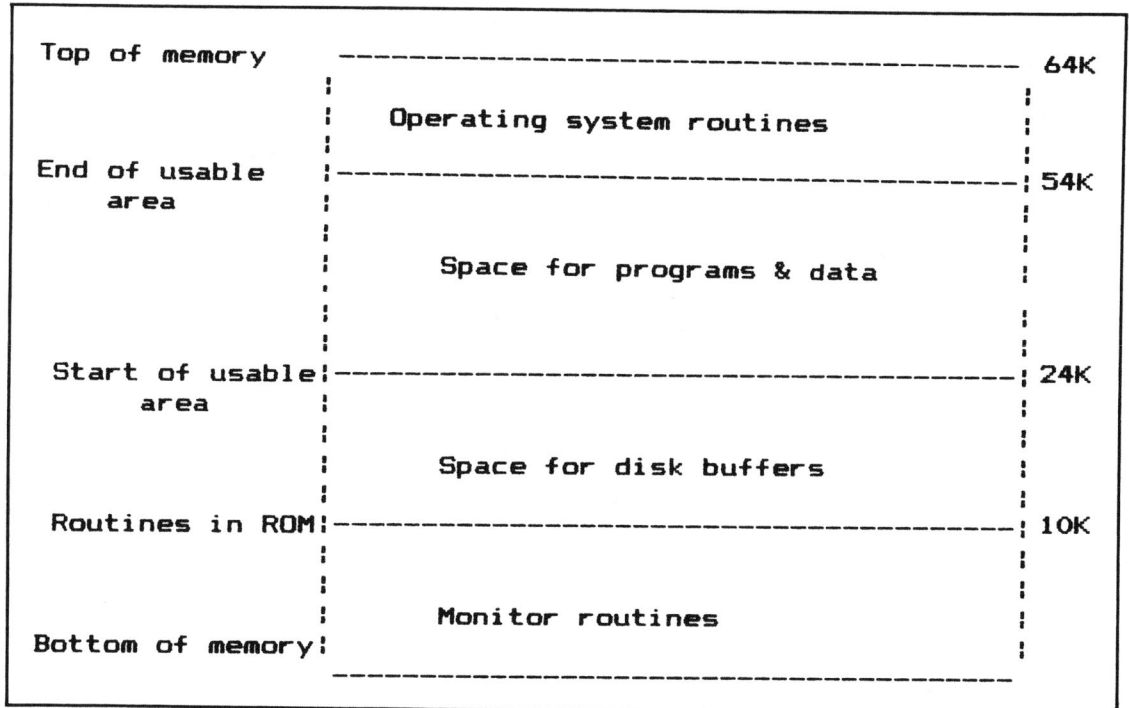

Fig. 1-2. A memory map

3

picture that tells you what parts of the computers memory are being used for what purposes. The map shown here is just an example, and although the one for the system that you are using will be different, the idea is the same. A memory map will tell you how much space is available in your system for you to store the program and the data in.

The numbers on the right side of the map show the approximate boundary locations for the various partitions. You would expect them to be different in your system.

One area of the map is labeled **Space for disk buffers**. Think of this space as a temporary area that is set aside for a single purpose. It is the area where information coming from the disk is placed so that the program can find it. It is also the place where information that is headed for the disk is put so that the operating system can find it. The size of this buffer area depends on the amount of space used by a sector on your system and the number of files that you have open at one time. In most systems you can have up to three files open, and the buffer area will be the standard sector size or 256 bytes. In some versions of Microsoft BASIC, the buffer area can be set to different sizes. This allows more information to be read from the disk and written to it at one time. This also allows the system to process several records at one time, but this is done at the cost of some memory space.

LANGUAGES

The language that you are using is a definite part of the overall system. Some languages let you do more than others do; some have special requirements or pose certain restrictions on the way that you will use the routines and examples in this book. The language you will probably use is a language called BASIC. In addition, it was probably written by the folks at MicroSoft. All the routines are in Microsoft BASIC release 5.2. For the most part, they can easily be changed to most other dialects of BASIC. Where we can, we will note the differences. If you are using Radio Shack equipment, you can use the routines almost entirely word for word, although there will be some differences in the screen formatting routines. If your particular version of BASIC is not covered here, don't despair; you can get a number of excellent books that will help you translate from one version to another. Drop down to your local computer store, or look through the listings of your favorite computer magazine to find the titles and prices that suit you best.

Chapter 2

Introduction to the Database Manager System

This chapter examines just what a typical database is and why a database is desirable. Two types will be presented in general and the type dealt with in this book will be examined specifically. The kinds of features you might want to see in your own program will then be investigated. Next you will be told how to look at your system and determine which features you can implement. Then the organization of the information to go on the disk is explored. Finally, the code that will make up part of the foundation necessary for an effective program will be presented.

DATABASES

What is a database, and why do you need one anyway? A database is just a collection of data, any data. It can consist of anything that is important to the task at hand. A collection of the titles of the songs and selections in your record collection is a database. A collection of recipes is a database. In short any grouping of data is a database. Why do you need one? Chances are that you have a database already. Some people have small books full of the titles of music that they have. When they want to hear a particular piece, they first look up their selection in the book; see what record it's on, and then play that record. This works if they know the title of the piece and the book is indexed according to the titles. If they can only remember the name of the group, they have to check in another book that has the same information, but is indexed according to the names of the groups. The desired information could just as easily be a recipe, or the names and addresses of your clients and what kind of equipment that they have. The key point is that all the data is similar because the same type of information is being recorded about each person, song, or group; and you will want to access the information quickly.

Types of Databases

Having established the desirability of having a database on your system, what kind of databases are available? There are two kinds of databases, and

5

the difference lies in the way they organize the data on the disk. One type of database is organized in a hierarchal way. Each field of the data may have subfields that fall under the main field. Several of these main fields make up a record. The advantage of this is that a reference to a particular main field will automatically include the associated subfields. In this type of database it is difficult for the program to keep track of all the pointers that indicate which subfield is under which main field, and which main fields make up which record. This type of database organization is found in environments where there are very fast processors to look after all the pointers. What are the advantages of this type? One advantage is that it is possible to avoid duplication of any piece of data. If you have several records that have fields that contain the same information, like the name of a particular city, they will have a pointer in that field that points to the location of this piece of data. This can save an enormous amount of space in a large system, such as a government license registry. Space is saved because each record is only long enough to store data that is not duplicated in any other record. Thus the information in a given record may bear little relation to any other, but all information is organized in a strict hierarchy.

The second type of database is called a *relational database*. In this type, the records all have the same file structure. If a field contains the same information in each record, the disk will have the same information duplicated many times. The maintenance of such a system is extremely simple when compared to the hierarchal system. The program merely concerns itself with the contents of each field in a given record, without worrying about the other records. To find the contents of a field in this type of database organization, each record in the file must be accessed and the appropriate field checked. To find the contents of a file organized in an hierarchal file, the field concerned is checked and if the desired value is there, it will contain pointers that will indicate which records are currently pointing to this field and this field value. Those pointers can then be followed back to reconstruct the original records.

The hierarchal system, then, is better suited to the maintenance of a large database where rapid searching for a particular record, based on the information in one or more fields, is required. A relational database is better suited to the maintenance of smaller databases.

It is much easier to design and implement a relational database in a microcomputer environment, than it is to implement a hierarchal database. This doesn't mean it can't be done, because it has been done well; but the programs that do it are written in assembly language and are too difficult for the average computerist to do. This book will examine the relational database, since it will be much easier to develop and will serve you in looking after almost anything you will want to store.

Figure 2-1 shows a chart of how a relational database is organized. Each record will be in a row, and the columns will be made up by the fields in the record. For the purpose of this illustration, our database will be one which looks after five things; the name, address, city, zip code and state of each of the persons on a mailing list.

You can see in this chart that each record has the same organization as all the other records in the database. Each field stores its data in the same manner and contains data that is the same type in each record although the contents of each field may have a different value. In record 1 the value of the contents in the state field is MA, while in records 2, 3 and 4 the value is PA. The type of data is all the same, but the contents are different in one field. This illustrates some of the points of a relational system; the program can count on the data being of the same type and being in the same place in each record. Thus the fields in each record have the same relationships to each other as the corresponding fields in the other records do. You can also see that it is quite possible for each record to contain the same data as any other record, and in the chart above most of them do. While this does waste some space, it makes the maintenance of such a database very easy. For instance, in order to delete a field, you merely have to erase its contents, and to change data, you only have to modify the contents of one or more fields. You will find this easier than

Mailing List Database

Field: →	Name	Address	City	Z.C.	State
Record 1	Jones	123 Any	Bost	021	MA
Record 2	Mudd	234 Here	Phil	171	PA
Record 3	Lee	89 West	Phil	171	PA
Record 4	Lee	23 East	Phil	171	PA

Fig. 2-1. The organization of a relational database.

trying to develop a program that will keep track of the many pointers that would be necessary in a hierarchal database.

FEATURES OF THE DATABASE MANAGER SYSTEM

Now that the type of database has been established the features to be implemented in the system will be examined. Some basic decisions that will affect how the program is written will be made. Since the success of this program will depend to a large degree on how well you can adapt the code to your system, make sure you go over the next section of the book carefully. Prepare a list like the one we have shown, and make lots of notes!

Examining Your System

First, you must look at how your particular system stores data on the disk. You will recall the earlier discussion of how the operating system stores data on a disk. You must now determine if your system allows the use of random access disk operations. This is by far the norm. To find out, consult the manuals that came with your system. In all likelihood they will describe two methods of operation. First there is the sequential mode. In this mode, data is placed on the disk as it becomes available. If you have 50 records, the first one is written, then the second; then the third, until you have written the 50th record. This requires that if the information you want is on the 45th record, you must read the preceding 44 records first. This is not a practical way of doing things. Random access is much more efficient. The system should be able to look at any of the records on the disk by having the program state which record it wants to look at. If, in this mode of operation, the program instructs the computer to read record 45, it will do so without looking at any of the other records. This is not to say that you can't build a database system that uses sequential accessing, because you can. It's simply not a practical way of doing things. The time involved will make the operations too slow, and the increased disk wear will give you maintenance headaches.

Assuming that you are allowed by the makers of your system to utilize random access, the next thing to determine is whether or not you can have variable length records. A variable length record is a record whose length is adjusted so that it uses only the space required by the amount of data to be stored. If your recipe records only take up 125 bytes of space, you will only use that much per record. Some systems will allow you to use as little as two bytes in a record and as much as 4096 bytes. Most systems will require that you use 255 byte records, so the Database Manager uses this type of disk access. This means that you will waste some space, but in the end, that could be an advantage. Using this procedure will simplify operations since the calling procedures for variable-length random-access records may be confusing.

Now take a look at what you want your system to accomplish. First, it must be able to write information onto the disk, read it, and provide some way to change and delete it. It must also provide a way to search for specific information that may be on the disk. It should have a way of reporting the information back in a manner that you can easily change. It would also be important to be able to sort the data to reflect current requirements for reporting. The system should also present you with choices for various operations via a menu. Most importantly, at the time that you create a file, you must be able to define just what information goes into it.

In order to see how much you can do with your machine, you must first take a look at what it offers. Get out the owner's manual for your computer and turn to the section that describes the features you can use. Write down the commands you have to use to accomplish the following procedures, if indeed you can do them at all.

Your Computer's Home Survey

1. Home the cursor and clear the screen.
   Your System:

2. Erase a line or part of a line.
   Your System:

3. Display characters in inverse video or half intensity.
   Your System:

4. Display characters on a status line, usually the 25th line of a display terminal.
   Your System:

5. Set up programmable special function keys if you have them.
   Your System:

6. Address the cursor to a particular spot on the screen.
   Your System:

Now, use your BASIC manual and find out how to do the following.

1. How to do error trapping so that you can recover from BASIC error conditions. These are sometimes unavoidable and unless you can prevent your program from crashing the program will be harder to convert.
   Sample statement: ON ERROR GOTO
   Your System:

2. How to use the intrinsic string functions, the most important of which is the ability to place a new group of characters within a string that already exists. You will also need to know about the LEFT$ and RIGHT$ functions.
   Sample statement: MID$(X$,4,7)=Y$
   Your System:

3. What the maximum length of your strings is. For most BASICs this is 255 bytes.
   Your System:

4. What fielding statements are required for random access files.
   Sample statement: Field #2,200 AS B$
   Your System:

5. How to direct print statements to the printer or the screen. For the most part it will be as simple as using LPRINT instead of the PRINT statement.
   Sample method: Poking the IO BYTE
   Your System:

6. How to open and close random files.
   Sample statement: OPEN "R", CLOSE #1
   Your System:

7. Whether or not you have a swap command that will let you sort easily.

   Sample statement: SWAP A$(X),A$(X+1)

   Your System:

8. Whether the index variable is checked and incremented at the beginning or end of a for-next loop. This will determine the final value of the variable when used as a counter.

   Your System:

9. How to access a character input at the keyboard without the return or enter key having to be pressed and without echoing the character to the screen.

   Sample statements: INKEY$,CIN,PIN,INPUT$(X)

   Your System:

Most of today's computers and terminals provide a way to tell the cursor where to go. This allows you to set up the program to present information in a pleasing manner. Being able to input information at the same spot on the screen is a great advantage. Some machines also allow you to highlight certain portions by using a reverse video technique. This turns on a block of text where the letters are black on white instead of white on black. Other features may also be available to you, such as being able to use special function keys that take on certain functions depending on what part of the program you are in. Because there are a great number of different protocols and ways of doing things, this book must have a standard system. In this standard system I will assume that you can tell the cursor where you want it to go. Other than that I will assume you have an ordinary terminal display. The terminal I use is a Heathkit H-19, so the protocols that I will be illustrating are the ones required for that terminal. They can easily be adapted for use on other equipment, and I'll show you how.

So what we have arrived at is that we want a database system that will do the following:

The Database Management System that will be presented in this book will do the following:

1. work with your disk drives
2. use 255 byte records
3. allow you to create different datafiles
4. allow you to add, change, delete, and modify records
5. allow you to search the database and find record(s) based on the contents of one or more fields
6. allow you to sort the records you have found based on the contents of one or two fields
7. allow the use of an addressable cursor

DATA ORGANIZATION

To organize your data you need to know how the data is to be organized on the disk. You need to know the kind of files that will be used and what kind of information will be stored there. You need to know how many records you can put on a disk, and how to organize them so that you can have different data in different databases that are all used by the same program.

If your system offers you the use of variable length records, you can set up a mechanism in the program that will count how much space each field takes and add these values together to get the total record length. You can then use this information to establish the record length on the disk. Since this is a relational database, if you accurately define one record in the database, you have done so for the rest. This technique will save space on the disk and allow you to have more records per disk. How many records? That depends on the size of your disk. If you are using a dual disk system, you can store the data on one disk, and the programs on the other. In the Heath system that this series of programs was developed on, I can use 90K for program storage on an initialized disk. If you have records that are 200 bytes long and you can use variable length records, you can store 90,000/200, or 450 records.

Using variable length records has a major disadvantage: you cannot add a field later because all the space is taken up. There are a number of ways to avoid this. You can set up an empty field, if you can foresee the inclusion of more data in a record at a later date. You can use a program to bring data from one database to another, and by setting up the new field in the new database, transfer the fields you wish. You can use 255 byte records, and redefine the database by duplicating the specifications that you already have, and then adding an extra field at the end. If you have not exceeded the 255 byte limit and have not changed any parameters of the original fields, you are away to the races!

Now that you have some idea of the format of your data files, it must be determined how to set them up so that you can use the same programs to create and maintain different data in different databases? The answer is to create a separate parameters file that will act as a sort of dictionary. Whenever the program needs to look at a field for any reason, it will consult the dictionary and from it, the program will be able to tell where the field is in the record structure, what kind of data it contains, how long it is, whether or not there is a range limit imposed on it by the user, and whether or not it is stored in a compressed mode. Since this dictionary file is likely to be small in comparison to the database, you can store it in a sequential file on the disk that contains the program. This will leave more space on the data disk for our datafile and give the program access to the dictionaries of more than one database. Also we can write other programs that need only consult this dictionary to find out everything they need to know about a particular database in order to perform specific tasks, such as label making. In this way we add to the flexibility of our system.

The information concerning each record must be transferred to and from the disk. Most BASICs that allow random access allow the user to specify a certain number of fields in each record. Each field is assigned a variable name, and when a particular record is accessed, the information within the record is assigned to the variables. The way that this is done is as follows. First BASIC sets aside a 255 byte area in memory called a disk buffer. The field statements assigns portions of this area to certain variables. To do this each variable is assigned a pointer that tells it where its information begins in the buffer. BASIC will assign all the information from the start of that area character by character, until the start of the next variable is reached. When the information is retrieved by the get command, the assigning of the information is done automatically. When the put command tells the program to place the information back to the disk, all the information that is currently stored in the field variables, will be transferred to the buffer and thence to the disk. In order to protect the variables from getting lost, it is important that they not be used outside of a field statement or a LSET or RSET statement. Figure 2-2 shows the fields graphically.

You will encounter a problem if you use this method. You don't know at the start of the program how long the fields are to be because they haven't been created yet. You could get that information from the data dictionary, but you would have to substitute it into the field statements and that leads to a lot of code. There is a much easier way. Since any string variable in BASIC can be 255 bytes long, why not simply field a single variable, and then use the string functions of MID$, RIGHT$, and LEFT$ to take the string apart and find the information that we want? This would work provided we copied the information from the field string into a temporary string prior to use and put any new information back into the field string prior to putting it back on the disk. This technique works for both those systems that use variable length random-access records and those that use fixed length ones. In order for this to work well, you must depend on the data dictionary to indicate where each field starts in the string, how long it is, and whether the data is numeric or alphanumeric. Since you can use three types of numeric data: integer, single precision, or double precision, you can take advantage of the fact that they can be stored in 2,4 or 8 bytes respectively by converting them into strings. Thus you can save space on the disk. You will need routines to separate the information from the string and also to repack it. A graphic representation is shown in Fig. 2-3.

The data dictionary will have to store several pieces of information about each of the data fields in our data base. In order to place this information onto the disk and to recall it easily, it will be stored

```
            [ Buffer area 255 bytes long:->]
       ---------|---------------------------|-------------    -------
      |1|2|3| | | | | | | | | | | | | | | | | |<-> | |    |N|
       ---------|---------------------------|-------------    -------
               |                           |
               |                           |
       -----------------           -----------------
      | Fielded Var:1 |           | Fielded Var:2 |
       -----------------           -----------------

           EXAMPLE CODE
           ============

    10 OPEN "R",1,"FILE"
    20 FIELD #1, Var:1 AS A$, Var:2 AS B$, Var:N AS N$
```

Fig. 2-2. The use of more than one field.

in a sequential file. To do this, the data will be organized in arrays. This is shown in Fig. 2-4.

As the chart shows, the table is made up of an array that holds the relevant values for each field in the database. You will program the computer to dump each value into a sequential file when you create the database and also to recover this information when needed. Since you know which values

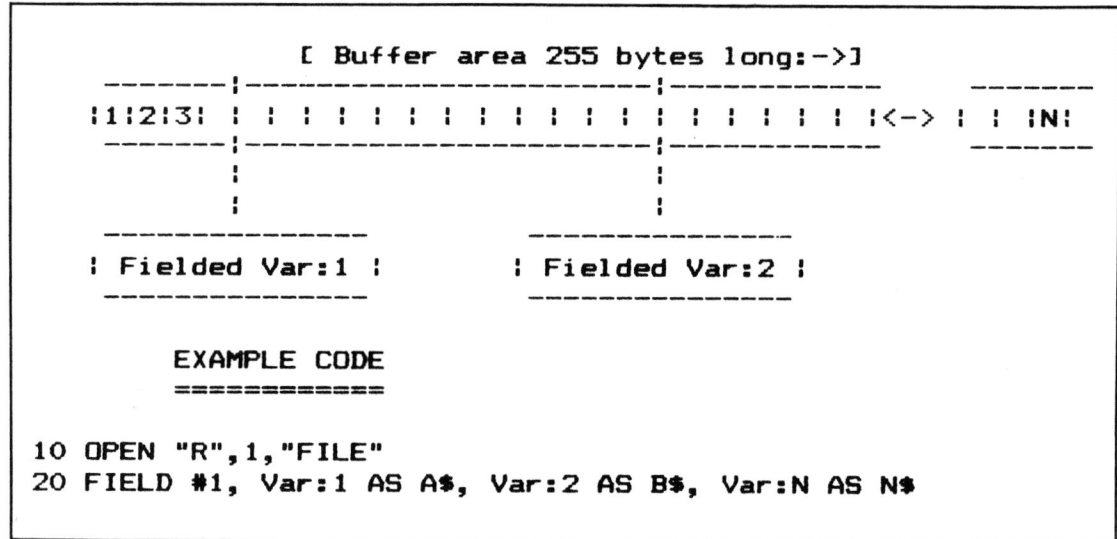

Fig. 2-3. Using a single fielded string variable.

```
------------------------------------
: Value to : Variable : One for
: be held  :   Name   : each field
------------------------------------
: Field    :  F$(X)   : ----->
: Name     :          :
------------------------------------
: Field    :  T$(X)   : ----->
: Type     :          :
------------------------------------
: Minimum  :          :
: Data     :  MI(X)   : ----->
: Value    :          :
------------------------------------
: Field    :  L(X)    : ----->
: Length   :          :
------------------------------------
: Field    :          :
: Starts   :  SA(X)   : ----->
: At       :          :
------------------------------------
: Maximum  :          :
: Data     :  MA(X)   : ----->
: Value    :          :
------------------------------------
```

Fig. 2-4. The organization of the data dictionary.

are relevant to which field, you can write a number of programs to make use of the data in the database. This will expand the utility of the system.

Thus, you need a program to create and maintain a database, the parameters of which are contained in another file. The database file is to be kept on a separate disk—ideally, in a random access format with 255 byte fixed length records. We should also enable the user to use one disk for everything, in case he only has a single drive or in case his requirements for a particular database are limited. The various programs required to accomplish these tasks will now be examined.

First, you will need to make up a table of subroutines that you will be able to use with all the sections of the program. Since the programs will have to be quite lengthy to accomplish all that you want, you will have to break them up into smaller programs. This will allow you to have the necessary memory space available for storing of record numbers and field values, and for the in-memory sorting routine. The storage of record numbers and field values, and the sorting could all be done on disk, but this is really only necessary if the database is going to be holding a lot of records (1000 or more). For most of us it is easier and certainly quicker to use the computer's memory for these operations.

GROUNDWORK FOR THE INPUT ROUTINES

One of the first subroutines that must be developed is the one that looks after all the input for our program. If you can develop this sufficiently, it will be able to do many things. It will be able to position the cursor and check whether or not the characters entered are valid for the type of data you want. This subroutine can incorporate both upper and lower range checking for numerical data and length checking for character data.

Take a look at the lines of BASIC code in Listing 1. Note that for the sake of clarity, each statement appears on a separate line. For your convenience in inputting the program, Appendix A contains the complete program listing using the conventional colons between statements.

This block of code sets up the control sequences used by the H-19 terminal. First in line 25 we set the line length to 255 spaces. This is necessary so that the graphics that are available with this machine will function correctly. When a graphics

LISTING ONE

```
25 WIDTH 255
30 CLEAR 3500
35 E$=CHR$(27)
        CS$=E$+"E"
        RV$=E$+"p"
        ER$=E$+"q"
        GM$=E$+"F"
        EG$=E$+"G"
        BC$=E$+"y5"+E$+"x4"
        CO$=E$+"x5"
        DC$=E$+"Y"
        S1$=RV$+DC$
        SB$=S1$+STRING$(80," ")+EG$
        CH$=E$+"H"
39 GOTO 60
40 PRINT E$+"x";CHR$(49)
45 PRINT DC$;CHR$(56);CHR$(32):PRINT
50 PRINT RV$:PRINT "    PRESS f1 to exit to menu    "
55 PRINT ER$:X1=0:GOSUB 80:PRINT
56 RETURN
60 DL$="ERA":REM #######    DELETE CODE    #######
65 DA$="":FOR I=8383 TO 8391:DA$=DA$+CHR$(PEEK(I)):NEXT I
70 DEFDBL M,N,O,T
75 GOTO 475
```

line contains some control characters, such as the escape character, these characters will not be printed. But the counter that determines whether or not you are at the end of the line will consider the unprintable characters in its total. Thus when it reaches 80 columns, it will issue a carriage return and line feed, and your graphics will be displayed incorrectly.

Next we set up an area to keep our string variables in. This is done by using the clear command with a numeric argument after it. In this case line 30 sets up an area of 3500 bytes. Some BASIC dialects will allot this dynamically, and the clear command is not required. In the sorting part of the program, most of the fields are kept in the string format. It is desirable then, to have approximately two-thirds of the available free memory space reserved for string space. You can determine the amount of free memory space available for your use, by typing **PRINT FRE(0)**. This will return the amount of memory space only if you do it prior to issuing any clear commands. Areas that have been reserved for string space by a previous clear command, will not be counted. Those areas can be checked by typing **PRINT FRE(A$)**.

Line 35 assigns a whole series of variables. The escape character is defined as E$. With the H-19 terminal, all the control sequences begin with the escape character. Thus when the terminal receives an escape, it will look to see if the character following is one that, together with the escape, will signal it to perform a special function. If it is, the sequence is trapped; the function completed; and control passed back to the program. If not, the escape character is passed on to the program. By placing these routines in variables at the start of the program, you need only use the variable representing the desired action instead of typing in the complete sequence. This saves time and memory space. It also prevents typing errors, and by having them at the start of the program, BASIC will find them more quickly. The C$ routine will clear the screen and home the cursor on the H-19. The other routines are as follows.

RV$ — Reverse video
ER$ — Exit reverse video
GM$ — Start graphics
EG$ — Exit graphics
BC$ — Turn on the block cursor
CO$ — Turn the cursor off
DC$ — Direct cursor addressing
S1$ — Turn on reverse video and cursor addressing combined
SB$ — Draw a graphics line
CH$ — Home the curosr without erasing the

You can see that by defining the most commonly used routines ahead of time, you can save yourself a lot of extra work. Note that you can build routines by using already defined variables as their building blocks. You will find that the program will execute them faster than if you used separate routines on the same line. You should only do this if speed is important or if the routine is to be used more than once or twice. Otherwise, you will use up valuable memory space. For example, the lines from 40 to 56 represent a subroutine that will enable the 25th line on the H-19, send the cursor there, and print a message. It is composed of both predefined variables such as E$ and DC$, and CHR$ routines. Because it is a subroutine that is called often, this is an acceptable way of doing things.

Line 60 sets up a string for use in checking with the operator when it is necessary to delete records from the database. This code must be entered in order for the deletion routines to work. By having to enter this code, accidental or unauthorized deletions will be prevented. The REM statement indicates that the rest of the line should be ignored as far as executing goes. REM lines are used by the programmer to make a note of what is happening in a particular section of code.

Line 65 is a routine that can only be used as printed by users of HDOS, the Heath Disk Operating System. When you bring up HDOS, you must input the correct date. This date is stored in memory locations 8383 to 8391. By peeking at those

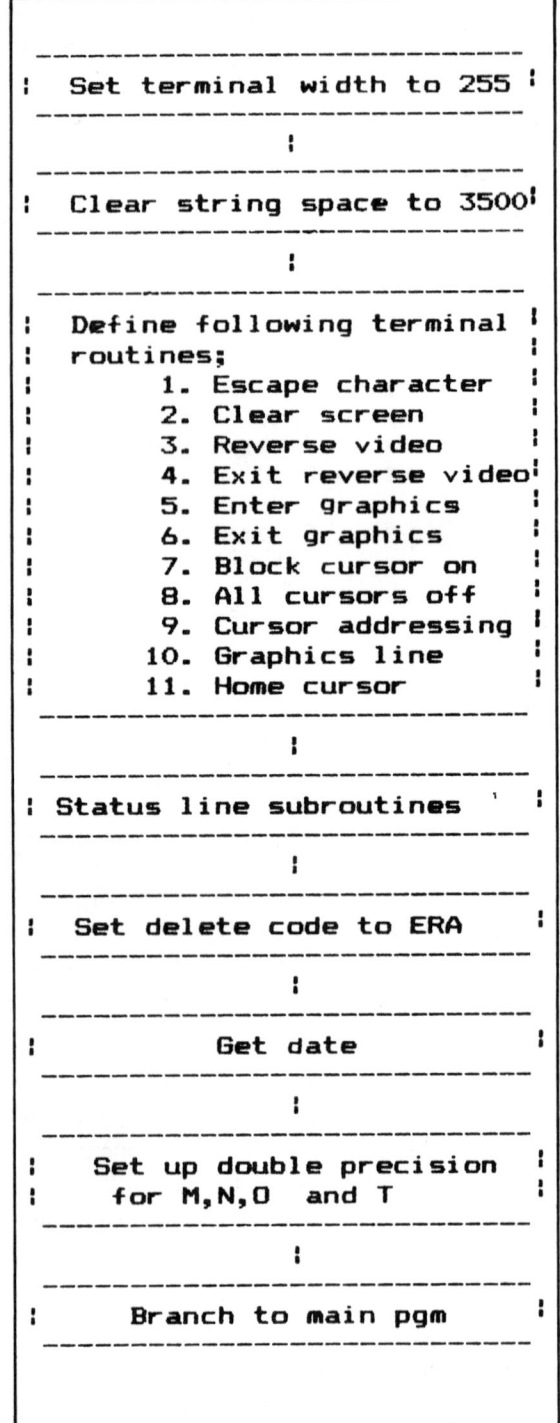

Fig. 2-5. Chart of the initial routines.

locations and recovering the values stored there, the program has access to the correct date also. Radio Shack owners can simulate this by using the appropriate part of the TIME$ provided to them. Users of other systems should request the date from the operator at this point in the program and store it in the variable DA$.

Line 75 is a line that will define all variables beginning with the letters M,N,O, and T to be double precision. In MBASIC, a double precision variable is one that will store a number that is accurate to 14 significant figures. To do this it requires 8 bytes of memory space. By defining these variables at the start of the program, we will again save space and time. If we hadn't done so, we would be required to append the pound sign, #, after each variable (for example, M#) to tell the program that we wanted it to be considered a double precision rather than single precision variable. Note that once it is defined, another DEF statement is required to change the type. We can use the variable M%, which is an integer, and M!, which is a single precision variable, without the danger of having the program confuse them. To the program, M%, M!, and M# are all different. If we hadn't used this statement, the program would have considered the variable M without a %, !, or # to be M!, but because we have defined it as a double precision variable, it will consider M to be M#.

This block of code is shown in flowchart form in Fig. 2-5.

Programming Your Own Computer

Wherever we can, we will provide simplified flowcharts like this so that you can more easily follow the program logic. Also, if you are programming in another language, you will be able to use the flowcharts to assist you.

If you have not yet figured out which routines are available in your particular system to duplicate the preceding functions, don't despair. If your system doesn't allow for them, you may not need them. Of the routines above, the most important are the clear screen, cursor addressing, and cursor homing routines. You can get by without the graphics and reverse video capabilities. These aren't really necessary, but they do make the program easier to use and nicer to look at. You should try to make your program as aesthetically pleasing as you can. You will find that it will reduce operator fatigue.

Chapter 3

Data Input Routines

Now you are ready to add to the foundation that you have established in Chapter 2. Remember to keep a sharp eye out for the areas to change to make the routines work with your system. I will explain where to look so that you won't get lost!

The next block of code, will provide you with another way of addressing the cursor to where you want it and a way to check the incoming characters from the keyboard to provide range checking for data entry. Some ways of displaying error messages to the operator will also be presented. Listing 2 shows the code for these routines.

Line 80 of this listing represents the subroutine for determining the proper location for the cursor. The user assigns an integer value to the variable X1. This value is divided by 80 to determine the line that it represents, and the remainder is the column on that line. In this way, any number from 1 to 1920 can represent a particular spot on the terminal screen. The row, represented in H%, and the column, represented in C%, have the number 32 added to them as required by the Heath H-19 terminal, and then are sent out to the screen. If you are using a screen of different dimensions, you need to change the number 80 to whatever your screen width is. The positioning routine will also have to be changed to represent your system. If you are using the TRS-80, the whole line can be replaced with a print@ statement.

Line 90 sets the variable XO$ to a null value. This ensures that any previous value assigned to it is erased.

Lines 95-100 are a part of the input routine. In general, all data entering the program is channeled through this routine. In line 95 we set up a string of 255*s. These will represent the number of character positions allowed for entry of a single record. By changing the asterisk into some other character, you can make the input routine display whichever character you'd like to see. Line 100 prints a portion of the asterisk string that corresponds to the length of the data field being input. It also causes the terminal bell to ring. This is the CHR$(7). If you do not wish to have the bell feature or if your computer

LISTING TWO

```
 80 H%=INT(X1/80):C%=X1-(H%*80)
    PRINT DC$;CHR$(H%+32);CHR$(C%+32):RETURN
 85 '
 90 XO$=" "
 95 X2$=STRING$(255,"*")
100 GOSUB 80:PRINT LEFT$(X2$,X2);CHR$(7):GOSUB 80
101 PRINT BC$
105 X$=INPUT$(1)
110 IF LEN(XO$)=0 AND X$=CHR$(13) THEN XO#=-1:RETURN
115 XO#=0
120 IF X$=CHR$(27) THEN 215
125 IF X$=CHR$(9) THEN 85
130 IF X$=CHR$(8) OR X$=CHR$(127) THEN X6%=1:GOTO 165
135 IF X$=CHR$(13) THEN 150
140 XO$=XO$+X$:IF LEN(XO$)>X2 THEN PRINT CHR$(7):X6%=2:GOTO 165
145 PRINT X$
    IF X2=1 AND LEN(XO$)=1 AND C=1 THEN 155 ELSE GOTO 105
150 IF X3=0 AND X4=0 THEN PRINT CO$;:RETURN
155 XO#=VAL(XO$)
    IF XO#>=X3 AND XO#<=X4 THEN PRINT CO$;:C=0:RETURN
160 X3$="OUT OF RANGE"
    GOSUB 185
    GOTO 85
165'
170 Z1%=LEN(XO$)-X6%
    IF Z1%<1 THEN 85
175 XO$=LEFT$(XO$,Z1%)
180 GOSUB 80
    PRINT LEFT$(X2$,X2)
    GOSUB 80
    PRINT XO$;
    GOTO 105
185 X5=X1
190 FOR L%=1 TO 3
195    X1=(320+(80-LEN(X3$))/2)
       GOSUB 80
       PRINT RV$;X3$;ER$;CHR$(7)
200       FOR L1%=1 TO 100
          NEXT L1%
205    X1=320
       GOSUB 80
       PRINT E$+"1";
210 NEXT L%
    X1=X5
    PRINT BC$
    RETURN
```

doesn't have one, delete this portion of the code.

Line 101 will cause the cursor on the H-19 terminal to be seen as a solid block. With the H-19 you can have either the solid block cursor or the blinking underlined cursor. You can set the terminal to come up under either mode. This can later be changed in software. The purpose of having the cursor changed to a block format is that the user's eye is drawn to it when we want him to enter a piece of data. Notice the semicolon (;) that is at the end of the line. This is to prevent the terminal from issuing a carriage return and skipping down a line. You will see this at various places within the program.

Line 105 allows the program to examine a character typed by the user without echoing it to the terminal. By doing this, the character can be examined and any special actions that may be necessary can be performed.

One of these actions is illustrated in line 110. Here the program is checking for the condition that will exist if the return or enter key has been pressed as the first character. In this case the program will return from this subroutine to the place it was called from, with the value in XO# set to -1. The program will check to see if the value of -1 has been assigned to XO# and take whatever action is then required.

Line 115 will erase any previous value in XO#.

Line 120 checks to see if the input character is an escape. If it is, the user has pressed one of the special function keys. On the H-19 terminal there are eight special function keys. If the user presses the f1 key when an asterisk is showing, he is placed back at the menu. If he pushes the red special function key, the program copyright is printed and the program stops. If you have programmable function keys on your system, the proper lead-in code may be substituted for the CHR$(27) escape code that is here.

Line 125 checks for the presence of a tab or CTRL-I. If it is found, the data inputed for the present question is disregarded, and the input sequence starts again. This will let you reenter the data when you realize you have made a mistake.

Line 130 checks for the pressing of either the backspace or delete keys on the H-19 terminal. If they are pressed, the last character is erased and an asterisk takes its place. The current valid data is reprinted to the screen. If your terminal uses different codes for these keys, you must replace the values that are here. These are the normal ASCII values however, and really no change should be necessary.

Line 135 detects the pressing of the return or enter keys. This will cause the routine to end and program execution to be returned to the calling segment of the main program.

Line 140 adds the new character to the variable XO$ and checks to see if the length collected so far is greater than that allowed for this data field. If it is, the terminal bell is activated, and the extra character is deleted.

Line 145 prints the character that was entered by the user. If the length of the data field had been specified to be one character, and the information being sought is not data but an answer to a question (for example, Y/N) the routine is terminated without the return or enter key being pressed. Otherwise, the routine will await the pressing of the return or enter keys so that the user can look at what he has typed to see if a mistake was made. Thus he will have a chance to edit his response before the program continues. If the input was a simple yes or no response to a question or the inputting of a single number as from the menu, the program will execute without delay. This will require less effort on the part of the user and speed up the program.

Line 150 checks to see if the data being input is supposed to be alphanumeric or numeric. If both X3 and X4 are equal to zero, the program assumes that we want alphanumeric character data here. Accordingly it turns the cursor off and returns to the calling segment of the program.

Line 155 assigns the numeric value of the string variable XO$ to the numeric variable XO#. It then checks to see if the value is within the range specified by the values of variables X3 and X4. X3 represents the lower limit and X4 represents the higher limit. If all is correct, then the routine exits here.

Line 160 is an error routine, which is activated when the test in line 155 fails. X3$ represents the current error message, the subroutine at 185 is called to display the message; and the entry process is started again.

Lines 170 to 180 are the lines that enable the program to execute a backspace and delete routine whenever the backspace or delete keys are pressed or when the input is greater than the allowable

```
---------------------------                                  :
: Calculate cursor position :                 ---------------------------
: and place it there       :                 : Character is not one of  :
---------------------------                  : the above so add it to   :
              :                              : the rest we have collected:
---------------------------                  : and check its length.    :
:      Set X0$ to zero     :                 : If it is too long, ring  :
---------------------------                  : bell, delete last charact.:
              :                              ---------------------------
---------------------------                                  :
:    Set up string of      :                 ---------------------------
:      asterisks           :                 : Character is OK, print it :
---------------------------                  ---------------------------
              :                                              :
---------------------------                  ---------------------------
: Print appropriate length :                 : If this is a one charact. :
: of asterisks             :                 : field - see if we can     :
: Ring terminal bell       :                 : return without entering   :
---------------------------                  : a carriage return         :
              :                              ---------------------------
---------------------------                                  :
:   Turn on block cursor   :                 ---------------------------
---------------------------                  : See if this is an alpha - :
              :                              : numeric field; if so then :
---------------------------                  : return with value is X0$  :
:   Get keyboard input     :                 : and with cursor off       :
:     without echoing      :                 ---------------------------
---------------------------                                  :
              :                              ---------------------------
---------------------------                  : Field is not an alpha -   :
: Return with -1 in X0# if :                 : numeric one, so put value :
: character typed was a CR :                 : into variable X0#         :
---------------------------                  ---------------------------
              :                                              :
---------------------------                  ---------------------------
:     Set X0# to zero      :                 : See if value is within    :
---------------------------                  : range. if so return with  :
              :                              : cursor off                :
---------------------------                  ---------------------------
: If user typed an escape  :                                 :
: then we have a function  :                 ---------------------------
: pressed - branch and do  :                 : Value is not with range,  :
: what is required         :                 : place error message in    :
---------------------------                  : X3$ - call error display  :
              :                              : routine                   :
---------------------------                  ---------------------------
: If user typed a CTL-I or :                                 :
: tab then he wants to     :                 ---------------------------
: abandon this input - go  :                 : Backspace routine -       :
: and start input routine  :                 : subtract one character    :
: again                    :                 : replace with asterisk     :
---------------------------                  : display corrected string  :
              :                              ---------------------------
---------------------------                                  :
: If user pressed backspace:                  ---------------------------
: or delete key - he wants :                  : Error display routine -   :
: to erase the last charact.:                 : Save cursor position.     :
: Go and do it             :                  : Flash error message three :
---------------------------                   : times and ring bell.      :
              :                               : Return when done.         :
---------------------------                   : Recover cursor position   :
: If user has pressed the  :                  ---------------------------
: return or enter key then :
: he has finished with     :
: entry. Go and check it   :
---------------------------
```

Fig. 3-1. Chart of the input routines

space. The rightmost character in the entry is replaced with an asterisk and the corrected entry is reprinted.

Lines 185 to 210 are the routines that display an error message. First the current cursor position is placed in variable X5. Next a for-next loop is set up to display the error message three times. The error message in variable X3$ is centered in row 4 and written in reverse video. The terminal bell is also activated. Next a short pause is set up in line 200 by the use of another for-next loop. This will allow the user time to read the message. Line 205 erases the entire contents of row 4. The loop is executed the three times, causing a blinking effect and getting the users attention, which is what is desired! After execution of the loop, the cursor is positioned where it was when this routine was called and reenabled so that data input can continue. Control is then passed back to the calling segment.

This segment of code is shown in flowchart form in Fig. 3-1.

You will note that the method of positioning the cursor as described in line 80 is much easier to adapt to different terminals and systems than the method described in the first section of code. You are free to use either routine, or both.

Those of you who do not have an INPUT$ function can probably simulate it in a variety of ways. For instance the INKEY$ function in Radio Shack's version of Microsoft will do the same. Other dialects have PIN or CIN functions that are similar. You will have to consult your manual to see which one is available to you.

You will also note that the error messages always appear on the same line on the terminal. This is done so that the user will be used to seeing the same thing happen at the same place. Hopefully there is much less chance of him getting lost that way. Since the user will probably be you, it pays to take the steps necessary to make life easier for yourself!

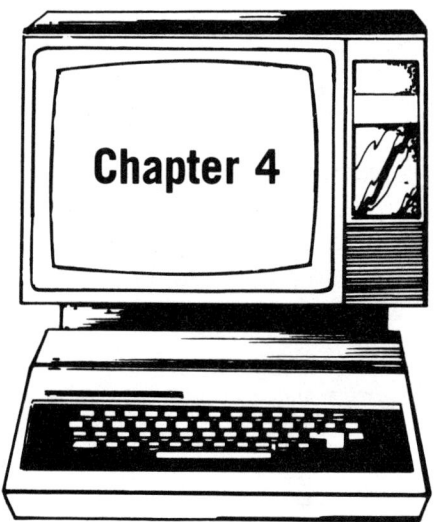

Chapter 4

Essential Subroutines

This chapter looks at the use of special function keys if you have them. It also shows how to trap errors by having the input routine check for data in a certain range or of a specific length, and how to alert the operator to these errors. It presents a menu that makes use of the reverse video routines.

SUBROUTINES FOR SPECIAL
FUNCTION KEYS, ERROR TRAPS, AND THE MENU

The next few sections of code will be used to set up the main menu and establish several more subroutines that the program will make use of. Listing 3 shows the code for these routines.

Lines 215-230 form the subroutine called from line 120. The purpose is to see which special function key has been pressed. We do this by checking the value of the next character input. In actuality, pressing any special function key sends out two characters in rapid succession. Line 120 traps the escape or lead character; line 215 traps the next one. If key f1 was pressed, the second character will be an S. In this case, the program will close all open files and go back to the menu. If the key pressed was the red topped key, the second character will be a Q. In this case the program will jump to a routine that displays the copyright information. If neither one of these keys is pressed, the subroutine terminates in line 230, and returns to the calling line.

Lines 235-240 comprise a subroutine that takes the information in variable X1$ and displays it at the beginning of row three on the screen. The message is displayed in reverse video. Note the use of the variables ER$, and RV$, used to toggle the reverse video function of the terminal.

Line 245 will erase any information on rows three or four. We use this in conjunction with lines 235-240 in order to remove old information that may be present there.

Lines 255-290 are used to display the menu and sign-on information on the screen. This routine is composed of two parts: first the background information, which is a subroutine starting at line 3105, is called; then the specific information for the menu is presented. Note the use of the variable

LISTING THREE

```
215 X$=INPUT$(1)
220 IF X$="S" THEN CLOSE:GOTO 500
225 IF X$="Q" THEN GOSUB 2935
230 RETURN
235 GOSUB 245
        X1=160
        GOSUB 80
        PRINT RV$;X1$;ER$
        X1=245
        C=1
240 RETURN
245 X1=160
        GOSUB 80
        PRINT E$+"1"
        X1=240
        GOSUB 80
        PRINT E$+"1"
        RETURN
250 '
255 PRINT CS$;
256 GOSUB 3105
260 PRINT S1$"% "STRING$(80," ")DC$"%?Main Option List"ER$CH$
265 GOSUB 3100
270 PRINT DC$"& "E$"F"STRING$(80,"a")EG$
271 PRINT DC$")D1       Create a File"
272 PRINT DC$"*D2       Input Data"
273 PRINT DC$"+D3       Query the Database"
274 PRINT DC$",D4       Review this file's parameters"
275 PRINT DC$"-D5       Set Data Disk Drive"
276 PRINT DC$".D6       Exit"
290 RETURN
295 PRINT CS$;
296 PRINT CO$;
300 PRINT RV$;"CREATE Database";ER$;TAB(60);RV$;DA$;ER$
305 PRINT:PRINT:PRINT
310 PRINT "1 = Filename";TAB(30)"2 = Date";TAB(55)"3 = # of Fields"
315 PRINT STRING$(79,95)
320 PRINT " Field #:- ";TAB(50);" Space left :- "
325 PRINT:PRINT
330 PRINT "4 = Field Name:- ";TAB(40);"7 = Field Length:- "
335 PRINT "5 = Field Type:- ";TAB(40);"Field Starts at :- "
340 PRINT "6 = Min Value :- ";TAB(40);"8 = Max Value    :- "
341 PRINT BC$
345 RETURN
```

DC$. The two characters next to the DC$ are enclosed in quotation marks and their values are translated into row and column information. This takes up little space and less memory than assigning the position to go to the variable X1 and then calling the subroutine in line 80. It is not as readable though and determining the characters requires more planning time.

Lines 295-345 represents the screen mask used for getting the data used to create the file

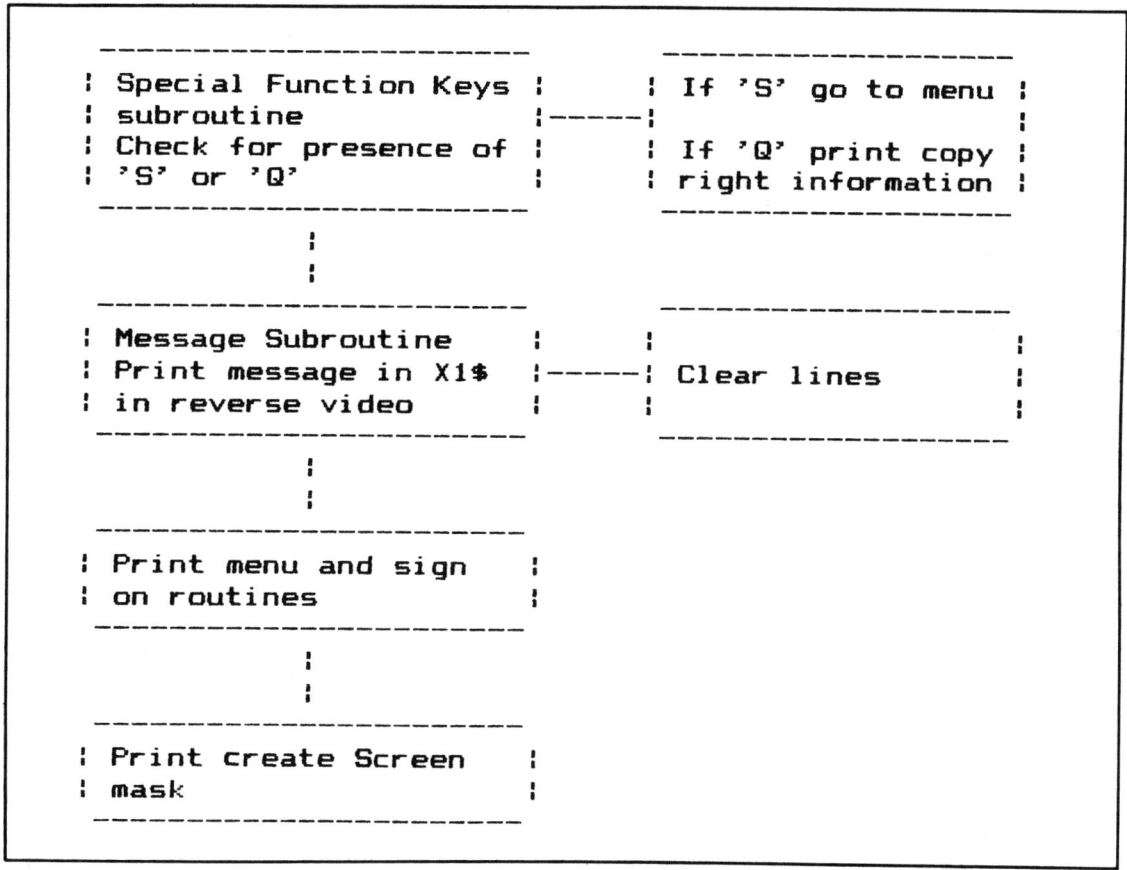

Fig. 4-1. Chart of the routines included in Listing 3.

parameters. By presenting screen masks, you need only be concerned with addressing the cursor to the specific areas of the screen where the data is accepted. This saves time.

If you do not have an addressable cursor on your system, you will have to rewrite this and other sections of the code to ask for information a line at a time. This will require more time and more code, but it will work. Figure 4-1 shows this section of the code in flowchart form.

SUBROUTINES FOR SCREEN AND INPUT CONTROL

Listing 4 shows the code that creates the appropriate screen mask, allows input concerning the file parameters, and finally clears the screen.

There are a number of subroutines in listing four. The first of these consists of lines 350 to 395. This is a screen mask that is used to form the background for the input of data into the database. Since the program does not know how much data is to be entered, and since you must design it to allow for all eventualities, the only practical way to do it is to have the data entered line by line. The information that you will display in this subroutine will let the user know about important parts of the database currently in use. We start off in line 350 by erasing the screen and homing the cursor. Next, in line 351, the cursor is turned off so that it does not distract the user while the program prints out the rest of the screen. Line 355 prints a heading in reverse video to tell the user what this portion of the program is responsible for. Line 360 spaces down four lines so that there will be room to print any error messages or queries for more information.

LISTING FOUR
============

```
350 PRINT CS$;
351 PRINT CO$
355 PRINT RV$;"DATABASE INPUT";ER$
360 PRINT:PRINT:PRINT:PRINT
365 PRINT "Filename   :- ";TAB(40)
    "Date Created  :- "
370 PRINT "# of Fields:- ";TAB(40)
375 PRINT STRING$(79,95)
380 PRINT
    "Date of Update :- "
385 PRINT "Rec # :- "
390 PRINT:PRINT
391 PRINT BC$
395 RETURN
400 X1=738
        X2=4
        X3=0
        X4=0
        GOSUB 85
        F$(X)=XO$
        GOSUB 80
        PRINT F$(X)
        RETURN
405 X1=818
        X2=2
        X3=0
        X4=0
        GOSUB 85
        T$(X)=XO$
        GOSUB 80
        PRINT T$(X)
        RETURN
410 X1=898
        X2=10
        X3=-9999999999
        X4=9999999999
        GOSUB 85
        MI(X)=XO#
        GOSUB 80
        PRINT MI(X)
        RETURN
415 X1=778
        X2=3
        X3=1
        X4=256
        GOSUB 85
        L(X)=XO#
        GOSUB 80
        PRINT L(X)
        RETURN
420 X1=938
        X2=10
        X3=-9999999999
        X4=9999999999
        GOSUB 85
        MA(X)=XO#
        GOSUB 80
        PRINT MA(X)
        RETURN
425 X1=335
        X2=7
        X3=0
        X4=0
        GOSUB 85
        F$=XO#
        GOSUB 80
        PRINT F$
        RETURN
430 X1=392
        X2=2
        X3=1
        X4=127
        GOSUB 85
        F=XO#
        GOSUB 80
        PRINT F
        RETURN
435 X3$="NOT ALLOWED"
        GOSUB 185
        RETURN
440 X1=738
        GOSUB 80
        PRINT "     "
445 X1=818
        GOSUB 80
        PRINT "   "
450 X1=898
        GOSUB 80
        PRINT "           "
455 X1=778
        GOSUB 80
        PRINT "    "
460 X1=858
        GOSUB 80
        PRINT "    "
465 X1=938
        GOSUB 80
        PRINT "           "
470 RETURN
```

Lines 365 and 370 print out four headings for the information of the user. The program will later request the name of the database and then go and find it. Once determined, the other information will be printed. It is sometimes vital to know when a database was created and when it was last updated. This is particularly true when there are a number of similar ones in use. The number of fields information also serves as a reminder of how much input the program is expecting.

Line 375 simply prints a line of equal signs to act as a delimiter on the screen. Next the program spaces down a row in line 380, prints out the Rec #:- prompt in line 385, and turns the cursor on in line 391. The record number is the current record being written to, and will be displayed by another section of the program.

Lines 400-430 are each subroutines. They all have a similar construction. The first value, X1, is the spot on the screen where this information is to be accepted. X2 is the value that represents the total length of the input string. X3 is the minimum numerical value that we will allow to be accepted here. If the input value requested is to be a string value, X3 and X4 are both set to 0. X4 is the maximum numerical data value that will be accepted here. If the numerical value is either below X3 or higher than X4, the input routine described in listing two will catch it, display an error message, and let the user reenter the value. The value of XO$ or XO# is assigned to the variable you are concerned with, and displayed at the correct place. Then control returns to the section of the program that called the routine. Look over the routines here, and note that all numerical values have a length of 10 if they are double precision.

Line 435 is called if the user tries to change the value of the date. This is not allowed in the present program because I want the date of the last update to remain unchanged. This helps the operator keep track of when he last updated the file.

Lines 440 to 470 are a collection of lines that clear the old information from the previous entry from the screen. This keeps the screen clear of everything except the needed questions and prevents any confusion about what was entered to what record or parameter file.

Again, look at the simplified flowchart shown in Fig. 4-2, to get a feel for the program logic displayed in listing four.

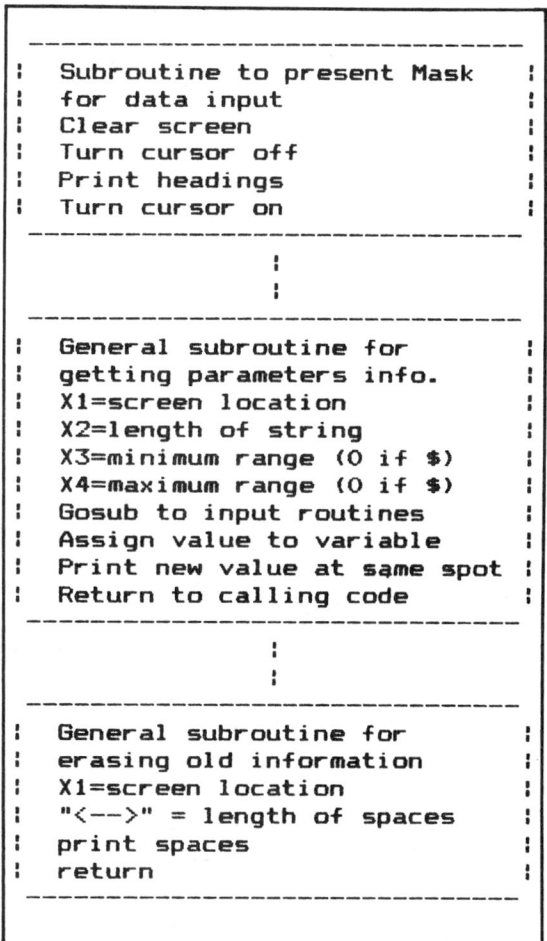

Fig. 4-2. Chart of the routines included in Listing 4.

THE MENU

You are now ready to take a look at the beginning of the main program, but to do so the order in which the material is presented will be reversed. Because the first four program listings have consisted mainly of subroutines it didn't really matter if the flowcharting appeared before the code or after it. In regular programming, however, the flow charts prepare the way for the code. Therefore, they will be presented before the code in the rest of the book.

The first thing that the program should do on the screen is to present a menu. Depending on the type of features you have with your system, this can be done in a number of ways. If you have a terminal that does not allow the use of an addressable cursor, you will have to present the choices in the following manner:

Joe's Database

1. Create a file
2. Data functions (input, change, delete)
3. Query the database
4. Review
5. Set data disk
6. Exit

Input your choice

The program will have to print each line and then wait at the bottom for you to input your choice. If you have cursor addressing, you can do the same thing, but upon receiving a choice you can go back and highlight the entire line or just the chosen number. This confirms the choice. If you have reverse video, you can put the title line in reverse video for emphasis.

Setting the correct data disk drive could be crucial in your system. If the program must know which drive the data disk is on, you must tell it. If the system is like Radio Shack, it will search all the drives to find the file. If you do not designate the drive, the file will be written to the first disk with available space, usually the one in drive 0. You will probably want the data file on drive 1 because with the programs and the disk operating system on drive 0, there probably won't be any room left.

After getting the menu choice from the user, the program must branch out to the appropriate line to do whatever is required, or it must load a program to do it if you wish to make the program a collection of smaller ones. Making the program a collection of various smaller programs may be a good idea. Because you are going to be sorting records in memory, it would be best to have as much memory available as possible for this job. The disadvantage is that all subroutines that are made use of by different segments of the program must be available to those segments. Thus you will use a larger amount of disk space for the storage of all the separate programs than you would to store one large one. The choice is yours. In this book we will present the program as a single large one, and you can make whatever adjustments are required to break it down. To assist you in this, you will find a note of all the subroutines called by a particular section.

The flowchart for this section of code appears as shown in Fig. 4-3. Listing 5 shows the code for these routines.

```
  ----------------------
  : Program begins here  :
  : First present the    :
  : menu                 :
  : If no data disk is   :
  : specified then assume :
  : it to be drive 0     :
  : (Drive A: in CP/M)   :
  ----------------------
             :
             :
```

Fig. 4-3. Chart of the routines included in Listing 5.

```
            ----------------------
            : Get choice from user :
            ----------------------
                       :
                       :
       ------------------------          -------
       : If Choice = 1        :  : S/R : : line :
       : GOSUB  creation code :          : 540  :
       ------------------------          -------
                       :
                       :
       ------------------------          -------
       : If Choice = 2        :  : S/R : : line :
       : GOSUB data functions :          : 980  :
       ------------------------          -------
                       :
                       :
       ------------------------          -------
       : If Choice = 3        :  : S/R : : line :
       : GOSUB query functions:          : 1705 :
       ------------------------          -------
                       :
                       :
       ------------------------          -------
       : If Choice = 4         : : S/R : : line :
       : GOSUB review parameter:         : 2630 :
       ------------------------          -------
                       :
                       :
       ------------------------          -------
       : If Choice = 5        :  : S/R : : line :
       : GOSUB set data drive :          : 480  :
       ------------------------          -------
                       :
                       :
       ------------------------          -------
       : If Choice = 6        :  : S/R : : line :
       : GOSUB exit           :          : 495  :
       ------------------------          -------
                       :
       ------------------------
       : On return redisplay  :
       : Menu                 :
       ------------------------
```

Fig. 4-3. Chart of the routines included in Listing 5 (continued from page 26).

LISTING FIVE
============

```
475 PRINT CS$
        GOSUB 3160
476 IF DK$="" THEN DK$="SY0:D"
477 GOTO 500
480 GOSUB 3100
        PRINT RV$DC$"'D Data Disk is on "ER$CH$
481 PRINT DC$")D1      SY0:"
        PRINT DC$"*D2      SY1:"
        PRINT DC$"+D3      SY2:"
483 PRINT DC$"6C";BC$;
        DE$=INPUT$(1)
        PRINT CO$
484 IF VAL(DE$)<1 OR VAL(DE$)>3 THEN PRINT DC$"6C "
        GOTO 483
485 TP=ASC(DE$)-8
        TP=CHR$(TP)
        PRINT DC$TP$"D"RV$DE$ER$DC$"6C";
486 IF VAL(DE$)=1 THEN DK$="SY0:D"
487 IF VAL(DE$)=2 THEN DK$="SY1:D"
488 IF VAL(DE$)=3 THEN DK$="SY2:D"
489 RETURN
495 PRINT CS$
        PRINT E$+"x";CHR$(49)
        PRINT DC$;CHR$(56);CHR$(32)
        PRINT E$+"1"
        X1=0
        GOSUB 80
        SYSTEM
500 CLOSE
        GOSUB 250
505 PRINT DC$"6C";BC$;
        DE$=INPUT$(1)
        PRINT CO$
507 IF VAL(DE$)<1 OR VAL(DE$)>6 THEN PRINT DC$"6C "
        GOTO 505
508 T1=ASC(DE$)-8
        T1$=CHR$(T1)
        PRINT DC$T1$"D"RV$DE$ER$DC$"6C";
510 XO#=VAL(DE$)
513 GOSUB 40
515 ON XO# GOSUB 540,980,1705,2630,480,495
520 GOTO 475
```

First the menu is presented by calling the subroutine at line 3160 in line 475. This will present the background information. Next we set up a drive default value in line 476. Here we have said that the default data disk drive will be drive 0. Thus if the user does not change the drive number, the system will assume it to be drive 0. Note that in the Heath Zenith system using HDOS, this drive is set as SY0:. In Radio Shack it would be :0, in CP/M, A:.

The GOSUB 3100 in line 480 prints some lines in reverse video for visual effect. These can be skipped if desired. The lines from here to 489 are a subroutine that is selected when the user wishes to change the data disk. The choice of three drives is given to the user; his answer is checked to make sure it is within the range in line 484; and the proper drive is then set.

Line 495 is the subroutine that exits from the program. The screen is erased, including the 25th line, and then control is passed to the operating system. If you are not using the 25th line, you can leave out all the statements between PRINT CS$ and SYSTEM.

Line 505 checks the user response to the menu. It is checked for the proper range, and then the appropriate action is taken in 515. The GOSUB 40 in line 513 presents the **Press f1 to exit to menu** message on the status line. Again, it can be deleted if not required.

Line 515 will branch to whichever routine is called for, and when the program finishes that routine, control will return to the menu routine via line 520.

Chapter 5

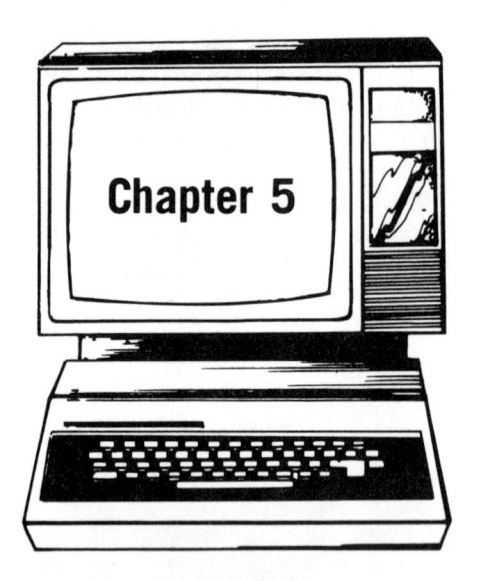

The Database Parameter File

This chapter presents the coding of the portion of the program that sets up the data dictionary. It also looks at the way in which the program sets up certain fields that can use the values of other fields as data. Along the way you will learn some things about the use and manipulation of strings that you might not have been aware of.

SETTING UP THE DATABASE PARAMETER FILE

In listing six you will be looking at the code required to create a database parameter file. You will recall that the file is to store the information that will allow any program to determine which fields are present within the database, what they contain, and where to find them. Also it will tell the program what type of information is within each field and if there are range limits to enforce.

In addition you will be adding more information to the parameters file. You will want to record the creation date of a particular file, the last date it was updated, what it is called, and the number of fields in use. You have already developed some subroutines to display a screen mask so that you need only place the cursor at a predetermined spot to accept the data. If you do not have a terminal with cursor addressing, you will have to ask the questions repetitively to get the data: the process is slow and not quite as elegant, but it will have the same results.

The first problem is to differentiate among the various types of data available to a field. The first of these is the alphanumeric data set. This includes all letters, numbers, and punctuation marks: simply a literal copy of whatever you enter. Data of this type is stored on the disk in ASCII and can be viewed by looking at the database file with a text editor.

Numeric data has three subsets of data. First, there is the integer data set. Integer data is considered to be a numeric expression that is positive and between 0 and 32767. Note that it cannot contain any decimal points. Some BASICs also allow the inclusion of numbers from 0 to -32767 as integers, and some allow from 0 to approximately 64000. Your manual will tell you what is available to you. For our purposes though, we will define an integer as any whole number between 0 and +32767.

The second type of numerical expression is the single precision number, which is accurate to six significant figures. It can contain decimal points and can be either positive or negative.

The third type available to us is the double-precision numeric expression. These numbers are accurate to 14 significant figures. These different types of numeric data can be stored on the disk in different ways. The quickest way is simply to convert the value into a string by using the STR$ function and storing the data in ASCII format. This will give you the ability to read the data from the database file by using a text editor.

There is one serious drawback to this system. You will recall that we are working with records of a set length, 255 bytes. Each field within that record must also have a set length. The problem lies in determining how much to allow for each numeric data field. We could allow 5 spaces for each expected integer type, 7 for each single-precision type, and 14 for each double-precision expression. When you consider this, keep in mind that you will soon eat up your 255 bytes. This is according to Murphy's first law of storage dynamics which states "The amount of record space required for any record will be no less than one byte more than what can be stored in any given format." Put into plain English it means that the record you want most to save will use one more byte than your system will allow you to use!

We can restrict Murphy somewhat by using some of the built-in functions of Microsoft BASIC. These functions will take numeric expressions and convert them into packed strings. There are, of course, corresponding functions to convert these strings back. How much space is saved? An integer, which would normally use five bytes of storage in ASCII format, is now saved in two bytes. A single precision number, which would have taken up 7 bytes, is saved in four bytes, and a double precision number is trimmed from 14 bytes to eight.

You may be wondering how such miracles happen. Actually it is quite simple. All data is stored within the computer, and on the disk as a seris of *bit patterns*. This is because the computer, (sometimes called a "fast idiot"), can only understand whether something is on or off. There is no middle ground. To a computer the letter A looks like 01000001. In this format there are eight bits in the pattern. Eight bits make up one *byte*. In simplified terms it can be said that the computer assigns a weight or value to each bit in the pattern. This weighting looks like this: 128,64,32,16,8,4,2,1. This is called the *binary* number system.

If each bit in the A pattern that is represented by a 1 is assigned a value according to the weight table, the result is 0,64,0,0,0,0,0,1. When these values are added together, the total is 65. 65 is the decimal representation of the letter A. All the letters, numbers, and punctuation marks can be represented by using only 7 bits of the 8 bit byte. The left-most bit is then used as a *parity* check bit in some systems. This bit is either a 1 or a 0 depending upon how many of the other seven bits are on or off. If the system is using *even parity*, the eighth bit is either a 1 or a 0 depending on which is required to make the total number of 1s in all eight bits an even number. If odd parity is being used, a 1 or 0 is used as required to make the number of 1s an odd number. The computer checks to see if the parity is odd or even and if the bit is correct in some systems. If there is an error in the setting of the parity bit, the computer knows that the piece of data is wrong and is not to be trusted.

All this discussion of bits and bytes brings us to a simple fact. If 7 bits can represent any number up to 256, how many bits are necessary to represent a number up to 32767? The answer is that 15 can. BASIC then stores the integer number into two bytes as a 16 bit word. This conversion is done by the built-in function of MKI$(X%), which is used to make the integer expression in the brackets into an integer string. To retrieve the number, the function CVI (X$) is used. This means to convert the string expression within the brackets into an integer. Now if we follow up on this, we can store.

A single precision expression can be stored in four bytes by using three bytes for the number and the fourth byte to indicate whether it is a positive or negative value, and where the decimal point should be. The function names for these conversions are MKS$(X) for converting into a string, and CVS(X$) to convert the string back into a single precision expression. A double precision expression can be stored in eight bytes total, and the functions are MKD$(X#) and CVD(X$) respectively.

The space requirements can be fixed by asking the user to indicate which type of numeric expression he wants to use. I have chosen to have the user enter an A for alphanumeric data, DI (Digital Integer) for integer numeric data, DS for single precision data and DD for double precision. If these seem a little strange to you, change them into whatever pleases you. Remember that the rest of the program will need to know what you are using as indicators.

You need to keep track of how much space is being used by the fields so that you don't run over. Therefore the program will include a routine to count the spaces and tell how much is left to use.

A flowchart of the routines required is shown in Fig. 5-1. When reading the flowcharts remember that the numbers in the boxes on the right are the starting line numbers for subroutines called by this section of code. Listing 6 shows the code for these routines.

Now lets take a look at the code in detail. Line 540 sets DI$ equal to DA$. Since the date was entered into DA$ when the system was brought up, both variables now have today's date.

Line 545 calls the earlier subroutine to set up the screen so you can enter the information. Line 550 prints the data and 555 goes to that subroutine that asks for the name of the file. If the user had entered this part of the program in error or just wished to exit without going through the routine of creating a database, he can enter a null, (caused by just pressing the return or enter key without entering anything) and be placed back at the menu. This response is checked for by line 560.

Line 565 will ask the user for the total number of fields in this database. If the user were to enter a null, line 570 would detect this and cause the program to back up one step to the point where the filename was being requested.

Line 575 will cause the program to branch to line 2345 if an error condition is detected. This error trapping is not a feature of all BASICs and you should check to determine if it is available in yours. Error trapping allows the programmer to test for error conditions and then have the program take corrective action. For example, the erase command in line 580 will cause an error to occur if an attempt is made to erase an array that does not yet exist. The program allows for this error to happen, and then takes corrective measures by ignoring the error and proceeding with line 585. This is done because, if this is the first time through the procedure, no dimensioning has occurred. The arrays are dimensioned to hold the information about each of the fields, but the number of fields is not known until the user indicates the value.

Error trapping occurs frequently throughout the program. If your BASIC does not allow an array to be erased (Radio Shack doesn't for instance), you will have to set up a routine to initialize a flag variable to tell the program that this is the first time through and no dimensioning has occurred yet. In this case, no attempt will be made to clear unwanted data out of the array. If this is not the first time through, the program could branch to a routine that sets all the variables in the arrays to zero if they are numeric and to nulls if they are strings.

Line 590 sets the variable that will count how many characters have been used to zero. 595 sets the field number to one and 600 prints the field number on the screen for the user. Line 605 will return the name of the field. This name is used by the user to refer to the field when necessary, and it is limited to a total length of four characters. Line 610 returns with the value that indicates the data type. The program will set the field length if the data is numeric and will set the minimum and maximum amounts to zero if the data is alphanumeric. These routines are in lines 612 to 618.

Line 620 keeps a check on the starting location of the field by adding one to the current value of the character total. This total is adjusted in line 625 and checked in line 630. If the user attempts to go over the 255 byte length limit for the record, an error message is flashed and the attempt is prevented.

```
+--------------------------------+
| Save the date in DA$ so we     |
| will know when this file was   |
| created.                       |
+--------------------------------+
                 |
+--------------------------------+   -----
| Go and print the screen mask   | S/R | 295 |
+--------------------------------+   -----
                 |
+--------------------------------+
|         Print the date         |
+--------------------------------+
                 |
+--------------------------------+   -----
|      Ask for the filename      | S/R | 425 |
| If a null entry then return    |
+--------------------------------+   -----
                 |
+--------------------------------+   -----
|    Ask for number of fields    | S/R | 430 |
| If a null entry go to          |
| ask for filename               |
+--------------------------------+   -----
                 |
+--------------------------------+
| Set up error routines calls    |   ------
| Erase old arrays if required   | S/R | 2345 |
| Dimension new arrays           |   ------
+--------------------------------+
                 |
+--------------------------------+
| Set character counter to 0     |
| Set field counter to one       |
+--------------------------------+
                 |
+--------------------------------+   -----
| Get field data                 |
|   Name                         |   | 400 |
|   Type                         |   | 405 |
|   Minimum                      | S/R | 410 |
|   Length                       |   | 415 |
|   Maximum                      |   | 420 |
+--------------------------------+   -----
                 |
+--------------------------------+   -----
| Allow any changes              |
| If all OK then erase inputs    | S/R | 440 |
| and go back for next field     |
+--------------------------------+   -----
```

Fig. 5-1. Chart of the routines included in Listing 6.

LISTING SIX
==========

```
540 DI$=DA$
545 GOSUB 295
550 X1=360
        GOSUB 80
        PRINT DA$
555 GOSUB 425
560 IF X0#=-1 THEN RETURN
565 GOSUB 430
570 IF X0#=-1 THEN 555
575 ON ERROR GOTO 2345
580 ERASE F$,T$,MI,L,SA,MA
585 DIM F$(F),T$(F),MI(F),L(F),SA(F),MA(F)
590 SU=0
595 X=1
600 X1=491
        GOSUB 80
        PRINT X
605 GOSUB 400
610 GOSUB 405
        IF T$(X)="A" THEN MI(X)=0
                        X1=898
                        GOSUB 80
                        PRINT MI(X)
612 IF T$(X)<>"A" THEN GOSUB 410
615 IF T$(X)="DI" THEN L(X)=2
                        X1=778
                        GOSUB 80
                        PRINT L(X)
616 IF T$(X)="DS" THEN L(X)=4
                        X1=778
                        GOSUB 80
                        PRINT L(X)
617 IF T$(X)="DD" THEN L(X)=8
                        X1=778
                        GOSUB 80
                        PRINT L(X)
618 IF T$(X)="A" THEN GOSUB 415
620 SA(X)=SU+1
        X1=858
        GOSUB 80
        PRINT SA(X)
625 SU=SU+L(X)
630 X1=545
        GOSUB 80
        PRINT 255-SU
        IF SU>255 THEN X3$="Out of Range"
                            GOSUB 185
                            GOTO 615
635 IF T$(X)="A" THEN MA(X)=0
        X1=938
        GOSUB 80
```

```
        PRINT MA(X)
        GOTO 640
636 GOSUB 420
640 X1$="Line to Change ?"
        GOSUB 235
        X2=1
        X3=0
        X4=8
        GOSUB 85
645 IF X0#<1 THEN 675
650 CH=X0#
655 SU=SU-L(X)
660 ON CH GOSUB 425,435,430,400,610,410,415,420
665 SU=SU+L(X)
670 GOTO 640
675 GOSUB 440
680 X=X+1
        IF X<F+1 THEN 600
```

Lines 640 to 670 allow the user to adjust any entries he has made concerning the field presently being defined. He may change any of the field parameters and the program will update the various counters as required. Once all is correct, line 680 will cause the program to loop back to get the information for the rest of the fields.

ESTABLISHING THE BASIS
FOR MATHEMATICAL CAPABILITIES

It would be helpful if you had the ability to make the contents of a certain field the results of some mathematical relationship between two or more preceding fields. Then you could designate certain fields as subtotal fields, and others as total fields. You could use them to keep track of sales tax and other goodies. Actually, it is not that difficult to arrange such a thing. Since you already know everything about any field, you can set up a routine to tell the program that one or more of them are *special* fields, and must be treated differently than the others.

This can be done by setting up special field strings that will contain the name of the field to receive the results of the calculations. This type of field will be called a *target* field. The field contributing the data will be called the *source* field. You can use as many source fields as you need.

The string would look like this:

```
:1--4-:1--40:1--40!
```

In this string the first four spaces are the name of the target field; the fifth space is blank; the next four spaces are the name of the first source field; the fifth is the operator (+,—,*,/), which serves to indicate how the information in the source field affects the information already in the target field. The program need only retrieve the name of the source field, get the data from it, and perform whatever operation is specified by the operator. To do this successfully, you must include the ability to check each entry to ensure that it is a valid field name or a valid operator. If you don't, the program will crash or give you that most feared of all bugs, **UNPREDICTABLE RESULTS.** This generally means that the program will get so confused, even the programmer can't guess what will happen to it! Look at what a flowchart shown in Fig. 5-2 will indicate about the routines. The code for this flowchart is shown in Listing 7.

Looking at the code you can see that the screen is cleared and the title is displayed by line 685. 690 spaces down four lines to allow for the message and error lines. The subroutine referred to in line 692 is one that will print all the field names we have used on the bottom of the screen.

Line 695 sets the marker for the first occurrence of a source string field name in the spe-

```
+--------------------------+       ------
| Clear screen and get     |       
| ready to accept data     | S/R | 3060 |
| Print out the valid      |       
| list of field names      |       ------
+--------------------------+
             |
+--------------------------+
| Set up the specials      |
| strings                  |
+--------------------------+
             |
+--------------------------+       ------
| Get target field name    | S/R | 2340 |
| and check it             |       ------
+--------------------------+
             |
+--------------------------+
| Get source field name    |
| and check it             |
+--------------------------+
             |
+--------------------------+
| Get operator and         |
| check it                 |
+--------------------------+
             |
+--------------------------+
| If needed get more       |
| source fields            |
+--------------------------+
             |
+--------------------------+
| When all done then       |
| print file to disk       |
+--------------------------+
```

Fig. 5-2. Chart of the routines included in Listing 7.

LISTING SEVEN
=============

```
685 PRINT CS$;
        PRINT RV$;"Specials";ER$
690 PRINT
        PRINT
```

```
              PRINT
              PRINT
    692 GOSUB 3060
    695 Y1=6
    700 FOR Y=1 TO 9
    705     SP$(Y)=""
            FOR Y%=1 TO F*5
                    SP$(Y)=SP$(Y)+" "
            NEXT
    710     X1=160
            GOSUB 80
            PRINT "Special #:-";Y
    715     X1=400
            GOSUB 80
    720     PRINT "Target Field:-"
            PRINT "Source Field:-"
            PRINT "       Action:-"
    725     X1=415
            GOSUB 2340
            X2=4
            X3=0
            X4=0
            GOSUB 85
            IF X0#=-1 THEN 800 ELSE MID$(SP$(Y),1,4)=X0$
    726     GOSUB 735
            IF X0=-1 THEN 725

    730     X1=495
            GOSUB 2340
            X2=4
            X3=0
            X4=0
            GOSUB 85
            IF X0#=-1 THEN 790 ELSE MID$(SP$(Y),Y1,4)=X0$
    731     GOSUB 735
            IF X0=-1 THEN 730
    734     GOTO 755

    735     FOR X5%=1 TO F
    740             IF X0$=F$(X5%) THEN X0=0
                                       RETURN
    745     NEXT X5%
    750     X3$="INVALID FIELD"
            GOSUB 185
            X0=-1
            RETURN
    755     X1=575
            GOSUB 2340
            X2=1
            X3=0
            X4=0
            GOSUB 85
            MID$(SP$(Y),Y1+4,1)=X0$
    760     IF X0$="+" OR X0$="-" OR X0$="*" OR X0$="/" THEN 770
    765     X3$="INVALID ACTION"
```

```
             GOSUB 185
             GOTO 755
770          Y1=Y1+5
775          X1$="MORE"
             GOSUB 235
             X2=1
             X3=0
             X4=0
             GOSUB 85
             IF XO$="Y" OR XO$="y" THEN 780 ELSE 790
780          X1=495
             GOSUB 80
             PRINT "        "
             X1=575
             GOSUB 80
             PRINT "     "
785          GOTO 730
790          Y1=6
             NEXT Y

800 OPEN "O",1,F$
805 PRINT #1,F$;",";D1$;",";DA$;",";F
810 FOR X=1 TO F
815     PRINT #1,F$(X);",";T$(X);",";MI(X);L(X);SA(X);MA(X)
820 NEXT X
825 FOR Y=1 TO 9
830     PRINT #1,SP$(Y)
835 NEXT Y
840 CLOSE 1:RETURN
```

cials string line. Line 700-705 sets up nine of these special string lines. If you wish you could change the number of specials here to some other value. I have found nine to be more than enough for most uses. Line 710 to 720 print out the mask and 725 gets the name of the target string. If a null value is entered at this point, the routine is terminated and the file written out to the disk. The program checks to see if the field name entered is a valid one in lines 735 to 750. In these lines the name that has been entered is checked against the array that holds the valid names. If the name matches one of them, the routine returns with a value of zero in XO; if not, an error message is dislayed and the value of −1 is returned in XO. This subroutine is used many times in the program.

Line 730 gets the source field name. It is also checked in the routine at 735, unless it is a null value. If it is a null value, the entry for this string is terminated and the program starts to get the data for the next special string. Line 755 gets the information about the operation desired. If it is valid, it is entered into the string and the program moves to line 775. Here the program asks if you have any more source fields for this target field. If you don't the program goes to the next special string and asks for the target field name again after erasing the old information using line 780. If you do have another source field to add, then you can do so in line 730.

After all the information for the special fields in entered, the program starts to write information to the disk. This is done in the routine that starts in line 800. Note the syntax for opening a sequenial file for outputting. This is the same as in Radio Shack BASIC. Note in line 805 that this BASIC requires the explicit writing of commas after each string expression. The information stored here is the file name, the creation date, and the date when the file was last written to. The last two are the same because you have just created the file. In line 815 the arrays are written out. These contain the specific information about each field. Finally, the information about any special fields is written out to the disk.

This ends the routines used for creating a database parameters file. If you have modified any of the routines so that they will run on your system, you should have no problems as long as the information can be accessed by the rest of the program and the file contains the proper data. The areas to watch out for are the methods of writing to the disk, the cursor addressing, and the storage format.

Chapter 6

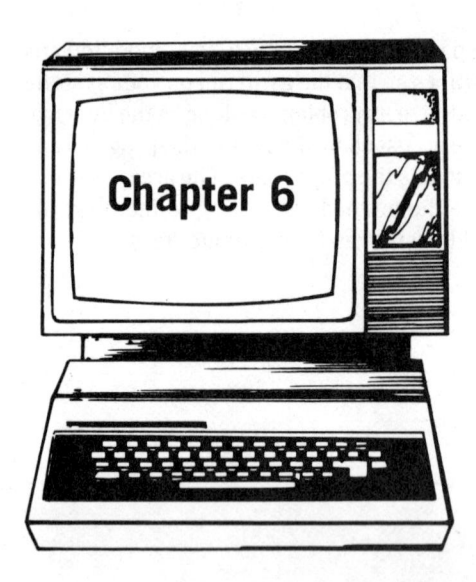

Dealing with the Data File

This chapter deals with the subroutines required to allow you to store and recover the actual data files in the database, how to use the special fields, and how to change the data.

SUBROUTINES TO EXECUTE THE MATHEMATICAL OPERATIONS

Now that you have a way for the program to make up the "specials", you need to tell it how to use them. After all, if the program can create the little beasties, it can look after keeping them current!

The subroutines in this next section of code are used by the program to look after the requirements of the special section. The program must be able to take the special strings apart and identify the fields involved. It then must get the values from those fields and execute the mathematical operations as required by the user. To do this, the strings will be taken apart in the same order as they were created. Starting with the first specials string, the target string will be located first. Then the first source string will be located and its associated value determined. Finally the indicated action will be taken. This linear processing of the strings imposes a somewhat unnatural flow on the operations.

For example, if the target field were to store the results of an operation that took a value from field one, multiplied it by the value in field two, and then added the value of field three, you would have to do it in this fashion: you will first add the contents of field one to the target field; then you will multiply this total by the contents of field two, and finally you will add the contents of field three. The specials string would look like the following if viewed using a text editor (assuming the target field to be four).

FOUR ONE+TWO *THRE+

The space after the word four is there because the first field is the target field and has no operator. The space after the words one and two are there

40

Starting with   Four = 0
                One   = 4
                Two   = 6
                Three = 10

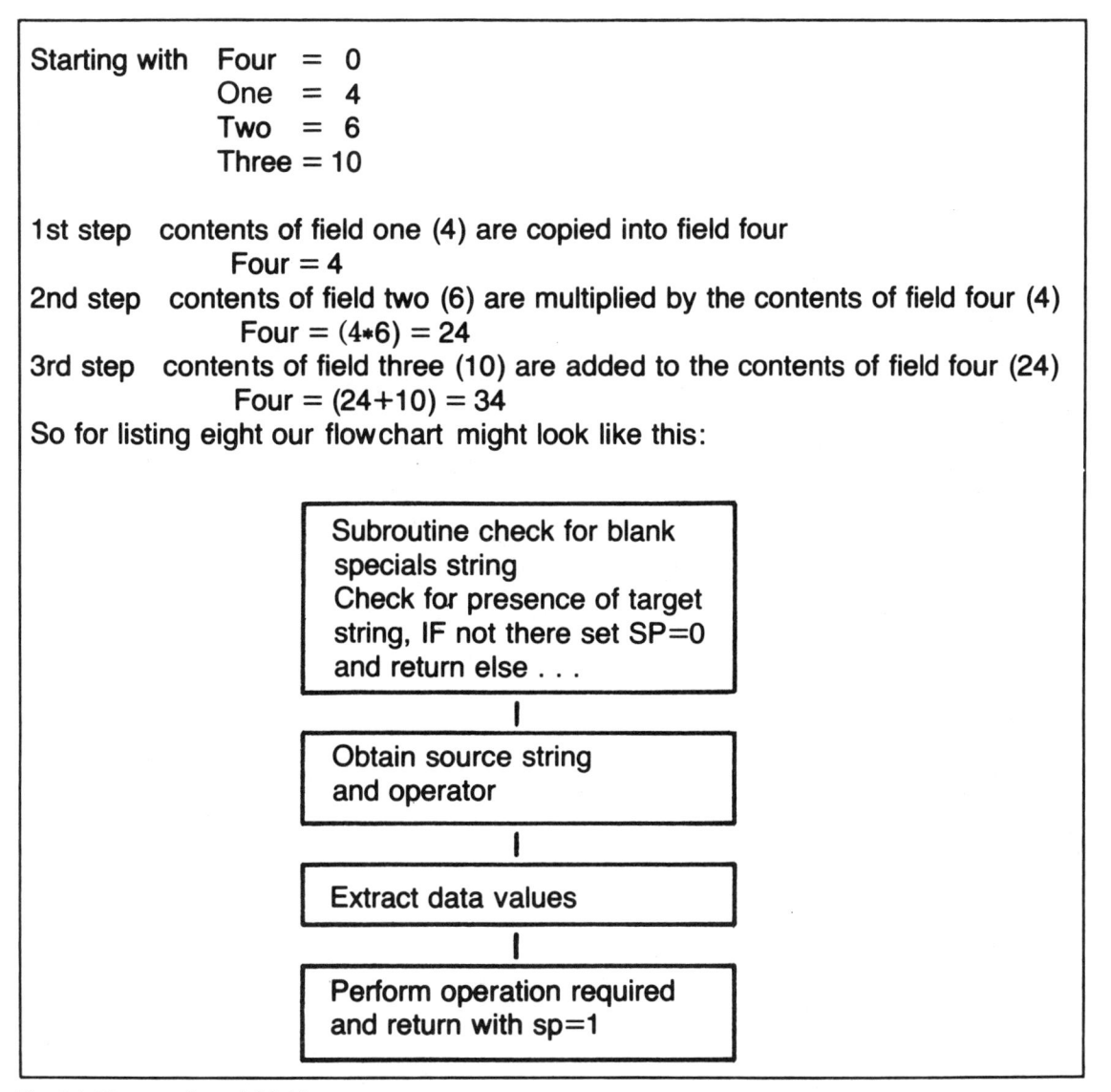

1st step   contents of field one (4) are copied into field four
           Four = 4
2nd step   contents of field two (6) are multiplied by the contents of field four (4)
           Four = (4*6) = 24
3rd step   contents of field three (10) are added to the contents of field four (24)
           Four = (24+10) = 34
So for listing eight our flowchart might look like this:

```
+---------------------------------------+
| Subroutine check for blank            |
| specials string                       |
| Check for presence of target          |
| string, IF not there set SP=0         |
| and return else . . .                 |
+---------------------------------------+
                    |
+---------------------------------------+
| Obtain source string                  |
| and operator                          |
+---------------------------------------+
                    |
+---------------------------------------+
| Extract data values                   |
+---------------------------------------+
                    |
+---------------------------------------+
| Perform operation required            |
| and return with sp=1                  |
+---------------------------------------+
```

Fig. 6-1. The use of special fields.

because there is room for four characters in the field name and only three are being used. The + sign indicates that the contents of one are added into four; the * after the two indicates that the contents of two are multiplied by what is now in four. The THRE is for field three, but there is not enough room for more than four characters so I'm assuming that when this file was created, field three was given the name THRE. The contents of this field are then added to four. The step-by-step procedure is shown in Fig. 6-1. The code for this procedure is shown in Listing 8.

In line 845 we see the beginning of a subroutine that will do two things: first, in line 850, it checks to see if there is anything to do in the specials string. If there is not, it branches to line

LISTING EIGHT

```
845 FOR Y%=1 TO 9
850     IF MID$(SP$(Y%),1,4)="" THEN 865
855     IF MID$(SP$(Y%),1,(LEN(F$(X))))=F$(X) THEN 870
860 NEXT Y%
865 SP=0:RETURN
870 Y1=6
875 TN=0
880 FOR L%=1 TO 5*F
885     IF MID$(SP$(Y%),Y1,1)="" THEN 950
890     TP$=MID$(SP$(Y%),Y1,4)
        FOR X1%=1 TO F
895         IF LEFT$(TP$,LEN(F$(X1%)))=F$(X1%) THEN 905
900     NEXT X1%
902     GOTO 950
905     IF RIGHT$(T$(X1%),1)="I" THEN NU=CVI(MID$(A$,SA(X1%),L(X1%)))
910     IF RIGHT$(T$(X1%),1)="S" THEN NU=CVS(MID$(A$,SA(X1%),L(X1%)))
915     IF RIGHT$(T$(X1%),1)="D" THEN NU=CVD(MID$(A$,SA(X1%),L(X1%)))
920     IF MID$(SP$(Y%),Y1+4,1)="+" THEN TN=TN+NU
925     IF MID$(SP$(Y%),Y1+4,1)="-" THEN TN=TN-NU
930     IF MID$(SP$(Y%),Y1+4,1)="*" THEN TN=TN*NU
935     IF MID$(SP$(Y%),Y1+4,1)="/" THEN TN=TN/NU
940     Y1=Y1+5
945 NEXT L%

950 SP=1
    RETURN
955 FOR X=1 TO F
960     GOSUB 845
965     IF SP=1 THEN RETURN
970 NEXT X
975 Y5=0
    RETURN
```

865 and returns. If there is, it checks the target string in line 855 and then branches to the routines starting at 870.

In line 870, we set the pointer Y1 to the beginning of the source field, and then in lines 905 to 935, the values of the source fields are found and the required operations performed. The routine returns to the calling section of code with the correct value in the target field.

THE MENU FOR USING THE DATA FILE

In the next section of code we will set up a menu to allow the user to enter data into the database, change data already there, delete data, or repack the database. The ADD section will be examined to see how to add a record.

When you develop this piece of code, you will see how the program looks first at the data parameters file to find the correct specifications for the fields. It is this technique that gives the program its flexibility. In order to find the next available sector for data entry, we need only ask BASIC which sector was most recently written to and add one to that value. This is done by using the LOF ( ) function. The previously written input routines will do all the data checking that are required if the correct parameters obtained from the data dictionary are passed to them.

```
---------------------------------
: Present the user with a menu  :
: to allow him to choose to     :         ------
: 1. add to the database        : S/R : 3105 :
: 2. Change data already there  :     : 3100 :
: 3. delete data                :       ------
: 4. repack the database        :
---------------------------------
                :
                :
---------------------------------           -----
: Branch to choice              : S/R : 795 :
---------------------------------           -----
                :
                :
---------------------------------
:   Choice is   ADD             :
---------------------------------
                :
                :
---------------------------------           ------
: Get file name                 : S/R : 2345 :
---------------------------------           ------
                :
                :
---------------------------------
: Consult data dictionary for   :
: the chosen file               :
---------------------------------
                :
                :
---------------------------------           ------
: Present user with each field  : S/R : 3060 :
: in turn                       :           ------
---------------------------------
                :
                :
---------------------------------
: Accept value entered and      :
: check it for matching type    :
: Correct range and length      :
---------------------------------
                :
                :
---------------------------------
: Locate next available record  :
: and enter new data into it    :
---------------------------------
                :
```

Fig. 6-2. Chart of the routines in Listing 9.

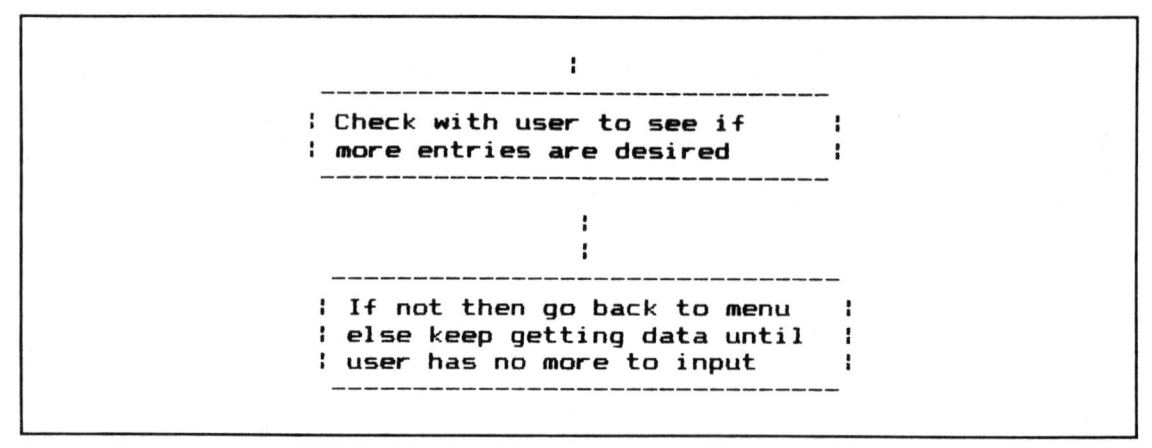

```
                                    :
           ----------------------------------
           : Check with user to see if      :
           : more entries are desired       :
           ----------------------------------
                                    :
                                    :
           ----------------------------------
           : If not then go back to menu    :
           : else keep getting data until   :
           : user has no more to input      :
           ----------------------------------
```

Fig. 6-2. Chart of the routines in Listing 9 (continued from page 44).

Figure 6-2 shows the process in flowchart form. The code is shown in Listing 9.

In this section of code, the menu is presented in lines 980 to 998, and the user's choice is accepted. In line 1000 program control branches to whatever routine is required.

Line 1015 is the start of the add routines. Line 1035 obtains the name of the desired file. Line 1032 checks for a previously entered filename and displays it, if it is available, to avoid having the user type it in again. Once the correct file is obtained the appropriate data parameter file is opened in line 1045. Line 1050 brings in part of the information. Line 1055 prints the date this file was created and the date it was last updated. Line 1060 erases the old arrays if they exist. New arrays are dimensioned to reflect the current number of fields in this file. In lines 1070 to 1095, all the other parameter information is read in and placed in the appropriate array so that the program can access it.

Line 1096 prints out the field descriptors (names) that you have assigned to this file. In line 1115, the actual database files are opened. Line 1120 fields the buffer string to 255 bytes. In line 1125 a string called A$ is set up. This string is filled with 255 spaces in line 1125. This is done to make sure no extraneous information is in the string. A$ will hold the data values for each field in the record that we are adding. This is done by placing the function MID$ on the left side of an equation. This causes the characters in the specified string to be filled with whatever is placed on the right side of the equation. In order for this to operate correctly, the string that the MID$ refers to, A$ in this case, must already be formed. Otherwise, BASIC will respond with an illegal function call error.

In line 1155 BASIC determines which record was the last one written to and adds one to this number to come up with the numbers of the next available record. This is then stored in the variable R. Line 1160 displays the number of fields in each record. Line 1165 prints the record number this record will be written to. Line 1170 erases the line that starts at cursor position 810 and presents each field descriptor and asks for a data entry for it.

The parameters from the data dictionary that are specific to the field in use are transferred to the input routine in lines 1180 to 1205. Line 1210 makes sure the X1$ is the correct length by adding nulls if required.

Line 1215 takes X1$ and places as much of it as will fit into A$. You should note that this process starts with the leftmost character of X1$ and continues until the space is used up. Any remaining part of X1$ is discarded. Line 1230 trims A$ again if required, and then the LSET function in line 1235 places it into the buffer B$. The put function in line 1240 writes the buffer to the disk. The value of R is now increased to reflect the increased record number. Line 1245 asks the user if he has any more data to enter. If he does, the whole process is repeated starting at line 1130. When he is done the

LISTING NINE
============

```
980 ' (* NOTE THE APOSTROPHE IS USED AS A REMARK FLAG*)
985 GOSUB 3105
990 PRINT S1$"% "STRING$(80," ")DC$"%?Data Records Section"ER$CH$
991 GOSUB 3100
        PRINT DC$"& "E$"F"STRING$(80,"a")EG$
992 PRINT DC$")D1     Add a record to Database"
993 PRINT DC$"*D2     Change a record in Database"
994 PRINT DC$"+D3     Flag a record for Deletion"
995 PRINT DC$",D4     Repack records in Database"
996 PRINT DC$"6C";BC$;
        DE$=INPUT$(1)
        PRINT CO$
997 IF VAL(DE$)<1 OR VAL(DE$)>4 THEN PRINT DC$"6C "
        GOTO 996
998 CH=VAL(DE$)

1000 ON CH GOSUB 1015,1260,1465,1605
1005 CLOSE
        GOSUB 795
1010 RETURN

1015 GOSUB 350
1020 X1=40
        GOSUB 80
        PRINT "ADD"
1025 GOTO 1105
1030 ON ERROR GOTO 2345
1032 IF F$<>"" THEN X1=415
        GOSUB 80
        PRINT F$
        X0$=F$
        GOTO 1045
1035 X1=415
        X2=7
        X3=0
        X4=0
        GOSUB 85
        IF LEN(X0$)=0 THEN RETURN
1040 F$=X0$
1045 OPEN "I",1,F$
1050 INPUT #1,F$,DI$,DB$,F
1055 X1=458
        GOSUB 80
        PRINT DI$
        X1=538
        GOSUB 80
        PRINT DA$
1060 ERASE F$,T$,MI,L,SA,MA
1065 DIM F$(F),T$(F),MI(F),L(F),SA(F),MA(F)
1070 FOR X=1 TO F
1075     INPUT #1,F$(X),T$(X),MI(X),L(X),SA(X),MA(X)
```

```
1080 NEXT X
1085 FOR Y=1 TO 9
1090     INPUT #1, SP$(Y)
1095 NEXT Y
1096 GOSUB 3060
1100 CLOSE
     RETURN

1105 GOSUB 1030
1110 IF LEN(XO$)=0 THEN RETURN
1115 OPEN "R",1,DK$+F$+".DAT"
1120 FIELD #1,255 AS B$
1125 A$=STRING$(255," ")
1130 SU=0
1135 FOR X=1 TO F
1140     FOR Y=1 TO L(X)
1145         X$=X$+" "
1150     NEXT Y
1155 R=LOF(1)+1
1160 X1=495
     GOSUB 80
     PRINT F
1165 X1=735
     GOSUB 80
     PRINT R
1170 X1=810
     GOSUB 80
     PRINT E$+"K"
1175 X1=810
     GOSUB 80
     PRINT F$(X)
     GOSUB 845
     IF SP=0 THEN 1180 ELSE XO#=TN
     GOTO 1180
1180 IF T$(X)="A" THEN X2=L(X) ELSE X2=10
1185 IF SP=1 THEN X1=X1+5
     GOSUB 80
     PRINT XO#
     GOTO 1195
1190     X3=MI(X)
         X4=MA(X)
         X1=X1+5
         GOSUB 85
         X1$=XO$
1195 IF RIGHT$(T$(X),1)="I" THEN X1$=MKI$(XO#)
1200 IF RIGHT$(T$(X),1)="S" THEN X1$=MKS$(XO#)
1205 IF RIGHT$(T$(X),1)="D" THEN X1$=MKD$(XO#)
1210 FOR X9=1 TO L(X)
         X1$=X1$+" "
         NEXT
1215 MID$(A$,SA(X),L(X))=X1$
1220 SU=SU+L(X)
1225 NEXT X
1230 A$=LEFT$(A$,SU)
```

```
1235 LSET B$=A$
1240 PUT #1,R
     R=R+1
1245 X1$="MORE"
     GOSUB 235
     INPUT XO$
     IF LEFT$(XO$,1)="Y" OR LEFT$(XO$,1)="y" THEN 1130 ELSE 1255
1250 SU=0
     GOTO 1165
1255 CLOSE 1
     RETURN
```

file is closed to ensure that the data is saved. Data written to the disk is not recognized until the file is closed. You then return to the menu.

If you cannot use the MID$ function of your BASIC on the left side of an equation, you will have to write a routine to simulate this. For example, you could set A$ to a null value and simply add the data in string form as it is input by the user. Then use LSET B$=A$ to transfer the information into the buffer. The method of adding is A$=A$+X1$. Most extended BASICs allow the use of the MID$ function on the right side of the equation. If yours doesn't, check the manual to see how it simulates this function. One of the typical ways is to use the LEFT$ and RIGHT$ functions to break the string apart and then pull the appropriate characters off one end or the other. You will need to do this in the next section of code, which enables you to correct or change a piece of data.

Chapter 7

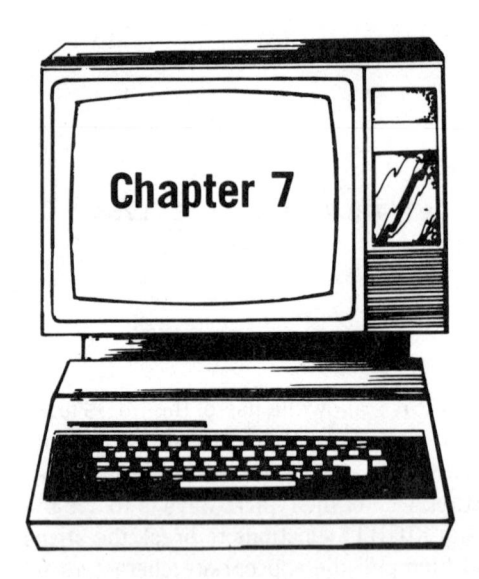

Changing the Data File

After getting all the information into the database, it is inevitable that there will be some things that have to be changed! Some data has a finite life span after which it is no longer useful, and the space it takes up is better employed holding more current data. This chapter will describe how to make changes to data already in the file and delete unwanted data. Ways to recover the valuable disk space that the old data took up will subsequently be examined.

ROUTINES TO CHANGE THE DATA

This section will examine what is required to make changes to the data already in the database. Essentially you must be able to identify the old data and then replace it with the new. Along the way, you should present the user with the old data, allow him to choose whether or not to change it, and if he does want to change it, allow him to substitute new data. This involves an important process in any database system: the finding of the desired record to modify.

There are two main ways of locating a record without going through the process of searching the entire database. The first is by having an index available. The index points to a record for a given key field. That is, if you enter the value for a key field, the computer searches a list until it matches the value and then, by the position of the key in the list or by means of a parallel list, it reads the record number that contains that particular piece of data.

The second way is to have the user input the record number. Then the program can go directly to it.

The advantage of the first method is that you do not need to know what the record number is; you only need to know what values are stored in the key fields. The disadvantage of such a system is that it can take a lot of memory to maintain such an index. You must devote memory space and disk space to store the actual key field data. You must have an efficient sorting routine to order the key list so that it can be searched with a binary sort. If you don't, you will have to search it sequentially, and if you are going to do that, you might as well not bother and

```
---------------------------------     -----
: Print screen mask              :     : S/R : 350 :
---------------------------------     -----
                :
                :
---------------------------------
: Print heading                  :
---------------------------------
                :
                :
---------------------------------     ------
: Get filename and open data     :     : S/R : 1030 :
: dictionary                     :     ------
---------------------------------
                :
                :
---------------------------------
: Open database file             :
---------------------------------
                :
                :
---------------------------------
: Get record # from user         :
---------------------------------
                :
                :
---------------------------------     -----
: Ask for field descriptor       :     : S/R : 735 :
: and check it for validity      :     -----
---------------------------------
                :
                :
---------------------------------
: Get data and print it          :
---------------------------------
                :
                :
---------------------------------
: Ask for and get new data       :
: and insert it into buffer      :
---------------------------------
                :
                :
---------------------------------     -----
: Make any required changes to   :
: any specials fields that are   :     : S/R : 955 :
: affected                       :     -----
---------------------------------
```

Fig. 7-1. Chart of the routines in Listing 10.

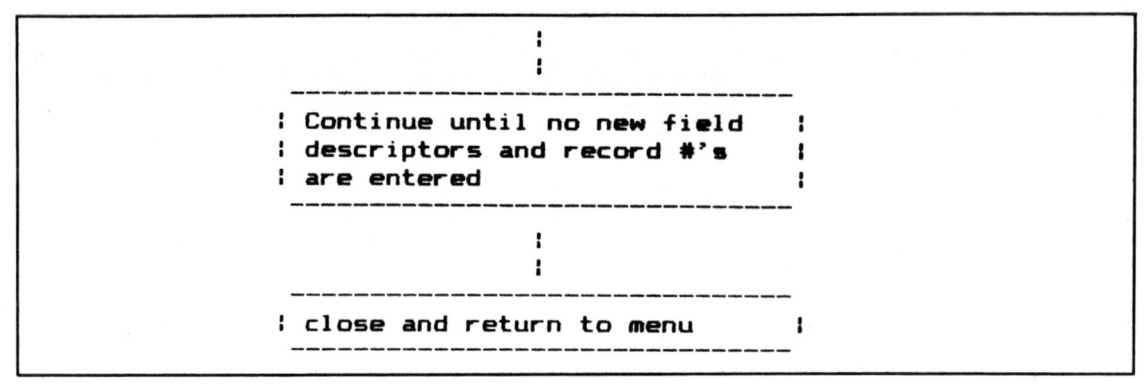

```
          :
          :
 ------------------------------------
 : Continue until no new field      :
 : descriptors and record #'s       :
 : are entered                      :
 ------------------------------------
          :
          :
 ------------------------------------
 : close and return to menu         :
 ------------------------------------
```

Fig. 7-1. Chart of the routines in Listing 10 (continued from page 49).

search the actual database. If you do use a keyed index list, you will have to decide which field will be the key field. In practice you will actually find that the fields that are not key fields are just as important.

The advantage of the second method is that it is faster than the first—if you know the record number. If you make a mistake that would require correction on input, the program is going to tell you the number of the record that you are working on so that you can make a note of it. If you notice the mistake on the printout, you can program the system to print out the record number there also. If you want, you can always use the query portion of the program to search the database for the record anyway.

In this database program the user must know the number of the record that he wants to change. This is in keeping with the limited space for program and data storage available in a microcomputer environment. If you want, you can make up a program to construct an indexed list for your database. All you need to do is consult the data dictionary to get the values for the key field specified, and then extract the values and place them into memory in an array. The array will have to include a space for each record number also. Next simply sort the array and write it to the disk. When you need to find a record quickly, simply bring the list back in from the disk, search it using a binary search, and read the corresponding record number. You now have the record number required by the program. By making a separate program you can have it on a separate disk and only bring it in as required. Figure 7-1 shows the flowchart for this procedure. Listing 10 shows the code.

Line 1260 calls the screen mask subroutine. Again, if you are using a terminal that does not allow cursor addressing, you will have to redo the way the program presents these masks. Line 1265 sets the data variables to zero, and 1270 prints the heading so that the user knows where he is in the program.

Line 1275 calls a subroutine that does two things: first it will ask for a filename, and then it will open the data dictionary that was created for that particular file. It will also read the information from the dictionary file into the appropriate arrays.

Line 1280 looks after getting the database file open and fielding the buffer string.

In line 1295 you are asking the user for the record number to look for. If the user inputs a record number that is less than 1, the program assumes he is finished with this section of the code, closes the files, and then returns to the menu. Otherwise the appropriate record is accessed and the program moves to ask for the field descriptor.

Line 1325 prints the question and gets the response. If a null value is entered here, the program reverts to asking for the record number again. If an entry is made, the program uses the subroutine at line 735 to check its validity. This routine will return with the value in X5% pointing to the correct element of the array for this field descriptor. Lines 1328 to 1375 will retrieve and print the old information from the buffer string.

Lines 1380-1410 ask the user to enter the new

LISTING TEN
==========

```
1260 GOSUB 350
1265 A$=""
     X1$=""
1270 X1=40
     GOSUB 80
     PRINT "CHANGE"
1275 GOSUB 1030
     IF X0$="" THEN CLOSE
                    RETURN
1280 OPEN "R",1,DK$+F$+".DAT"
1285 FIELD #1,255 AS B$
1290 X1=495
     GOSUB 80
     PRINT F
1295 X1=735
     X2=3
     X3=0
     X4=LOF(1)
     GOSUB 85
     R=X0#
     IF R<1 THEN CLOSE
     RETURN
1300 GET #1,R
1305 A$=B$
1310 SU=0

1315 '
1325 X1$="Field Descriptor ?"
     GOSUB 235
     X2=4
     X3=0
     X4=0
     GOSUB 85
1326 IF X0#=-1 THEN LSET B$=A$
     PUT #1,R
     CLOSE
     GOTO 1295
1327 GOSUB 735
     IF X0#=-1 THEN 1325 ELSE X=X5%
1328 X1=810
1330 GOSUB 80
     PRINT E$"1"
     GOSUB 80
     PRINT X;F$(X)
1335 X1$=MID$(A$,SA(X),L(X))
1340 IF RIGHT$(T$(X),1)="I" THEN X9=CVI(X1$)
                                 GOTO 1360
1345 IF RIGHT$(T$(X),1)="S" THEN X9=CVS(X1$)
                                 GOTO 1360
1350 IF RIGHT$(T$(X),1)="D" THEN X9=CVD(X1$)
1355 X2$=X1$
     GOTO 1365
```

```
1360 X1=X1+8
        GOSUB 80
        PRINT X9
        GOTO 1370
1365 X1=X1+8
        GOSUB 80
        PRINT X1$
1370 X1=X1-8

1375 '
1380 PRINT "New Value"
1390 Y5=1
1395 X1=X1+89
1405 IF T$(X)="A" THEN X2=L(X) ELSE X2=10
1410 X3=MI(X)
        X4=MA(X)
        GOSUB 85
1412 IF X0#=-1 THEN 1325
1415 IF T$(X)="A" THEN X1$=X0$
1420 IF RIGHT$(T$(X),1)="I" THEN X1$=MKI$(X0#)
1425 IF RIGHT$(T$(X),1)="S" THEN X1$=MKS$(X0#)
1430 IF RIGHT$(T$(X),1)="D" THEN X1$=MKD$(X0#)
1435 MID$(A$,SA(X),L(X))=STRING$(L(X)," ")
1440 MID$(A$,SA(X),L(X))=X1$
1445 IF Y5=0 THEN 1315
1450 IF Y5=1 THEN GOSUB 955
1455 IF SP=1 THEN Y5=0
                X0#=TN
                GOTO 1420
1460 LSET B$=A$
        PUT #1,R
        GOTO 1325
```

value for this field. Lines 1420 to 1460 put the new information back into the string. This information together with the rest of the buffer string will be written back to the disk when a null value is subsequently entered for the field descriptor question.

This routine allows the user to enter the filename, and the record number. The program then gets the old data, substitutes the new values, and writes the information back on to the disk. This procedure takes care of changes, but how do you handle the problem of deleting unwanted information?

DELETING DATA

The first step in deleting data is to find the desired record and flag for deletion. The record is not physically removed from the database, but it is marked in such a manner that the program will skip it during the querying section. A password is used to indicate to the program that the deletion is actually to take place. This password is defined in line 60 as you'll remember. This will prevent many mistakes by requiring the operator to stop and think for a minute. Also it will prevent an operator who does not know the code from deleting records that you don't want to be deleted. The choice is yours to leave it in or remove it.

The second step, repacking the records means to go through the database files, extract all the valid records, and write them to a new file. You will then have created a data file without any records that have been marked for deletion. This technique requires that the disk have enough space to write a second file of almost as long as the original data file.

```
-----------------------------------
: Print screen mask              :
-----------------------------------
              -----
        S/R : 350 :
              -----
                :
                :
-----------------------------------
: Set buffer variables to zero   :
-----------------------------------
                :
                :
-----------------------------------
: Print heading for user         :
-----------------------------------
                :
                :
-----------------------------------
: Go and get the filename to use :
: Open data dictionary and read  :
: in the data to the arrays      :
-----------------------------------
              ------
        S/R : 1030 :
              ------
                :
                :
-----------------------------------
: Open the database file         :
: Field the buffer string        :
-----------------------------------
                :
                :
-----------------------------------
: Ask user for the record #      :
-----------------------------------
                :
                :
-----------------------------------
: If the record <0 then close    :
: Go back to the menu            :
-----------------------------------
                :
                :
-----------------------------------
: Locate record                  :
: Show first three fields        :
-----------------------------------
                :
                :
-----------------------------------
: Ask for delete password        :
-----------------------------------
```

Fig. 7-2. Chart of the deletion procedure.

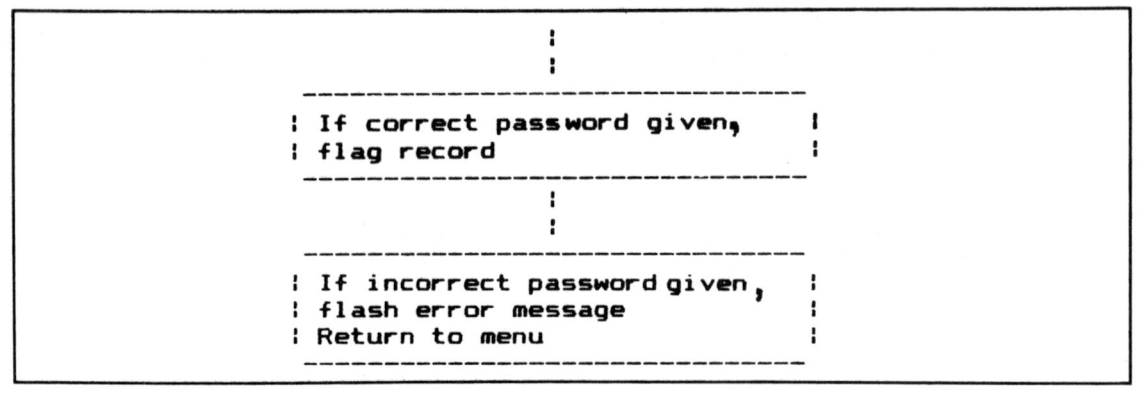

```
+------------------------------------+
|                                    |
|                                    |
| ----------------------------------|
| : If correct password given,      |
| : flag record                     |
| ----------------------------------|
|                :                   |
|                :                   |
| ----------------------------------|
| : If incorrect password given,    |
| : flash error message             |
| : Return to menu                  |
| ----------------------------------|
+------------------------------------+
```

Fig. 7-2. Chart of the deletion procedure (continued from page 53).

One way around this problem is to go through the database and whenever a delete flagged record is encountered, write the record following it into its space. This takes more time and involves a greater number of disk accesses, but it does make the file shorter. Another technique is to use the change part of the program to write valid information into a record that has been flagged. You can also write into the program a routine that will allow you to create a new database file with selected records from an existing file. So you have a number of ways to accomplish your aim.

The method used in this program is to first put all the records that have been marked for deletion at the end of the file. Then all records except those to be deleted are transferred to a new file. The moving of the flagged records to the end of the database file will speed up some of the record checking routines, and you will always have a good idea of where they are if you should want to use the change portion of the program to write good data to them. At the same time, you can create a new database file at any time and leave them out of the new file. If you were able to move the end-of-file marker in BASIC, as can be done using NEWDOS 80, it would be much easier because you could pack the flagged records into the end of the file and then move the EOF to the end of the last good record. That would effectively free up the record space.

If you wish to change the method of repacking, go ahead and do so. Depending on the abilities of your system, you may be able to come up with an easier way. The critical point is that the program uses the LOF value, which is the last sector written to in a particular file, to indicate where the next available sector is. Make sure you allow for this or you will have to rewrite more code than is in the repack section.

The flowcharts for these operations are shown in Figs. 7-2 and 7-3. The code for the two routines is shown in Listing 11.

Line 1470 makes sure that all files are closed

```
+------------------------------------+
|          REPACK ROUTINE            |
|          ===============           |
|                                    |
| ----------------------------------|
| : Print heading                   |
| ----------------------------------|
|                :                   |
|                :                   |
| ----------------------------------|
| : Ask user for filename           |
| ----------------------------------|
|                :                   |
|                :                   |
| ----------------------------------|
| : For each record in database     |
| : check for delete flag           |
| : If there; move all the others   |
|   up one                          |
|   Move delete flagged             |
| : one down                        |
| ----------------------------------|
+------------------------------------+
```

Fig. 7-3. Chart of the repacking procedure.

LISTING ELEVEN
==============

```
1470 CLOSE
1475 GOSUB 350
        A$=""
        X1$=""
1480 X1=40
        GOSUB 80
        PRINT "DELETE"
1485 GOSUB 1030
1490 IF LEN(XO$)=0 THEN RETURN
1495 OPEN "R",1,DK$+F$+".DAT"
1500 FIELD #1,255 AS B$
1505 X1=495
        GOSUB 80
        PRINT F
1510 X1=735
        X2=3
        X3=0
        X4=LOF(1)
        GOSUB 85
        R=XO#
        IF R=-1 THEN RETURN
1512 XO$=""
1515 GET #1,R
1520 A$=B$
        SU=0
1522 IF F>3 THEN F1=3 ELSE F1=F
1525 FOR X=1 TO F1
1530    X1=810
        X1=(X1+(X-1)*80)
        GOSUB 80
        PRINT E$+"K"
1535    GOSUB 80
        PRINT X;F$(X)
1540    X1$=MID$(A$,SA(X),L(X))
1545    IF RIGHT$(T$(X),1)="I" THEN X9=CVI(X1$)
                                        GOTO 1565
1550    IF RIGHT$(T$(X),1)="S" THEN X9=CVS(X1$)
                                        GOTO 1565
1555    IF RIGHT$(T$(X),1)="D" THEN X9=CVD(X1$)
                                        GOTO 1565
1560    GOTO 1570
1565    X1=X1+8
        GOSUB 80
        PRINT X9
        GOTO 1575
1570    X1=X1+8
        GOSUB 80
        PRINT X1$
1575    X1=X1-8
1580 NEXT X
1585 X1$="To DELETE enter DELETE CODE"
        GOSUB 235
```

```
            GOSUB 80
            PRINT "?"
1590 D1$=INPUT$(3)
            IF D1$<>DL$ THEN X3$="INVALID CODE"
            GOSUB 185
            RETURN
1595 A$=STRING$(25," ")
1600 LSET B$=A$
            PUT #1,R
            CLOSE
            X3$="Record Deleted"
            GOSUB 185
            RETURN

1605 '
1610 X5=1
1615 CLOSE
1620 PRINT CS$;
            X1$="Repack Routine - This routine repacks the Database"
            GOSUB 235
1625 PRINT
            PRINT
1630 PRINT BC$
            INPUT "FILE TO REPACK ";F$
1632 PRINT CO$;
1635 IF LEN(F$)=0 THEN RETURN
1640 ON ERROR GOTO 2345
1645 OPEN "I",1,DK$+F$+".DAT"
1650 CLOSE
1655 OPEN "R",1,DK$+F$+".DAT"
1660 FIELD #1,255 AS B$
1665 FOR Y%=1 TO LOF(1)
1670     GET #1,Y%
         A$=B$
         IF LEN(A$)<20 THEN A=LEN(A$) ELSE A=20
1672     IF LEFT$(A$,A)=STRING$(A," ") THEN GOSUB 1680
1675 NEXT Y%
1679 CLOSE:RETURN
1680 FOR X%=Y% TO LOF(1)-1
1682     GET #1,X%+1
         A$=B$
         PUT #1,X%
         LSET B$=STRING$(255," ")
         PUT #1,X%+1
1684 NEXT X%
1685 RETURN
```

and then prints the screen mask and the heading for the user. Line 1485 is the call to the subroutine that will get the filename, open the file and fill the data arrays.

Line 1500 opens the database file, and then line 1510 gets the number of the record to be deleted. If the user enters a zero for a record number here, the routine is terminated and he is returned to the menu. After getting the record data, the program will display the first three fields of data so that the user can make sure it is this record that he actually wants to delete.

To delete it, he must enter the correct code called for in line 1585. If the correct code is not entered, an error message is printed in line 1590 and the user is returned to the menu. If the correct code is entered, the first 25 bytes are blanked out. If the record length is less than 25 bytes, the entire record is blanked. The routine is then terminated, and the user is returned to the menu. The routine will only erase one record at a time. This helps prevent errors by ensuring that each record deleted was supposed to be deleted.

Line 1615 again ensures that the files are all closed; line 1620 tells the user he is in the repack routine. Line 1630 asks for the name of the file to repack. Line 1645 determines whether the file exists. Because no manipulations of data at the field level take place here, it is not necessary to consult the data dictionary. It is therefore not loaded in.

Lines 1665 to 1675 form a loop that checks each record for the existence of the delete flag. If the flag is found, control is passed to the routine in lines 1680 through 1685. This routine will "bubble up" the good records and move the deleted ones to the bottom of the file. If you have the ability to move the EOF and LOF pointers in your BASIC, move them to the position of the last good record after this routine is done. If you can't, you will find yourself with a file of the same length as the original one, but with all the deleted records at the end. Thus you can look at the last record when you want to add a record to the database, and use the change routines to convert this from a deleted record to a good record. To create a new database file that doesn't have any delete-flagged records, use the routine to split a file. This routine will be described later in this book.

Chapter 8

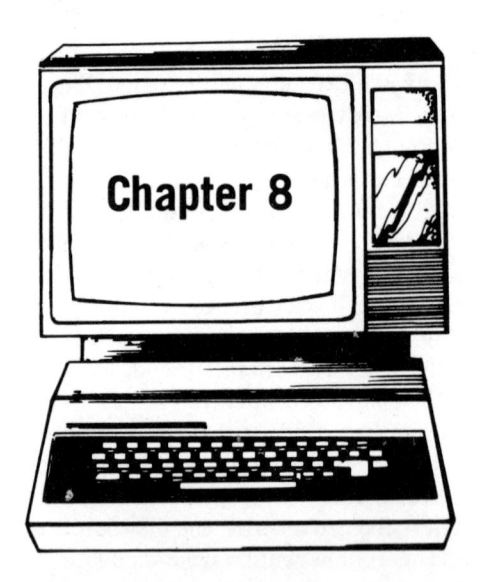

Accessing the Data

It is important that a database allow you to search for data. This chapter will explore the ways of looking for specific data. Then, once the data is found, you will start to look at where you can put it.

RETRIEVING INFORMATION

The heart of any database system is the ease with which you can find the information stored in it. A good system should allow you to make a search of all the records based on multiple criteria. That is, you should be able to ask the program to give you a list of records that meet one or more conditions. In that way you could get all the records that meet criteria A plus all those that meet criteria B.

In this system you will be able to search a record, find out whether or not it meets a condition and then search the same record again to see if it meets any other conditions you have set. It would be simple if you could do this using familiar expressions like *and* or *or*.

In a relational type database, records can be queried based on how value in a particular field or range of fields relates to a given value. Thus you could instruct the program to give you the records in which the value in the name field is equal to a given value of **Greene,** or in which the value in the dues field is greater than the given value of zero.

You need to ask the user what field to check for a value, what the given value to check for will be, and what kind of relationship between the values should be checked for. You then need to ascertain whether or not the user wishes to check the value of the same field or any of the other fields for a relationship with the same value or a different given value. The program must then go through the records one by one and do the checking. The program must also disregard any record that has been flagged as deleted.

This seems to be a tall order. The relational system must check each and every record to determine which fields meet the conditions that have been set. This is bound to slow down the query process to a certain degree. The greatest time loss occurs in two areas: one is the speed of disk accessing, which can be improved by going to faster disk drives or by going to a double density recording system. The second is in the area of conversion from the strings recorded on the disk to the values used by the program. Here little can be done because this is a result of the design of the BASIC in use. A computer with a faster CPU time may help here. You can also speed up the process by using a BASIC like CBASIC, which allows you to specify a larger than required disk buffer. If the disk buffer holds four records at a time, BASIC can process them just about four times as fast. You will have to consult your manual to see if this is available or not. If it is, remember that the space you take up for the larger disk buffer, will be subtracted from that available to your program for other purposes. For the purpose of this program, it is assumed that you cannot change the disk buffer from the 255 byte size that is typical of microcomputers.

You already have field descriptors with which the user can identify the field, and he will also supply the value to be searched for. What can be used to signify the desired relationship between the value in the field and the given value? You must use something that the computer can understand. One suggestion is to allow the user to enter complete words like *equal to*, *greater than*, *less than* and *not equal to*. I have found though, that the more you allow the user to enter, the greater the chance of error. There are a number of signs that the operator can use that are also understood by the computer. These are the relational operators described in your users' manual.

Most BASICs use a table similar to the following:

SYMBOL	MEANING
=	equal to
<	less than
>	greater than
< >	not equal to
≥ =	less than or equal to
≤ >	greater than or equal to

There is one other very useful function that would be desirable in the system. It would be the operator that would allow us to check for the presence of a specific group of characters anywhere within a field. Then you could use one of the fields to store the titles of several songs, and use this function to search for the occurrence of a particular song title in the group. Such a function is available in most BASICs and is called the instring function. Check your manual to determine the proper syntax for your system. In this program the $ symbol will be used to designate this function.

Now there is a way for the operator to indicate the relationship between a field and a given value. What if you want to allow him to indicate that there are other fields whose values must also be checked? You can do this by allowing him to use the words *and* and *or*, and having the program check for these values also.

Figure 8-1 shows this process in flowchart form. Listing 12 shows the code.

In an earlier listing you saw the use of a logical operator using the EOF construct. It was used to tell the program when the end-of-file marker had been detected so that the program would break out of a routine that read in sequential data without an error being detected. In the query section you will see the simulation of such a function. This is done by setting up a value for a true or false condition in line 1706. Notice also that the variable name is over two characters long. Extended Microsoft BASIC will allow the use of variable names up to 40 characters long. In some other versions you are restricted to use of two character names. In still others, you may use more than two, but only the first two characters are recognized. In the version this program is written in, all 40 characters are significant. This is a great boon to serious programmers, as a variable name of FIELD. DESCRIPTOR is much more readable than F$. However, if I had used the longer variables throughout this program, the translation to lesser forms of BASIC would be difficult indeed. I did do it in this section to show that it can and should be done, and also to make the logic more easily understood. If you are using a BASIC that requires two character variables, the variables TR and FA may be used in place of TRUE and FALSE.

```
              ----------------------------------
              ! Set true and false flags       !
              ----------------------------------
                              !
                              !
              ----------------------------------
              ! Clear variables                !
              ----------------------------------
                              !
                              !
              ----------------------------------
              ! Print screen mask              !
              ----------------------------------
                              !
                              !
              ----------------------------------
              ! Get filename and read in data  !
              ! dictionary                     !
              ----------------------------------
                              !
                              !
              ----------------------------------
              ! Print available field names    !
              ----------------------------------
                              !
                              !
              ----------------------------------
              ! Get field descriptor for field !
              ! to check value of              !
              ----------------------------------
                              !
                              !
              ----------------------------------
              ! Get operator (given value)     !
              ! to check against               !
              ----------------------------------
                              !
                              !
              ----------------------------------
              ! Get action (relationship) to   !
              ! govern query                   !
              ----------------------------------
                              !
                              !
              ----------------------------------
              ! Get AND OR if user is          !
              ! selecting another field for    !
              ! same search                    !
              ----------------------------------
                              !
```

Fig. 8-1. Chart of the routines in Listing 12.

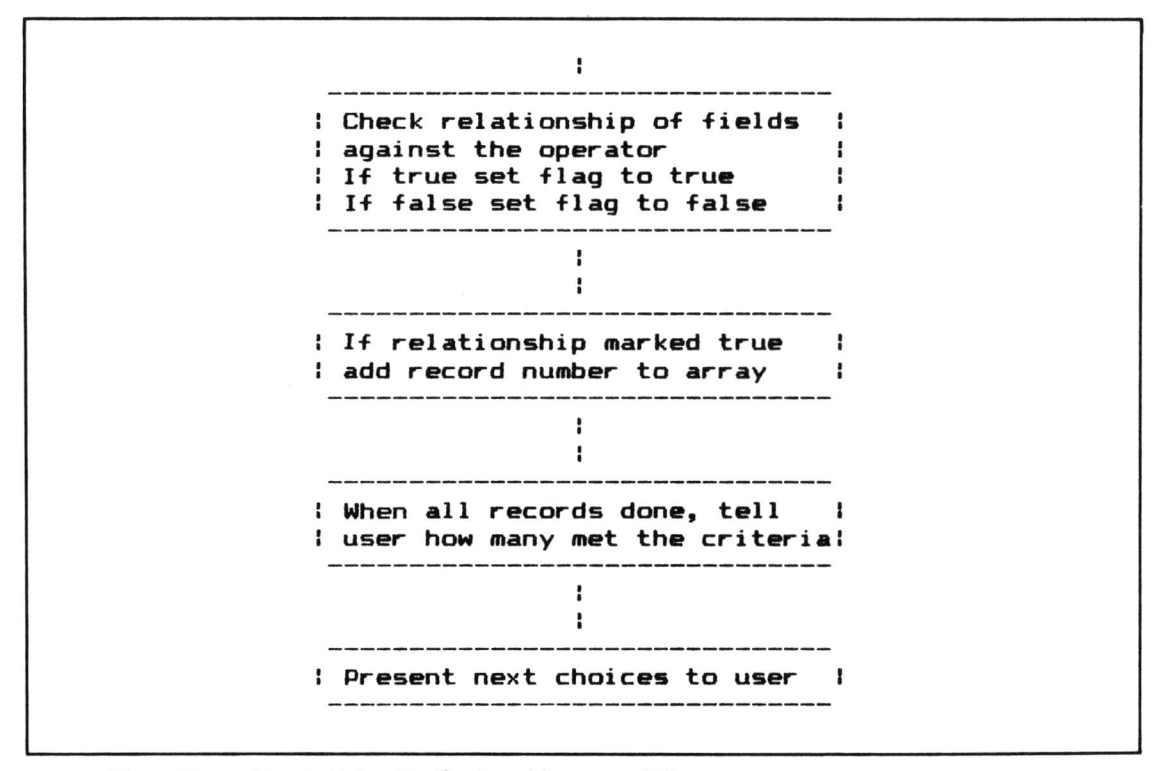

```
            :
------------------------------
: Check relationship of fields :
: against the operator         :
: If true set flag to true     :
: If false set flag to false   :
------------------------------
            :
            :
------------------------------
: If relationship marked true  :
: add record number to array   :
------------------------------
            :
            :
------------------------------
: When all records done, tell  :
: user how many met the criteria:
------------------------------
            :
            :
------------------------------
: Present next choices to user :
------------------------------
```

Fig. 8-1. Chart of the routines in Listing 12. (Continued from page 60.)

LISTING TWELVE
==============

```
1705 '
1706 TRUE=1
     FALSE=0
1710 AN$=""
     OP$=""
     N$=""
     N=0
1715 PRINT CS$;
     PRINT RV$;"Query";ER$TAB(50);RV$;DA$;ER$
     PRINT
1720 PRINT "Filename:-";TAB(40)"Date of last Update:-"
1721 PRINT BC$
1725 X1=171
     X2=7
     X3=0
     X4=0
     GOSUB 85
     F$=X0$
     IF X0#=-1 THEN RETURN
1726 PRINT CO$;
1730 ON ERROR GOTO 2345
```

```
1735 CLOSE
     OPEN "I",1,F$
1740 INPUT #1,F$,DI$,DB$,F
1745 ERASE F$,T$,MI,L,MA,SA,Q$
1750 DIM F$(F),T$(F),MI(F),L(F),MA(F),SA(F),Q$(3,F)
1755 FOR X=1 TO F
1760     INPUT #1,F$(X),T$(X),MI(X),L(X),SA(X),MA(X)
1765 NEXT X
1770 CLOSE
1772 GOSUB 3060
1775 X1=222
     GOSUB 80
     PRINT DB$
1780 OPEN "R",1,DK$+F$+".DAT"
1785 FIELD #1,255 AS B$
1790 Z=1
1795 PRINT
     PRINT
1797 PRINT "Field Descriptor"
     PRINT "Operator"
     PRINT "Action"
     PRINT "AND/OR"
1798 PRINT BC$
1799 FOR L4%=1 TO F
1800     X1=417
         GOSUB 2340
         X2=4
         X3=0
         X4=0
         GOSUB 85
         Q$(0,L4%)=X0$
         IF X0#=-1 THEN 1715
1805     GOSUB 735
         IF X0=-1 THEN 1800 ELSE X=X5%
1825     IF T$(X)="A" THEN X2=L(X) ELSE X2=10

1830     X1=497
         GOSUB 2340
         X3=MI(X)
         X4=MA(X)
         GOSUB 85
         Q$(1,L4%)=X0$
1835     X1=577
         GOSUB 2340
         X2=2
         X3=0
         X4=0
         GOSUB 85
         Q$(2,L4%)=X0$
1836     AN$=Q$(2,L4%)

1840     IF AN$<>"=" AND AN$<>"$" AND AN$<>"<>" AND AN$<>">" AND AN$<>"
         AND AN$<>"<=" AND AN$<>">=" THEN X3$="OUT OF RANGE"
         GOSUB 185
```

```
              GOTO 1835
1841     X1=657
         GOSUB 2340
         X2=3
         X3=0
         X4=0
         GOSUB 85
         Q$(3,L4%)=X0$
1842     IF X0$="" THEN 1845
1843 NEXT L4%

1845 IF AD=1 THEN 1865
1850 ON ERROR GOTO 2345
1855 ERASE R
1860 DIM R(LOF(1)+1)
1862 Z=1
1865 Y1=1
1870 GET #1,Y1
1875 A$=B$
1880 FLAG%=FALSE
1885 FOR L4%=1 TO F
1890     GOSUB 2000
1895     IF Q$(3,L4%)="AND" AND FLAG%=FALSE THEN 1955
1900     IF Q$(3,L4%)="OR" AND FLAG%=TRUE THEN 1955
1905     IF Q$(3,L4%)="" THEN 1955
1950 NEXT L4%

1955 IF FLAG%=TRUE THEN R(Z)=Y1:Z=Z+1
1960 Y1=Y1+1
         IF Y1<=LOF(1) THEN 1870
1965 PRINT
         PRINT" THERE ARE ";Z-1;" RECORDS THAT SATISFY THE QUERY"
1970 IF Z-1=0 THEN 1799
1975 X1$="Type 'P' to print records"
         GOSUB 235
         X2=1
         X3=0
         X4=0
         GOSUB 85
         IF X0#=-1 THEN RETURN ELSE GOTO 2115
1980 RETURN

2000 X0$=Q$(0,L4%)
         GOSUB 735
2001 N2$=RIGHT$(T$(X5%),1)
2003 N3$=Q$(1,L4%)
2005 N1$=MID$(A$,SA(X5%),L(X5%))
2006 IF T$(X5%)="A" THEN 2020
2007 IF N2$="I" THEN N1=CVI(N1$)
                              N=VAL(N3$)
2008 IF N2$="S" THEN N1=CVS(N1$)
                              N=VAL(N3$)
2009 IF N2$="D" THEN N1=CVD(N1$)
                              N=VAL(N3$)
2010 AN$=Q$(2,L4%)
```

```
2011 IF AN$="=" AND N=N1 THEN 2019
2012 IF AN$="<" AND N<N1 THEN 2019
2013 IF AN$=">" AND N>N1 THEN 2019
2014 IF AN$="<>" AND N<>N1 THEN 2019
2015 IF AN$="<=" AND N<=N1 THEN 2019
2016 IF AN$=">=" AND N>=N1 THEN 2019
2018 FLAG%=FALSE
     RETURN
2019 FLAG%=TRUE
     RETURN
2020 N$=Q$(1,L4%)
2025 AN$=Q$(2,L4%)
2026 IF AN$<>"$" THEN N1$=LEFT$(N1$,LEN(N$)) ELSE 2070
2030 IF AN$="=" AND N$=N1$ THEN FLAG%=TRUE
                               RETURN
2035 IF AN$="<" AND N$<N1$ THEN FLAG%=TRUE
                               RETURN
2040 IF AN$=">" AND N$>N1$ THEN FLAG%=TRUE
                               RETURN
2045 IF AN$="<>" AND N$<>N1$ THEN FLAG%=TRUE
                                 RETURN
2050 IF AN$="<=" AND N$<=N1$ THEN FLAG%=TRUE
                                 RETURN
2055 IF AN$=">=" AND N$>=N1$ THEN FLAG%=TRUE
                                 RETURN
2060 FLAG%=FALSE
     RETURN
2070 P%=INSTR(N1$,N$)
     IF P%>0 THEN 2019 ELSE 2018
```

The setting of the values to 1 and 0 is not quite the same as is used in the real error-detection case. This version of BASIC takes an expression to be false if its value is negative, and true if it is positive. To hold with convention the false value should be set at −1. However, since this is a simulation, it doesn't matter.

After setting the value of the true and false flags, line 1710 clears out the values of some of the variables that we will be using. Lines 1715 through 1721 write the screen mask and get the name of the file to query. If the filename is not available, line 1730 traps the resulting error. If the filename is correct, the data dictionary information is obtained in lines 1735 to 1770.

After printing out the range of field descriptors to be chosen from in line 1772, the file is opened and another mask is printed in line 1797.

In order for the program to know what values to check, you must get the user to enter some information. The user is prompted for the field descriptor to tell the field to check, the value to check against it, and the method of checking. Finally he is asked if there are any more checks to be made on this same record. If the user enters **AND** or **OR**, the program will loop to get another set of criteria to meet. The maximum number of times this loop occurs is the number of different fields that there are in the record. If there are ten fields, the user can ask for ten sets of criteria. There is nothing in the program to restrict the query to being set at only one condition per field. The user may instruct the program to check the same field in ten different ways if so desired.

Line 1840 makes sure that the action entered is a valid one, and the values entered for the field descriptors are also checked to make sure that they represent an existing field.

In line 1855 the array R is erased. Some BASICs, such as Radio Shack, do not allow this. If this is the case, you will have to take steps to zero out the values in this array. The array is used to store the record number of any record retrieved during the query process. Since the array may have been previously filled by an earlier query on the same or a different file, it is necessary to remove the values from the earlier search. This is done easily by the use of the erase statement and then by redimensioning the arrays in line 1860.

Line 1862-1890 set up the search routine. The data file is read in, record by record, and control is passed to line 2000. Lines 2000-2070 check the contents of the fields based on the user entries and determine whether or not the conditions have been met. If they have, the true flag is set. Otherwise, the false flag is set. When control returns to the routine at line 1895, the program will see whether or not more checks are required. If they are, control is passed back; otherwise the record number is entered into the array or the record is skipped as required.

The *or* and *and* constructs are set up so that the determination of true or false is made at the earliest opportunity to save time. If the *and* construct is required, the false flag is set as soon as a condition fails to match and the rest of the conditions, if any, are skipped. If the *or* construct is used, the true flag is set as soon as one of the conditions are met, and again the rest, if any are left, are skipped.

The evaluation then is from the first to the last entered, or left to right, in accordance with commonly accepted rules of implementation. This allows the user to choose almost any specific records desired; for example, all the club members who have Apples and have not paid their dues!!

With the exception of the variable names of four characters each, this routine should run on any of the disk based microcomputers.

SUBDIVIDING FILES

Now that you have a method of searching the database, you have two more things left to consider. One is how to present the information to the user, and the other is how to divide files into smaller ones. Every disk has a limit as to how much it can store. Murphy's laws dictate that aside from the absolutes of death and taxes, you must eventually face the time when the information you collect exceeds the storage of the medium on which to store it!

The storage problem will be considered first. You will recall I mentioned that in addition to deleting a record by marking it as empty, you could instruct the program to construct a new file, leaving out the marked records. Rather than just having it leave out deleted records, it made better sense to have it able to construct a file that would let you determine which records to include. The query section of the program already gives us the ability to select a group of records from all those in the database. It stores the record numbers so you can have only those records written to the disk in a new file. In this manner you can break-up files that are getting unmanageable.

You could, if desired, include a routine to flag the records that you have moved because they were deleted, but it would serve no practical purpose. In addition, it could be dangerous to do so, as vital information could be lost if the new file failed to write correctly. The choice is yours though. I did not want to include such a routine, but you may wish to.

When you write out the new file, you should write it out to a new disk and also copy over the parameters file from the present disk, giving it the same name as the new data file. If you are using a variable length file where you are forced by the operating system to keep track of the number of records in the file, you will have to update this information also. You are not required to do so when the record length is 255 bytes because the LOF function will do it for you by returning the number of the last record written to.

The flowchart of the routines to write the new file to disk, shown in Fig. 8-2, is simple. The code is presented in Listing 13.

Line 2115 sends control to the menu in line 2120. There, the program asks for a selection. If the selection is for the disk routines, control goes to line 2116, where the data file to read from, #1, and the data file to write to, #2, are opened. All the records that you have noted in the R array are

```
+-------------------------------+
! After the query process,      !
! include in the submenu the    !
! option to write a file to     !
! the disk                      !
+-------------------------------+
                :
                :
+-------------------------------+
! Get a record                  !
! from the record numbers       !
! stored in the R array         !
+-------------------------------+
                :
                :
+-------------------------------+
! Write it to the new file      !
+-------------------------------+
                :
                :
+-------------------------------+
! Continue till done            !
+-------------------------------+
                :
                :
+-------------------------------+
! Close and return to submenu   !
+-------------------------------+
```

Fig. 8-2. Chart of the routines in Listing 13.

```
                    LISTING THIRTEEN
                    ================

2115 GOTO 2120
2116 CLOSE
        OPEN "R",1,DK$+F$+".DAT"
        OPEN "R",2,F1$
                FIELD #1,255 AS B$
                FIELD #2,255 AS C$
2117 FOR Y=1 TO Z-1
        GET #1,R(Y)
        A$=B$
        LSET C$=A$
        PUT #2,Y
        NEXT Y
2118 CLOSE
        F2$=F$
        F$=XO$
        GOSUB 800
        F$=F2$
```

```
          OPEN "R",1,DK$+F$+".DAT"
          FIELD #1,255 AS B$

2120 X1$="1 = SCREEN, 2 = PRINTER, 3 = SORT, 4 = DISK"
          GOSUB 235
```

transferred to the new file in line 2117. Line 2118 opens the original file again and control goes back to the menu.

As you can see, the code is not complicated.

No information has been lost, and by returning to the menu, the program can now sort and print the information for the user.

Chapter 9

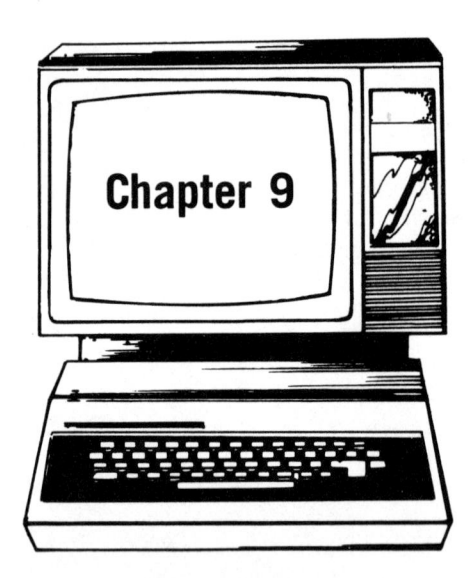

Reporting the Data

With so much information in the database files, it becomes important to be able to obtain the information that you want and to present it in a logical fashion. Reports should only contain information that is of value to the user for the purpose that he has in mind. This chapter looks at how to design a report format, and also how to sort the information. You will also see how you can use some functions of BASIC to trap errors that may occur when the program is running. Some of the errors are intentional—most are not!

There are at least two reporting options that should be offered to a database system user. First the system should be able to print out all the accumulated records in the database showing all the values in each record. This will provide the user with the ability to review the data to find errors. Secondly, the user should be able to specify the fields whose values he wishes to have printed out and determine the order in which those values should be printed. Inherent in this second objective is the desirability of being able to give each field a new name that is specific to a report. If the information is numeric, the user should be able to have it formatted so that decimal points and dollar signs can be aligned. Finally, having done all this, the user should be able to save a particular format and use it at a later date.

The implementation of the first point is easy. Since you can access the R array, which holds the desired record numbers, you merely have to read in each record from the disk and print out each field value along with its field descriptor, line by line. Alternatively, you could skip the use of the R array altogether and start at the first record and continue until the last one is done.

The second form is a little harder to do. You must find a way to assemble information about each field that you want to print. You will have to keep track of what the field descriptor is so that the program can find the information. You will need to know what the user wishes to call the field in the report, and where he wants it to go. Perhaps the easiest place to start in allowing the user some

```
      ---------------------------------
      : Display menu to user           :
      : 1 = Screen (print to screen)   :
      : 2 = Printer (Print to printer) :
      : 3 = Sort (Sort output)         :
      : 4 = Disk (Output to disk)      :
      ---------------------------------
                      :
                      :
      ---------------------------------
      : If screen selected open TT:    :
      : as the device                  :
      : If printer selected open AT:   :
      : as the device                  :
      : If sort - go-to sort routine   :
      : If disk print file to disk     :
      ---------------------------------
                      :
                      :
      ---------------------------------
      : Select a formatted report or   :
      : a general (page) report        :
      ---------------------------------
                      :
                      :
      ---------------------------------
      : If a page report, print out    :
      : each records values            :
      ---------------------------------
                      :
                      :
      ---------------------------------
      : If format report get from the  :
      : user,                          :
      : the report file (if available) :
      :   or                           :
      : report name                    :
      : Fields to print                :
      : New field names                :
      : Where to put field value       :
      : Format to print in (Numeric)   :
      ---------------------------------
                   ------
             S/R : 2445 :
                   ------
                      :
      ---------------------------------
      : Get report name to save report :
      : format under                   :
      ---------------------------------
                      :
                      :
      ---------------------------------
      :  Save report                   :
      ---------------------------------
                      :
                      :
      ---------------------------------
      : Do formated report             :
      ---------------------------------
                      :
                      :
      ---------------------------------
      : Back to menu                   :
      ---------------------------------
```

Fig. 9-1. Chart of the routines in Listing 14.

LISTING FOURTEEN
================

```
2122 S2=0
2125 X2=1
        X3=1
        X4=4
        GOSUB 85
        CH=X0#
        IF X0#=-1 THEN RETURN
2126 IF CH=4 THEN X1$="ENTER FILENAME TO BE SAVED UNDER"
        GOSUB 235
        X2=7
        X3=0
        X4=0
        GOSUB 85
        IF X0#=-1 THEN 2120
2127 IF CH=4 THEN F1$=X0$
        F1$=DK$+F1$+".DAT"
        GOTO 2116
2130 IF CH=3 THEN GOSUB 2405
        GOTO 2120
2135 IF CH=1 THEN F1$="TT:" ELSE F1$="AT:"
2140 IF CH=1 THEN PRINT CS$;
2144 IF CH=1 THEN WI=80
        GOTO 2150
2145 X1$="PAGE WIDTH ?"
        GOSUB 235
        X2=3
        X3=1
        X4=250
        GOSUB 85
        WI=X0#
        IF X0#=-1 THEN 2120
2150 X1$="1=FORMAT REPORT, 2=PAGE REPORT"
        GOSUB 235
        X2=1
        X3=1
        X4=2
        GOSUB 85
        C1=X0#
        IF C1=2 THEN 2160
2152 IF X0#=-1 THEN 2145
2155 GOSUB 2445
2157 IF X0#=-1 THEN 2150
2160 OPEN "O",2,F1$
        PG=1
2162 IF CH=2 THEN PRINT #2,CHR$(18)
        IF WI>80 THEN PRINT #2,CHR$(15)
2165 IF CH=2 AND C1=1 THEN OUT 252,12
2175 IF CH=1 THEN PRINT CS$
2180 PRINT #2,"FILE: ";F$;TAB(40)"DATE: ";DA$
2185 PRINT #2,"LAST UPDATE: ";DB$
2190 IF WI<1 THEN WI=80
```

```
              PRINT #2,STRING$(WI,95)
2195 PRINT #2,"RECORDS REQUESTED:"
2200 PRINT #2,
              PRINT #2,
              GOSUB 2800
2205 FOR Y=1 TO Z-1
2210    IF C1=2 THEN 2245
2215    GET #1,R(Y)
        A$=B$
2220    GOSUB 2570
        LI=LI+1
        GOSUB 2785
2225 NEXT Y

2230 IF TO=1 THEN PRINT #2,ELSE GOTO 2305
2235 PRINT #2,
        PRINT #2,STRING$(WI,95)
        GOSUB 3020
2240 GOTO 2305

2245 FOR Y=1 TO Z-1
2250     GET #1,R(Y)
         A$=B$
2255     PRINT #2,"REC #:-";R(Y)
2260     FOR X=1 TO F
2265             IF T$(X)="A" THEN PRINT #2,F$(X),MID$(A$,SA(X),L(X))
2270             IF RIGHT$(T$(X),1)="I" THEN
                        N=CVI(MID$(A$,SA(X),L(X)))
                        PRINT #2,F$(X),N
2275             IF RIGHT$(T$(X),1)="S" THEN
                        N=CVS(MID$(A$,SA(X),L(X)))
                        PRINT #2,F$(X),N
2280             IF RIGHT$(T$(X),1)="D" THEN
                        N=CVD(MID$(A$,SA(X),L(X)))
                        PRINT #2,F$(X),N
2285     NEXT X
2290     PRINT #2,
         PRINT #2
2295     IF CH=2 THEN 2300
2296     IF CH<>2 AND CH<>4 THEN CLOSE #2
         OPEN "O",1,F1$
         INPUT XO$
2300 NEXT

2305 PRINT #2
        CLOSE #2
2307 PRINT
2309 IF CH=4 THEN PRINT CS$
2310 INPUT "PRINTOUT COMPLETE - TYPE 'RETURN' TO CONTINUE";XO$
2312 PRINT CS$
2315 X1$="A=PRINT AGAIN, P=NEW HEADINGS, R=RESORT, E=EXIT"
        GOSUB 235
2320 X2=1
        X3=0
        X4=0
```

```
              GOSUB 85
              IF X0$="" THEN RETURN
2325 IF X0$="A" THEN 2160
2330 IF X0$="P" THEN 2135
2335 IF X0$="R" THEN 2115 ELSE RETURN
2340 GOSUB 80
        PRINT E$+"K"
        RETURN

2345 IF ERR=53 AND ERL=1045 THEN X3$="NO SUCH FILE"
                       GOSUB 185
                       RESUME 1035
2347 IF ERR=5 AND ERL=2562 THEN RESUME 2563
2350 IF ERR=5 AND ERL=580 THEN RESUME 585
2355 IF ERR=5 AND ERL=1855 THEN RESUME 1860
2360 IF ERR=5 AND ERL=2446 THEN RESUME 2447
2365 IF ERR=53 AND ERL=1645 THEN X3$="NO SUCH FILE"
                       GOSUB 185
                       RESUME 1630
2370 IF ERR=53 AND ERL=1735 THEN X3$="NO SUCH FILE"
                       GOSUB 185
                       RESUME 1725
2375 IF ERR=5 AND ERL=1910 THEN RESUME 1920
2380 IF ERR=5 AND ERL=1060 THEN RESUME 1065
2385 IF ERR=5 AND ERL=1745 THEN RESUME 1750
2390 IF ERR=10 AND ERL=1860 THEN RESUME 1865
2395 ON ERROR GOTO 0

2400 '
2405 X1$="FIELD TO SORT ON"
         GOSUB 235
         X2=4
         X3=0
         X4=0
         GOSUB 85
         K$=X0$
         IF X0#=-1 THEN ERASE TS$
         RETURN
2410 GOSUB 735
         IF X0=-1 THEN 2405 ELSE Y%=X5%
2430 X1$="1=HIGHEST AT TOP, 2=LOWEST AT TOP"
         GOSUB 235
         X2=1
         X3=1
         X4=2
         GOSUB 85
         IF X0#=-1 THEN 2405
2432 IF S2=0 THEN S2=1
         GOTO 2435
2433 GOSUB 3430
         GOTO 2440
2435 GOSUB 2830
2440 GOTO 2405
2445 ON ERROR GOTO 2345
2446 ERASE F1$
```

```
2447 DIM F1$(3,F)
2450 PRINT CS$;
     PRINT RV$;"REPORT FORMATING";ER$
2452 CLOSE #3
     X1$="REPORT FORMAT FILENAME TO READ ?"
     GOSUB 235
     X2=9
     X3=0
     X4=0
     GOSUB 85
     IF X0#=-1 THEN GOTO 2456 ELSE GOSUB 3350
     GOTO 2560
2455 PRINT
     PRINT
     PRINT
2456 GOSUB 3060
2460 PRINT "REPORT HEADING"
2465 X1=337
     X2=40
     X3=0
     X4=0
     GOSUB 85
     RH$=X0$
     IF X0#=-1 THEN RETURN
2470 X6=480
2490 F1=0
     LI=0
     PG=1
2492 X1=400
     GOSUB 80
     PRINT "FIELD      SUBHEADING            TAB>4!     FORMAT"
2493 PRINT STRING$(80,95)
2495 FOR X%=1 TO F
2505     X1=X6+(80*X%)
         X2=4
         X3=0
         X4=0
         GOSUB 85
         F1$(0,X%)=X0$
         IF X0#=-1 THEN 2560
2510     GOSUB 735
         IF X0=-1 THEN 2505 ELSE Y4%=X5%
2530     X1=X1+10
         X2=12
         X3=0
         X4=0
         GOSUB 85
         F1$(1,X%)=X0$
2535     X1=X1+31
         X2=3
         X3=5
         X4=WI
         GOSUB 85
         F1$(2,X%)=X0$
2540     IF T$(Y4%)="A" THEN 2550
```

```
2545        X1=X1+12
            X2=12
            X3=0
            X4=0
            GOSUB 85
            F1$(3,X%)=X0$
2550        F1=F1+1
2555 NEXT X%

2560 PRINT
            INPUT " TOTALS   (Y/N) ";X0$
            IF X0$="Y" OR X0$="y" THEN T0=1 ELSE T0=0
2561 ON ERROR GOTO 2345
2562 ERASE T9
2563 DIM T9(F1)
2564 X1$="REPORT FILENAME TO SAVE ?"
            GOSUB 235
            X2=9
            X3=0
            X4=0
            GOSUB 85
            IF X0#<>-1 THEN GOSUB 3365
2565 X0#=0
            X0$=""
            RETURN
2570 PRINT #2,
            PRINT #2,R(Y);
2572 FOR Y%=1 TO F1
2575     IF F1$(0,Y%)="" THEN RETURN
2580     FOR X=1 TO F
2585     IF F1$(0,Y%)=F$(X) THEN 2600
2590     NEXT X
2595     RETURN
2600        '
2601     IF T$(X)="A" THEN PRINT #2,TAB(VAL(F1$(Y%)));MID$(A$,
         )); SA(X),L(X
2602     IF F1$(3,Y%)<>"" THEN GOSUB 3000
                                    GOTO 2620
2605     IF RIGHT$(T$(X),1)="I" THEN N=CVI(MID$(A$,SA(X),L(X)))
              PRINT #2,TAB(VAL(F1$(2,Y%)));N;
              T9(Y%)=T9(Y%)+N
2610     IF RIGHT$(T$(X),1)="S" THEN N=CVS(MID$(A$,SA(X),L(X)))
              PRINT #2,TAB(VAL(F1$(2,Y%)));N;
              T9(Y%)=T9(Y%)+N
2615     IF RIGHT$(T$(X),1)="D" THEN N=CVD(MID$(A$,SA(X),L(X)))
              PRINT #2,TAB(VAL(F1$(2,Y%)));N;
              T9(Y%)=T9(Y%)+N
2620 NEXT Y%
2625 RETURN
```

discretion over where to place the value is to allow him to input a tab value. The program can then translate this value into a column number to start printing the field value at. Finally, you need to know how the user wishes the program to format the value if it is numeric in nature.

In order to keep track of all these things, you will use another array to store the values in. This array will be a string array as all the values required can be represented as strings, but not as numeric values. The program can then use these values to govern its action.

You also need to know how the operating system accesses the printer. In HDOS, the program can open a file called **TT:** for the screen or **AT:** for the printer and thereafter any print statements directed to the channel number that has been opened will be sent to that device. This makes switching easy as either the **TT:** driver or the **AT:** driver will be opened depending on the user's wishes. Other systems require the use of the LPRINT statement to direct printing to the printer. In such a case, duplicate print and LPRINT statements must be made, or some other form of rerouting must be used. TRS-80 Model III allows the changing of a route call to direct output to a printer or the screen. CP/M operating systems can be rerouted by poking the IOBYTE to the appropriate value. To determine what is available for your system, look in your operating manual. Figure 9-1 shows the flowchart of this process. The code is shown in Listing 14.

The subroutine in line 2120 in Listing 13 gives the user four choices. The disk writing routines have been covered already, and the sort routines will be discussed later. The other choices allow the user to direct the output to the screen or the printer.

Line 2122 is a flag that is used by the program to determine the ordering of the sort requirements that will be examined later also. Line 2125 gets the choice from the user and puts it in the variable named CH. Lines 2126-2127 prompt the user for the filename required to store the results on disk. Line 2130 directs the program to the sort routines.

Line 2135 determines whether the output will be written to the screen or to the printer depending on the choice of the user. All output in the report destined for either device is now written to the device opened under the name stored by F1$. If the report is to go to the screen, the device drive **TT:**, which is the HDOS terminal device driver, is loaded into the space provided by channel two. If the printer is desired, the printer driver called **AT:** is loaded. There are many printer drivers available under HDOS. In the early days there were not so many, and in order to get one to work with the HB, which is the development system for this program, I had to use the **AT:** driver. This driver was really developed to run an alternate terminal device, such as a DECWRITER II. Thus the use of the **AT:** driver name. However, all drivers can be renamed into any two character device driver, so it is not a problem to use any of the other printer drivers. Simply call the driver of your choice **AT:** and it will work.

Line 2144 sets the printer width to 80 characters. If your terminal normally uses a width that is different, change this statement to comply. Line 2145 asks the user to input a width value for the list device. Line 2150 allows the user to choose between two formats; either the formatted report in which the user decides which fields are printed where on a line, or the page format report whereby the program outputs each selected record one field value per line. If the formatted report is selected, control is passed to the subroutine at 2445, which will be examined in the next section.

If the page report is selected, line 2160 opens the list device, and lines 2180 to 2200 print out the header information. Lines 2245 to 2285 get each selected record and print out the information line by line. If any conversions are required for numerical values, they are handled in lines 2270-2280. When the printout is complete, the program allows the operator to reprint the information, re-sort it, give new headings to a formatted report, or exit to the main menu.

Lines 2345 to 2395 are examples of the error trapping routines used by the program. Depending on the error that occurred and the line where it happened, the program takes whatever action is required to avoid a crash. Some of the more common errors trapped are attempts to open nonexistent files and the erasing of arrays that haven't yet been dimensioned. If an error that has not been allowed for appears, it will show up in the normal manner via the statement in line 2395. If no error trapping routines are allowed for by your version of BASIC, you must write the routines that may result in errors in such a way that the error conditions will not arise. For example, erasing an array to set the values to zero can be done when you are through using that array. The statements that would redimension it must then also be deleted as well.

Lines 2400 to 2435 set up the sort parameters. The sort routines will start at line 2830.

Line 2445 is the beginning of the routine to allow the user to format his report. Line 2447 dimensions the start by setting up the F1$ array. Next, in line 2452, the user is asked if there is a previously defined report file that he wants to use, and if so, a branch is made to 3350 to read it in. Otherwise he is asked for the name of the report he is about to construct. Next the program will print out a number of questions that will allow the user to identify the field that he wants printed out, the name the field will have for the report, the location on the line to print it, and if it is a numerical value, the type of format he wishes it presented in. If the user enters a null value for the field descriptor. The program assumes he is finished. Otherwise it will loop until all fields have been defined.

Line 2560 asks if the user wishes the numerical columns to be totaled. If he does, the totals will be presented at the conclusion of the report, and formatted in the same manner as the columns they are the totals of. Totals are stored in the T9 array that is dimensioned in line 2563. After defining the report, the user is given the opportunity to save it for later use. Lines 2570 to 2590 read in each record and recover the information in the subroutines at lines 2600-2625 or 3000 depending on whether or not formatted numerical values are required.

The formatted report will be presented on a page-by-page basis with each page numbered. By defining a number of different report formats you can easily call up information and print a variety of reports from the same database file. There is no necessity to print all of the fields, only those that you require. You can choose to print only as many fields as will fit on the longest line allowed by your printer. You cannot squeeze a 200 character line onto a 132 character long line.

Line 2162 contains the CHR$(15) output. This forces an Epson printer to print out in condensed characters. If you are using a different printer, change this line to allow the appropriate command for your printer. The condensed printing is set to occur if a width of more than 80 characters is specified.

Line 2165 puts a form feed character out on port 252, which is the one that is standard as the printer port for Heath/Zenith Equipment. Again you may have to adjust this to your own equipment.

Chapter 10

Sorting and Other Final Touches

This is the final chapter that presents the main code. It will show you how to review how you created a particular file, examine the sorting routines in greater depth, and look at some of the odds and ends that haven't been presented yet. At the end of the chapter, there will be a review of some of the important points to consider when you are converting the program to another system.

REVIEWING THE PARAMETERS

This chapter will look at a way to see what you have used as specifications for your database. This is necessary because after a while you will certainly forget what you have done, and you may want to modify the file later.

In order to do this all you need to do is to access the parameters and print them out. The values should be presented to the user in much the same way as he entered them so that there is no misunderstanding of what relates to what. You can do this easily by first getting the name of the file to look at and then showing the original mask you used when you got the information. Against this mask you will print the values that were entered and the user can easily ascertain what is what. The flowchart is shown in Fig. 10-1. Listing 15 shows the code.

Line 2635 starts off by clearing the screen and printing the heading. Lines 2640-2650 print the rest of the heading and the screen mask. Line 2655 gets the name of the file to read and the routine at 1045 looks after reading the values into the array. Lines 2665-2700 print out each field's parameters as they were entered. After printing out a field, the program pauses waiting for the user to enter a Y to allow it to go to the next field. If the user doesn't enter a Y or y, the process terminates and the program returns to the main menu.

You could add some more code to this routine to get it to list the values to the printer along with the screen. That way you would have a hard copy record in case something happened to the disk with the parameter file on it. Since the database file is liable to be on a separate disk, this is one way to

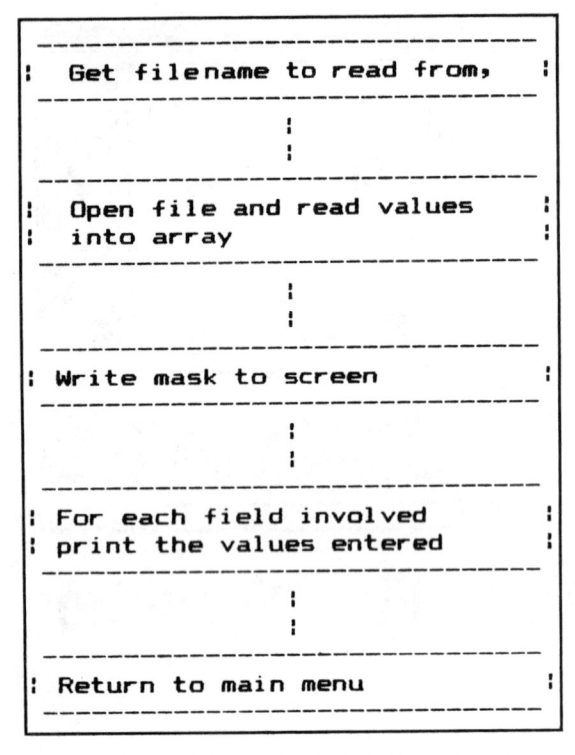

```
┌─────────────────────────────────────┐
│  Get filename to read from,         │
│─────────────────────────────────────│
│                :                    │
│                :                    │
│  Open file and read values          │
│  into array                         │
│─────────────────────────────────────│
│                :                    │
│                :                    │
│  Write mask to screen               │
│─────────────────────────────────────│
│                :                    │
│                :                    │
│  For each field involved            │
│  print the values entered           │
│─────────────────────────────────────│
│                :                    │
│                :                    │
│  Return to main menu                │
└─────────────────────────────────────┘
```

Fig. 10-1. Chart of the routines included in Listing 15.

insure the recovery of the information. The more you store on a disk, the more valuable it becomes. Good hard copy backup can be just as important as good soft copy backup!

SORTING ROUTINES

Computers can do sorting well because it involves repetitive routines. There are as many good sorting routines as there are types of machines, it seems. The best sorting routine would be one that requires little memory space overhead, can sort on the disk, and can do so instantly. If anyone finds such a routine please let me know—I'd like to have it! In practical terms, a sort that can be used with any machine is a compromise. While I have developed a machine language sort for this program that is very fast, it is written specifically for the configuration that I have. Thus it is not practical to publish it for those who aren't using a Heath/Zenith H-8/H-89 or H-90. The sort routine that I have included is in BASIC and should run on any machine that can make use of this database program at all. While not as fast as the machine language version, it is no slouch either. I have sorted in excess of 700

```
                LISTING FIFTEEN
                ===============

2630 '
2635 PRINT CS$;RV$"REVIEW";ER$;TAB(60);RV$;DA$;ER$
2640 PRINT
     PRINT
     PRINT
     PRINT
2645 PRINT " FILENAME   :- ";TAB(40)"DATE CREATED   :-":
     PRINT TAB(40) "DATE OF UPDATE :-"
2650 PRINT STRING$(80,"-")
     PRINT
     GOSUB 330
2655 X1=415
     X2=7
     X3=0
     X4=0
     GOSUB 85
     F$=X0$
     IF X0#=-1 THEN RETURN
2660 CLOSE
     ON ERROR GOTO 2345
     GOSUB 1045
```

```
2665 FOR X=1 TO F
2666     PRINT CO$
2670     X1=738
         GOSUB 80
         PRINT F$(X)
2675     X1=818
         GOSUB 80
         PRINT T$(X)
2680     X1=898
         GOSUB 80
         PRINT MI(X)
2685     X1=778
         GOSUB 80
         PRINT L(X)
2690     X1=938
         GOSUB 80
         PRINT MA(X)
2692     PRINT BC$
2695     PRINT
         PRINT
         PRINT"NEXT (Y/N)"
         INPUT NE$
         IF NE$="Y" OR NE$="y' THEN 2700 ELSE 2705
2700 NEXT
2705 RETURN
```

record in 8 minutes with it. It is a Shell Metzner algorithm that operates in BASIC. The main time hogs are the parts of BASIC that read the records from the disk into memory, and the string conversion required. If your particular BASIC is slow in these areas, the sort is going to be slow for you.

Essentially, the routine first loads the values of the field that you have selected to sort on, from records you have previously selected, into an array. This array is then sorted along with the array holding the record numbers. The value array is then discarded and the ordered record number array is used to determine the order of retrieval of the full records for reporting purposes. The processes make use of the swap function of Microsoft BASIC. This function swaps the array pointers only, not the values, so the sort is not held up by having to copy the values to temporary variables and then to each others place. If you have to use a temporary variable to hold a value in order to swap it, the sort will be slower. Even with all the handicaps of being written in BASIC, the sort is fast enough to be practical for use in this program. If you are using CP/M, you can always add SUPERSORT by Micropro to really make your sorts sing—so to speak!

Figure 10-2 shows the flowchart for the sort routine. Listing 16 shows the code.

In this sort, the idea is to divide the number of items to be sorted into two parts and starting at both ends, work towards the middle and compare as you go. In this manner the list gets sorted much faster than in a bubble sort where a value is simply bubbled up from some place in the list towards the top.

Line 2830 sets the array TS$ to the number of places required to hold all the selected field values. By allowing the user to select a second field to sort on, he is allowed much more flexibility. Since only the field values are stored in the array, you can sort more records than if we use the entire record. You will note though, that there is a finite limit to the sort. At some point you will amass a database file large enough to use up the memory available. You must then use the ability of the program to break up the file into smaller chunks to maintain your sorting ability. An alternative is to provide the program

```
 ----------------------------------
: Set up dimensioned array to     :
: hold value strings of sorting   :
: field                           :
 ----------------------------------
                 :
                 :
 ----------------------------------
: Get value for each record       :
 ----------------------------------
                 :
                 :
 ----------------------------------
: When array all filled up then   :
: do S/M sort                     :
: * Note * record numbers are     :
: sorted in parallel              :
: since both arrays are linked    :
 ----------------------------------
                 :
                 :
 ----------------------------------
: When done set sorted flag and   :
: return to the submenu so that   :
: the user can select a second    :
: sort if desired                 :
 ----------------------------------
                 :
                 :
 ----------------------------------
: If second sort desired then     :
: go through the array and look   :
: at any values which are         :
: identical                       :
: In such a case sort them        :
: based on the values in the      :
: field entered by the user       :
: for the secondary sort          :
 ----------------------------------
                 :
                 :
 ----------------------------------
: Return to menu so user can      :
: select output device            :
 ----------------------------------
```

Fig. 10-2. Chart of the sort routine.

with an interface to another utility that will allow the records to be sorted on the disk. There are lots of these coming out now. Almost every popular computer system has at least one or two. You can sort the database file with one of these utilities and then use the program to select and print those records that you want.

You can also make this sorting routine a separate routine called by the program and thus gives it much more memory to work with. There are many choices open to you.

Line 2840 calls the subroutine at 3500. This routine examines the field value and converts it to a string value if this has not already been done. This is done so as to allow a single string array to hold both string and numeric values.

Line 2855 to 2930 comprise the actual sort. The direction of the sort is chosen by the user, and lines 2885 and 2890 will make the swap, if required, based on the decision of the user.

The secondary sort beginning line 3430 allows the user to select another field to further sort the array. This routine will examine the order resulting from the first sort, and if it finds any two values that are the same, it will reorder them according to the value of the second field. This sort is a straight bubble sort, but it is unlikely that the number of matching values in the first array will be large. The time taken by this method of sorting is not likely to be great.

HOUSEKEEPING SUBROUTINES

There are a number of subroutines in the program that are called in various places. I shall present them now with an explanation of what they do. Since the flowcharting has already described their actions, I will skip that part of the procedure. Listing 17 shows the code for these subroutines.

The first subroutine, beginning at 2935 is a routine to let the user know who wrote the program. While I expect the reader to make use of this program for his own purposes, I would appreciate it if you would kindly allow my name to appear in this section and at the front. This helps protect my copyright, and besides, I like to see my name in print! You will note that the program will cease if

LISTING SIXTEEN

```
2830 DIM TS$(Z-1)
2835 FOR Y=1 TO Z-1
2840     GOSUB 3500
         TS$(Y)=T$
2850 NEXT Y
2855 N%=Z-1
     M%=N%
2860 M%=INT(M%/2)
2865 IF M%=0 THEN RETURN
2870 J%=1
     K%=N%-M%
2875 I%=J%
2880 L%=I%+M%
2885 IF XO#=1 AND T$(Y%)="A" AND TS$(I%)>=TS$(L%)
                     OR
         XO#=1 AND T$(Y%)<>"A" AND VAL(TS$(I%))>=VAL(TS$(L%)) THEN 2920
2890 IF XO#=2 AND T$(Y%)="A" AND TS$(I%)<=TS$(L%)
                     OR
         XO#=2 AND T$(Y%)<>"A" AND VAL(TS$(I%))<=VAL(TS$(L%)) THEN 2920
2895 SWAP TS$(I%),TS$(L%)
2900 SWAP R(I%),R(L%)
2905 I%=I%-M%
2910 IF I%<1 THEN 2920
2915 GOTO 2880
2920 J%=J%+1
2925 IF J%>K% THEN 2860
2930 GOTO 2875

3500 GET #1,R(Y)
     A$=B$
3503 IF T$(Y%)="A" THEN T$=MID$(A$,SA(Y%),L(Y%))
3505 IF T$(Y%)="DI" THEN T$=STR$(CVI(MID$(A$,SA(Y%),L(Y%))))
3510 IF T$(Y%)="DS" THEN T$=STR$(CVS(MID$(A$,SA(Y%),L(Y%))))
3515 IF T$(Y%)="DD" THEN T$=STR$(CVD(MID$(A$,SA(Y%),L(Y%))))
3520 RETURN

3430 ' SECONDARY SORT
3435 FOR Y=1 TO Z-2
3440     IF TS$(Y)=TS$(Y+1) THEN GOSUB 3525
3445 NEXT Y
3450 IF SW=1 THEN SW=0
     GOTO 3435
3455 RETURN

3525 GOSUB 3500
     T1$=T$
     Y=Y+1
     GOSUB 3500
     T2$=T$
     Y=Y-1
3530 IF XO#=1 AND T$(Y%)="A" AND T1$>=T2$
```

81

```
                        OR
         XO#=1 AND T$(Y%)<>"A" AND VAL(T1$)>=VAL(T2$) THEN RETURN
3535 IF XO#=2 AND T$(Y%)="A" AND T1$<=T2$
                        OR
         XO#=2 AND T$(Y%)<>"A" AND VAL(T1$)<=VAL(T2$) THEN RETURN
3540 SWAP TS$(Y),TS$(Y+1)
         SWAP R(Y),R(Y+1)
         SW=1
         RETURN
```

LISTING SEVENTEEN
==================

```
2785 IF LI<50 THEN RETURN
2790 PRINT #2,
         IF CH<>4 THEN CLOSE 2
         OPEN "O",2,F1$
2795 OUT 252,12
         PRINT #2,
         PRINT #2,
2800 PRINT #2,TAB((WI-LEN(RH$))/2);RH$;TAB(WI-10);"PAGE ";PG
2805 PRINT #2,
         PRINT #2,
2807 PRINT #2,"REC";
2810 FOR X8%=1 TO F1
2815 PRINT #2,TAB(VAL(F1$(2,X8%)));F1$(1,X8%);
2820 NEXT
2825 PRINT #2,
         PRINT #2,STRING$(WI,95)
         LI=1
         PG=PG+1
         RETURN

2935 PRINT CS$
         PRINT RV$;"COPYRIGHT 1980 BY"
2940 PRINT "GREG GREENE, 2022 DOUGLAS STREET"
2945 PRINT "VICTORIA, B.C. CANADA V8T 4L1"
2950 PRINT "PROGRAM MUST BE RE-RUN NOW"
2955 END

3000 IF RIGHT$(T$(X),1)="I" THEN N=CVI(MID$(A$,SA(X),L(X)))
         PRINT #2,TAB(VAL(F1$(2,Y%))) USING F1$(3,Y%);N;
         T9(Y%)=T9(Y%)+N
3005 IF RIGHT$(T$(X),1)="S" THEN N=CVS(MID$(A$,SA(X),L(X)))
         PRINT #2,TAB(VAL(F1$(2,Y%))) USING F1$(3,Y%);N;
         T9(Y%)=T9(Y%)+N
3010 IF RIGHT$(T$(X),1)="D" THEN N=CVD(MID$(A$,SA(X),L(X)))
         PRINT #2,TAB(VAL(F1$(2,Y%))) USING F1$(3,Y%);N;
         T9(Y%)=T9(Y%)+N
3015 RETURN

3020 FOR X8%=1 TO F1
3025     IF T9(X8%)=0 THEN PRINT #2,TAB(VAL(F1$(2,X8%)));T9(X8%);
                                                         GOTO 3050
```

```
3030      PRINT #2,TAB(VAL(F1$(2,X8%)))USING F1$(3,X8%);T9(X8%);
3050 NEXT X8%
3055 PRINT #2,
        PRINT #2,STRING$(WI,95)
        ERASE T9
        RETURN


3060 PRINT E$+"j";
3065 X1=1600
        GOSUB 80
3067 PRINT "FIELD DESCRIPTORS"
3070 FOR X7%=1 TO F
3075     PRINT F$(X7%);"-";L(X7%);" ";
3080 NEXT
3090 PRINT E$+"k";
3095 RETURN

3100 PRINT DC$")C"E$"1"
3101 PRINT DC$"*C"E$"1"
3102 PRINT DC$"+C"E$"1"
3103 PRINT DC$",C"E$"1"
        PRINT DC$"-D"E$"1"
        PRINT DC$".C"E$"1"
3104 RETURN

3105 PRINT CS$S1$" 8 Greg Greene & Associates Database"ER$CH$
3110 PRINT E$"y4";
3120 PRINT DC$"$ "GM$STRING$(80,"a")EG$CH$
3125 PRINT GM$DC$"% "STRING$(80," ")EG$
3130 PRINT DC$"& "GM$STRING$(80,"a")EG$
3135 PRINT S1$"'D Menu "ER$CH$
3140 PRINT DC$"4 ";GM$STRING$(80,"a")EG$
3145 PRINT S1$"5 Enter the Number"
3150 PRINT S1$"6 You Want ------> "ER$
3155 RETURN

3160 PRINT J$E$+"x"CHR$(49);DC$"8 "E$"1"K$
        RETURN

3350 OPEN "I",3,X0$+".RPT"
3352 INPUT #3,RH$,F1
3354 FOR L1%=0 TO 3
3356     FOR L2%=1 TO F
3358             INPUT #3,F1$(L1%,L2%)
3360     NEXT L2%
3362 NEXT L1%
3364 CLOSE #3
        RETURN

3365 OPEN "O",3,X0$+".RPT"
3366 PRINT #3,RH$;",";F1
3368 FOR L1%=0 TO 3
3370     FOR L2%=1 TO F
```

```
3372            PRINT #3,F1$(L1%,L2%)
3374    NEXT L2%
3376  NEXT L1%
3378  CLOSE #3
        RETURN
```

this section is activated because of the end statement at line 2960.

Line 3000 is the beginning of the subroutine that prints a formatted numeric expression on a formatted report. The numeric type is retrieved from the data dictionary, and based on it, the necessary conversion takes place. The array at the end of the lines, T9, is used to store the value in a totaling format so that the next subroutine can print it if desired by the user.

Line 3020 is the totals print subroutine. It is printed in the same format as the column that it was retrieved from. At the end of this subroutine, the array T9 is erased. Note that the customary **On error Goto** is missing. This is because we don't need to trap the error of erasing a nonexistent array, as the array has already been dimensioned at this point. If you are using an operating system that will not allow the use of an erase statement, just zero out the values in the array.

Line 3060 contains the command to remember where the cursor is positioned. The routine will then branch down to the 20th line on the screen and begin printing the current field descriptors in use. This helps the user keep track of what is in use and what isn't. Also the lengths of the fields are printed to assist him during the process of formatting a report.

Line 3100 is the routine to erase some of the lines used in the menu. This is because the menu is actually composed of two parts, a background part and a foreground part. When different choices are to be presented to the user, different foregrounds are used against the same background. Thus the foreground must be erased.

The routine at line 3105 is the actual background of the menu. A number of graphics routines are used here. You will have to modify them for your own menu display.

The routine at line 3350 will read in the structure of a report file previously made up. The routine at line 3365 will write out a new file to the disk for later use.

CONVERTING THE PROGRAM FOR YOUR MACHINE

This then is the program, and the reasons for writing it in the particular way in which I did. Let's go over some of the trouble areas that may arise in converting it to your particular machine.

Erasing. If you cannot use the erase command in your machine, you must dimension the arrays at some common point in the program where they will only be seen once by the program. This leads to several problems: first, you won't know the size of the arrays until you know which file you are going to work with, since the number of fields per file may change. Second, the main reason for erasing an array to save memory space that is no longer required. Some BASICs allow you to use the clear command to erase all or some of the variables.

If you have to put the array dimensioning statements at the beginning of the file, I suggest you do so right after you have received a legal filename and know how many fields are to be used. Then dimension all the arrays that require the number of fields as a limit. Keep track of the filename and if the user selects a new database, clear out the variables with the clear command and have the program redimension the arrays. You will also need to have the user reinput the data disk drive specification that is kept in DK$, because this variable will also be erased. If you are using Radio Shack TRS-80 equipment, the operating system will search for your data file on all mounted disks. Although this works well when you are reading, it is not good when you are writing because the system will write a new file to first available space on the first available disk. One way to avoid this is to poke the value of drive number to an unused memory location and have the program peek at it when required.

Graphics. Not all computers have the same

graphic capabilities as the Heath/Zenith H-19 terminal does. Some have more, some have less, and some are just different. Study the menu routine beginning at line 3105. The string statements with lower case a in them will print a solid line 80 characters wide, those with " " in them will print a broad band of spaces in reverse video. I recommend that you develop your own menu display if you are using a different system. The graphics available to you will be much more familiar and easy to work with, and you will be able to do it more quickly than if you tried to convert my program.

Cursor Addressing. Some of you will be able to use the translation routine at the beginning of the book with print@statements. Some will have to use horizontal and vertical tabbing. Whatever you must do, remember that this program is set up for a normal 80 column screen with 24 lines. This means that those with smaller screens will have to divide the information so that it is presented in smaller chunks. There will be some problems if you try to use the formatting routines with a 40 column screen. The fields may wrap around the screen and destroy information on the line below, and so on. These problems can all be overcome. The worst case solution is to ask a single question per screen, if the expected answer will fill the screen. In most cases allowing two lines of space between each question will suffice.

25th Line. If your system does not have a 25th line, simply ignore those parts of the program that make use of it. They are used to label the special function keys that allow the user to return to the menu. If you don't have a 25th line, it is unlikely that you have special function keys either, as they tend to go hand in hand.

Chapter 11

Additional Ways to Use the Data Files

No program is ever really finished, and this one is certainly no exception! Because of the modular construction of the main routines, it is not a problem to remove some of them and make the program do other things. This chapter tells how to make three new programs out of the main routines discussed already. These changes will allow us to prepare mailing labels, form letters, and a simple chart. The ideas expressed here will inspire you to use the program to do many other things!

MAILING LABELS

Now that you have the basic program, how can you expand on the system? One of the big things that a database manager is used for is to keep track of names and addresses that are parts of records used for other purposes. For instance, a file of all the people in your club would of course have name and address information included. The same is true of a file of accounts payable or receivable, or just about anything else. In almost every database, there is some information that would serve some purpose on a label. So to use the program to write information to a label, you need only replace the parts of the program that format the output. Why didn't I just include it in the regular program? There was not enough room. It is better to have a stand-alone type of program for this and other functions.

As you remember, the regular program consists of a number of parts, which in turn are composed of the routines shown in Fig. 11-1.

Essentially you can discard anything to do with writing to the database file, as all you will want to do with it is extract the information to put on the labels. You will need the querying and sorting routines, and the routines that allow you to enter a filename and specify a disk drive. You will also need to add routines to allow the user to tell the program how many lines are on his label and what field values should be printed there.

You must consider whether to print, one label or a number of labels across. For your purposes it should be sufficient to print the labels one across. If you were to try to print them several across, you

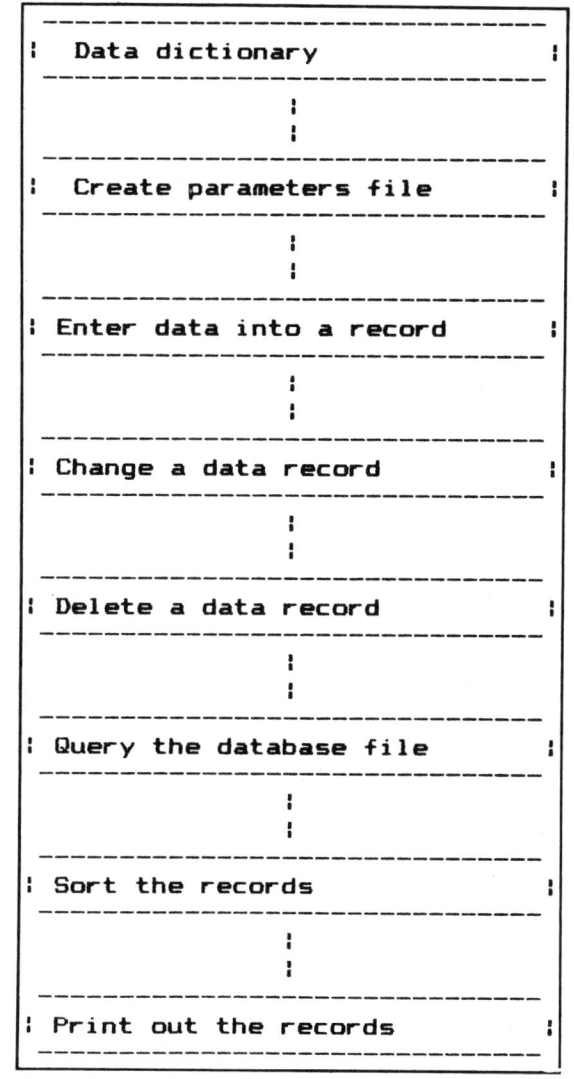

```
----------------------------
: Data dictionary          :
----------------------------
             :
             :
----------------------------
: Create parameters file   :
----------------------------
             :
             :
----------------------------
: Enter data into a record :
----------------------------
             :
             :
----------------------------
: Change a data record     :
----------------------------
             :
             :
----------------------------
: Delete a data record     :
----------------------------
             :
             :
----------------------------
: Query the database file  :
----------------------------
             :
             :
----------------------------
: Sort the records         :
----------------------------
             :
             :
----------------------------
: Print out the records    :
----------------------------
```

Fig. 11-1. Chart of the main routines in the regular program.

report files since you are going to change them.

You will substitute a routine that prints a blank label on the screen and then asks the user to input the fields in the position that he wants them printed. This allows the user to set up the number of lines on each label and the number of lines between each label. Next you will want to put in a routine that will print out each field value on a line. Since you already know how to get that value, this

```
---------------------------------------
: Assume records are selected         :
: and sorted by routines already      :
: developed for main program          :
---------------------------------------
                   :
                   :
---------------------------------------
: Start line = 2445                   :
: Ask user for number of print        :
: lines on the label                  :
---------------------------------------
                   :
                   :
---------------------------------------
: Ask user for the number of          :
: space lines between the lables      :
---------------------------------------
                   :
                   :
---------------------------------------
: Using the terminal graphics         :
: print out on the screen             :
: the boundaries of the label         :
---------------------------------------
                   :
                   :
---------------------------------------
: Allow user to place the field       :
: descriptors in the label as he      :
: wants them printed                  :
---------------------------------------
                   :
                   :
---------------------------------------
: When all lines accounted for        :
: print a label for each              :
: selected record                     :
---------------------------------------
```

Fig. 11-2. Chart of the routines in Listing 18.

would have to take memory space to store as many records as there are labels across before formatting the line to be printed. It is a good idea to keep things as simple as possible and to avoid using memory if you don't have to, so this program will print only one label across.

Since you can eliminate the routines that create, add, modify, or delete records you can shorten the program. You can also get rid of the routines that print the records and those that read in should not be a problem. Figure 11-2 shows a flowchart of the sections to be added. Listing 18 shows the code for these sections.

Line 2447 sends control to a routine at 3200 that asks the user how many lines there are in the label and how many there are between each label. Usually there are 8 lines per label and 1 line in between. This will vary with the label size. Some users may be making name and address labels; some may be making stock labels. After obtaining the required information, the program goes to line 600. Here the graphics abilities of the H-19 are used to draw a box, centered on the screen and 40 columns wide, that represents the label being created.

Lines 2460 to 2485 allow the user to enter a field descriptor on the line where he wishes to have the information printed out. If no information is to be printed, the user may just enter a blank line by pressing the return or enter key. Line 2470 calls a checking subroutine that will check the entry to determine if a valid field descriptor or blank line has been entered.

Lines 2500 - 2596 will print out the required information on each line of the label. Please note that in this version, only one field is printed per line. The actual printing is done by the subroutine in lines 2600-2625.

This is all there is to modifying the main program to be used as a label making program. You can see how, by just changing a few routines, you can make the program do any special job that you might wish to do.

LISTING EIGHTEEN
=================

```
2445  ' SET UP LABELS
2446  OPEN "O",2,"AT:"
2447  GOSUB 3200
2450  GOSUB 600
2455  X6=502
2460  FOR Y%=1 TO LD%
2465       X1=X6+(Y%*80)
            X2=4
            X3=0
            X4=0
            GOSUB 85
2470       GOSUB 800
2475       IF X0=-1 THEN 2465
2480       LA$(Y%)=X0$
2485  NEXT Y%
2490  PRINT
            PRINT
            PRINT
            PRINT
2500  INPUT "Set up Labels on Printer - press <RETURN> when ready";X0$
2515  FOR Y=1 TO Z-1
2520       GET #1,R(Y)
            A$=B$
2530       IF LS%=0 THEN 2570
2540       FOR X=1 TO LS%
                 PRINT #2,
            NEXT X
2570       FOR Y%=1 TO LD%
2575            IF LA$(Y%)="" THEN PRINT #2,
                 GOTO 2592
2580            FOR X=1 TO F
```

```
2585                    IF LA$(Y%)=F$(X) THEN GOSUB 2600
2590              NEXT X
2592      NEXT Y%
2595 NEXT Y
2596 CLOSE
     RETURN

2600 IF T$(X)="A" THEN PRINT #2,MID$(A$,SA(X),L(X))
2605 IF RIGHT$(T$(X),1)="I" THEN N%=CVI(MID$(A$,SA(X),L(X)))
        PRINT #2,N%
2610 IF RIGHT$(T$(X),1)="S" THEN N!=CVS(MID$(A$,SA(X),L(X)))
        PRINT #2,N!
2615 IF RIGHT$(T$(X),1)="D" THEN N#=CVD(MID$(A$,SA(X),L(X)))
        PRINT #2,N#
2625 RETURN

3200 ' LABEL LINES
3210 PRINT CS$;
3220 X1=410
        GOSUB 80
        PRINT "# of Lines on Label";TAB(50)"# of Lines Between"
3230 X1=500
        X2=2
        X3=0
        X4=30
        GOSUB 85
3240 IF X0#=-1 THEN 2405
3250 LD%=X0#
3260 X1=540
        X2=2
        X3=0
        X4=30
        GOSUB 85
3270 IF X0#=-1 THEN 3230
3280 LS%=X0#
3290 RETURN

600 PRINT CS$;
605 PRINT "LABELS"
620 PRINT
        PRINT
        PRINT
        PRINT
630 PRINT GM$
640 PRINT TAB(20)"f";
650 FOR X%=1 TO 40
660 PRINT "a";
670 NEXT
680 PRINT "c"
690 FOR X%=1 TO LD%
700 PRINT TAB(20)"`";TAB(61)"`"
710 NEXT
720 PRINT TAB(20)"e";
730 GOTO 751
735 FOR X5%=1 TO F
```

```
740       IF X0$=F$(X5%) THEN X0=0
          RETURN
745 NEXT X5%
750 X3$="INVALID FIELD"
          GOSUB 185
          X0=-1
          RETURN
751 FOR X%=1 TO 40
752 PRINT "a";
755 NEXT
760 PRINT "d"
770 PRINT EG$
          GOSUB 2965
775 RETURN
```

FORM LETTERS

Let's look at using the routines to form a simple text substitution program that substitutes information from the database files into form letters that you have prepared with an editor. This will allow you to use the stored information in one more way, increasing the flexibility of the system.

In order to do this, you will start with the same set of routines that you used as the basis of the label making program; that is, those routines that allow the user to query and sort the information in the database, but none of the ones that allow modification.

In place of the label making routines, you will substitute a routine to put the information into a form letter. How is this done? Let's start with the form letter itself. It forms a file that consists of data stored in a sequential format, with the information stored as ASCII. So you only have to read in the file one line at a time, check to see if there is a place in the line where some information must be substituted, make the substitution, and output the line to the printer.

There are some restrictions: When you are writing the letter you cannot tell how much of the line will be required by the field value. You must therefore make sure that you allow enough room for the substitution to take place. You must also devise a way to alert the program that a substitution is required.

The solution to this is to have the user, when entering the letter, surround the field name that corresponds to the desired value with backslashes, \ . The program can then search each line for the occurrence of such a string using the INSTR function and make the substitution. The user must be sure to enter the field descriptor exactly as the program will have it stored in the data dictionary. This means that if he uses a field descriptor of less than 4 characters, such as BAL, he must realize that the program has stored it as BAL , which is BAL with a space for the fourth character. Thus if he enters it in the letter as \ BAL \ , no substitution can take place as the program cannot find the match.

Figure 11-3 shows the flowchart for this procedure. Listing 19 shows the code for these changes.

Line 2445 is again the start of this routine. The name of the text file is obtained in line 2455, and the file is opened and the first line read in. Note that line 2470 sets the maximum number of lines in the text file to 30,000. I doubt that you will ever have cause to change it! Line 2586 adds backslashes to the field descriptor so that a match can be made by the INSTR function in line 2489. If a match is obtained, the program goes to the routine starting at line 2540. This routine identifies the value to be substituted, and line 2585 makes the insertion. Line 2580 makes sure that the length of the value substituted is at least 6 characters long so that the original field descriptor and accompanying backslashes are covered over.

This continues till all the lines of the text file are checked.

```
-------------------------------
: Text substitution            :
: starts   at line 2445        :
: Get name of text file to     :
: read form letter from        :
-------------------------------
               :
               :
-------------------------------
: Read in a line               :
: using the line input         :
: function of BASIC            :
-------------------------------
               :
               :
-------------------------------
: Check with the INSTR         :
: function for the presence    :
: of a field descriptor with   :
: back slashes surrounding it  :
-------------------------------
               :
               :
-------------------------------
: If such is found, make       :
: the value substitution       :
-------------------------------
               :
               :
-------------------------------
: Output the new line to the   :
: printer                      :
-------------------------------
               :
               :
-------------------------------
: Continue till each line is   :
: done - then back to the menu :
-------------------------------
```

Fig. 11-3. Chart of the routines in Listing 19.

SIMPLE GRAPHS

Graphs generally serve two purposes. One is to show a single variable and the other is to show more than one variable so that the user can make some comparisons between them.

The type of graph depends very much on the capability of the hardware that you have access to. If you have a graphics printer, you can make use of a bar chart. Otherwise you are restricted to using a chart that plots points on the paper.

Keeping in mind the objective of making this system as universal as possible, a set of routines that will enable the printer to output a set of points on the paper will be constructed. The program will use a maximum of three different variables. In order to allow the user to differentiate between them, they will be named (L), (H), and (N).

Each graph requires three sets of values: the scale for measurement on the horizontal axis, the scale on the vertical axis, and the values of the variable to be plotted. The database file can supply the values of the points. You can use the dates of the data records as the values for the vertical axis scale, and the horizontal axis will reflect the values being plotted.

A good way to demonstrate the system is to use stock market information as the basis of our chart. Market quotations generally have a low value, a high value, and a closing value. In addition they are recorded every day, so there are dates to order the records by. Since you have little control over the range of values assumed by the stock, the ability to modify or scale the range will be built into the routines.

You must remember that our printer will have a finite number of columns that it is able to print,

LISTING NINETEEN
================

```
2445 ' SET UP SUBSTITUTION
2446 CLOSE #2
        OPEN "O",2,"AT:"
2450 PRINT CS$
        PRINT
        PRINT
        PRINT
2455 INPUT "Filename for Text File ";F2$
```

```
2464 ON ERROR GOTO 2346
2467 FOR Y%=1 TO Z-1
2468     GET #1,R(Y%)
         A$=B$
2469     CLOSE #3:OPEN "I",3,F2$
2470     FOR X%=1 TO 30000
2475         IF EOF(3) THEN 2505
2480         LINE INPUT #3,X$
2485         FOR X1%=1 TO F
2486             IF LEN(F$(X1%))<6 THEN F$(X1%)="\"+F$(X1%)+"\"
2490             P=INSTR(X$,F$(X1%))
                 IF P>0 THEN 2540
2491         NEXT X1%
2492     PRINT #2,X$
2500     NEXT X%
2505     PRINT #2,CHR$(12)
2506 NEXT Y%
2510 CLOSE #2
     CLOSE #3
     RETURN
2540 IF LEN(X$)<80 THEN X$=X$+STRING$((80-LEN(X$))," ")
2550 IF T$(X1%)="A" THEN MID$(X$,P,(P+L(X1%)))=MID$(A$,SA(X1%),L(X1%))
2555 TE$=RIGHT$(T$(X1%),1)
     TN$=MID$(A$,SA(X1%),L(X1%))
2560 IF TE$="I" THEN NS$=STR$(CVI(TN$))
     GOTO 2580
2565 IF TE$="S" THEN NS$=STR$(CVS(TN$))
     GOTO 2580
2570 IF TE$="D" THEN NS$=STR$(CVD(TN$))
     GOTO 2580
2575 GOTO 2485
2580 IF LEN(NS$)<6 THEN NS$=NS$+STRING$((6-LEN(NS$))," ")
2585 MID$(X$,P,LEN(NS$))=NS$:RETURN
```

and that you cannot exceed this number. The routine in Listing 20 assumes that you are using a printer that prints 66 lines per sheet. This will give you enough space to present the performance of a single stock over a month. The program will be more flexible if it offers the user the option of plotting one, two, or three variables. Let's consider the flowcharts shown in Fig. 11-4. Listing 20 shows the code for these changes.

The routine at line 600 asks the user which field is to be used for each symbol. If the user is not using all three symbols, he may skip them by just pressing the return or enter key instead of entering a value. Line 2455 to 2500 go through all the selected records and determine the range of the chart. This is so that the graph will not extend beyond the range of the printer. The maximum usable printer width has been set to 70 columns. This leaves us 10 columns for the date to be printed in. Line 2502 requests the user to input a modifier, or scaling factor if it is apparent that the range is inappropriate. The resulting range is checked in line 2504. If it is more than 70, the user will be requested to enter a new modifier value, which, when the range is too large, will be a number between 0 and 1. In this manner the graph can be expanded or contracted to fit the situation at hand.

Lines 2510 to 2625 examine each record and print the symbol at its proper spot. This graph is meant to be a model upon which you can build. It is another example of the flexibility of the system. A much more sophisticated graphing program ex-

LISTING TWENTY
==============

```
600 PRINT CS$;
        PRINT
        PRINT CH$
601 PRINT
602 CR$(0)=""
        CR$(1)=""
        CR$(2)=""
        CR$(3)=""
605 GOSUB 2965
        PRINT CH$
610 PRINT "CHART PARAMETERS"
615 PRINT
        PRINT
620 PRINT "This section of the program will ask you what you wish on"
625 PRINT "your chart, please answer the questions as they are asked."
630 PRINT
        PRINT
635 PRINT " What is the field descriptor for the 'DATE' :-"
640 PRINT "                                      'HIGH VALUE' :-"
645 PRINT "                                      'LOW VALUE' :-"
650 PRINT "                                      'NEXT VALUE' :-"
652 X1=688
        X2=4
        X3=0
        X4=0
        GOSUB 85
        IF X0$<>"" THEN GOSUB 800 ELSE 654
653 CR$(0)=X0$
        IF X0=-1 THEN 652
654 X1=768
        GOSUB 85
        IF X0$<>"" THEN GOSUB 800 ELSE 656
655 CR$(1)=X0$
        IF X0=-1 THEN 654
656 X1=848
        GOSUB 85
        IF X0$<>"" THEN GOSUB 800 ELSE 658
657 CR$(2)=X0$
        IF X0=-1 THEN 656
658 X1=928
        GOSUB 85
        IF X0$<>"" THEN GOSUB 800 ELSE 660
659 CR$(3)=X0$
        IF X0=-1 THEN 658
660 PRINT
        PRINT "Thankyou"
665 FOR V%=1 TO 500
        NEXT V%
        RETURN

2445 ' SET UP CHART
2447 H=0
     L=0
```

```
2450 GOSUB 600
2455 FOR Y=1 TO Z-1
2460     GET #1,R(Y)
         A$=B$
2465     XO$=CR$(1)
         GOSUB 800
         X=X%
2470     GOSUB 2605
         HV=N
2475     IF Y=1 THEN L=HV
2477     IF CR$(2)="" AND HV<L THEN L=HV
2480     IF HV>H THEN H=HV
2485     XO$=CR$(2)
         GOSUB 800
         X=X%
2490     GOSUB 2605
         LV=N
2495     IF LV<L THEN L=LV
2500 NEXT Y

2501 PRINT CS$
         PRINT "CHART WILL BE FROM "INT(L)" TO "INT(H)
2502 INPUT "MODIFIER";MD
2503 IF MD=0 THEN MD=1
2504 IF INT(H*MD)-INT(L*MD)>70 THEN X3$="OUT OF RANGE"
                                GOSUB 185
                                PRINT CS$
                                GOTO 2501
2505 OPEN "O",2,"AT:"
         PRINT #2,CHR$(15)
         GOSUB 3200
2506 L1=INT(L*MD)
         H1=INT(H*MD)
2507 PRINT #2,TAB((L1+9)-L1)L;TAB((H1+9)-L1)H
2508 FOR X=(L1+10)-L1 TO (H1+10)-L1
         PRINT #2,TAB(X)".";
         NEXT X
2509 PRINT #2,
2510 FOR Y=1 TO Z-1
2515     GET #1,R(Y)
         A$=B$
2516     XO$=CR$(0)
         GOSUB 800
         PRINT #2,MID$(A$,SA(X%),L(X%));
2518     IF CR$(2)="" THEN 2535
2520     XO$=CR$(2)
         GOSUB 800
         X=X%
2525     GOSUB 2605
         N=INT(N*MD)
         N=N+10
2530     PRINT #2,TAB(N-L1)"L";
2535     IF CR$(3)="" THEN 2555
2540     XO$=CR$(3)
         GOSUB 800
```

```
              X=X%
2545      GOSUB 2605
              N=INT(N*MD)
              N=N+10
2550      PRINT #2,TAB(N-L1)"N";
2555      IF CR$(1)="" THEN 2580
2560      X0$=CR$(1)
              GOSUB 800
              X=X%
2565      GOSUB 2605
              N=INT(N*MD)
              N=N+10
2570      PRINT #2,TAB(N-L1)"H";
2580      PRINT #2,
2585 NEXT Y
2596 GOTO 2305
2605 IF RIGHT$(T$(X),1)="I" THEN N=CVI(MID$(A$,SA(X),L(X)))
2610 IF RIGHT$(T$(X),1)="S" THEN N=CVS(MID$(A$,SA(X),L(X)))
2615 IF RIGHT$(T$(X),1)="D" THEN N=CVD(MID$(A$,SA(X),L(X)))
2625 RETURN
```

pressly set up for stocks which will chart the highs, lows, closing, volume, and 20 week moving on an Epson MX-80® printer is available from the author. This graph is a bar graph and makes use of the built in graphics of this printer. The graph takes the form of those that are printed in papers such as *The Wall Street Journal* and uses a single 8½ by 11 inch sheet of paper no matter what the range of the stock. All scaling is automatic to make the best use of the space.

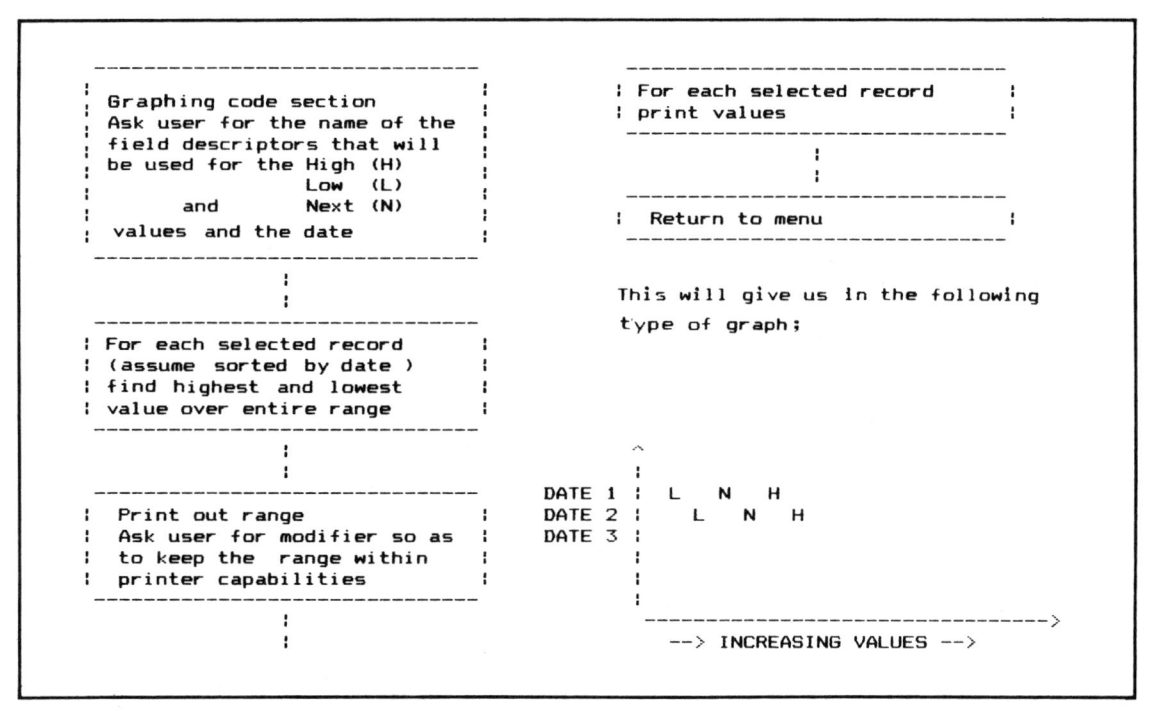

```
---------------------------------       ---------------------------------
: Graphing code section         :       : For each selected record      :
: Ask user for the name of the  :       : print values                  :
: field descriptors that will   :       ---------------------------------
: be used for the High (H)      :                       :
:                  Low  (L)     :                       :
:        and       Next (N)     :       ---------------------------------
: values and the date           :       : Return to menu                :
---------------------------------       ---------------------------------
                :
                :                       This will give us in the following
---------------------------------       type of graph;
: For each selected record      :
: (assume sorted by date )      :
: find highest and lowest       :
: value over entire range       :
---------------------------------
                :
                :                                ^
---------------------------------       DATE 1 :   L    N    H
: Print out range               :       DATE 2 :      L    N    H
: Ask user for modifier so as   :       DATE 3 :
: to keep the  range within     :              :
: printer capabilities          :              :
---------------------------------              ----------------------------->
                :                               --> INCREASING VALUES -->
                :
```

Fig. 11-4. Chart of the routines in Listing 20.

Appendix A
The Database Manager Program Listing

```
                    PROGRAM LISTING
                    ===============
25 WIDTH 255
30 CLEAR 3500
35 E$=CHR$(27):CS$=E$+"E":RV$=E$+"p":ER$=E$+"q":GM$=E$+"F":EG$=E$+
   "G"
36 BC$=E$+"y5"+E$+"x4":CO$=E$+"x5":DC$=E$+"Y":S1$=RV$+DC$
37 SB$=S1$+STRING$(80," ")+EG$
38 CH$=E$+"H"
39 GOTO 60
40 PRINT E$+"x";CHR$(49)
45 PRINT E$+"Y";CHR$(56);CHR$(32):PRINT
50 PRINT RV$:PRINT "    PRESS f1 to exit to menu    "
55 PRINT ER$:X1=0:GOSUB 80:PRINT
56 RETURN
60 DL$="ERA":REM ******* DELETE CODE *******
65 DA$="":FOR I=8383 TO 8391:DA$=DA$+CHR$(PEEK(I)):NEXT I
70 DEFDBL M,N,O,T
75 GOTO 475
80 H%=INT(X1/80):C%=X1-(H%*80):PRINT E$+"Y";CHR$(H%+32);CHR$(C%+32);
   :RETURN
85 '
90 XO$=""
95 X2$=STRING$(255,"*")
100 GOSUB 80: PRINT LEFT$(X2$,X2);CHR$(7):GOSUB 80
101 PRINT BC$
```

```
105 X$=INPUT$(1)
110 IF LEN(X0$)=0 AND X$=CHR$(13) THEN X0#=-1:RETURN
115 X0#=0
120 IF X$=CHR$(27) THEN 215
125 IF X$=CHR$(9) THEN 85
130 IF X$=CHR$(8) OR X$=CHR$(127) THEN X6%=1:GOTO 165
135 IF X$=CHR$(13) THEN 150
140 X0$=X0$+X$::IF LEN(X0$)>X2 THEN PRINT CHR$(7):X6%=2:GOTO 165
145 PRINT X$;:IF X2=1 AND LEN(X0$)=1 AND C=1 THEN 155 ELSE GOTO 105
150 IF X3=0 AND X4=0 THEN PRINT CO$;:RETURN
155 X0#=VAL(X0$):IF X0#>=X3 AND X0#<=X4 THEN PRINT CO$;:C=0:RETURN
160 X3$="OUT OF RANGE":GOSUB 185:GOTO 85
165 '
170 Z1%=LEN(X0$)-X6%:IF Z1%<1 THEN 85
175 X0$=LEFT$(X0$,Z1%)
180 GOSUB 80:PRINT LEFT$(X2$,X2):GOSUB 80:PRINTX0$;:GOTO 105
185 X5=X1
190 FOR L%=1 TO 3
195 X1=(320+(80-LEN(X0$))/2):GOSUB 80: PRINT RV$;X3$;ER$;CHR$(7)
200 FOR L1%=1 TO 100:NEXT L1%
205 X1=320:GOSUB 80:PRINT E$+"1";
210 NEXT L%:X1=X5:PRINT BC$:RETURN
215 X$=INPUT$(1)
220 IF X$="S" THEN CLOSE:GOTO 500
225 IF X$="Q" THEN GOSUB 2935
230 RETURN
235 GOSUB 245:X1=160:GOSUB 80:PRINT RV$;X1$;ER$:X1=245:C=1
240 RETURN
245 X1=160:GOSUB 80:PRINT E$+"1":X1=240:GOSUB 80:PRINT E$+"1":RETURN
250 '
255 PRINT CS$;
256 GOSUB 3105
260 PRINT S1$"% "STRING$(80," ")DC$"%?Main Option List"ER$CH$
265 GOSUB 3100
270 PRINT DC$"& "E$"F"STRING$(80,"a")EG$
271 PRINT DC$")D1        Create a File"
272 PRINT DC$"*D2        Input Data"
273 PRINT DC$"+D3        Query the Database"
274 PRINT DC$",D4        Review this file's parameters"
275 PRINT DC$"-D5        Set Data Disk Drive"
276 PRINT DC$".D6        Exit"
290 RETURN
295 PRINT CS$;
296 PRINT CO$;
300 PRINT RV$;"CREATE Database";ER$;TAB(60);RV$;DA$;ER$
305 PRINT:PRINT:PRINT
310 PRINT "1 = Filename";TAB(30)"2 = Date";TAB(55)"3 = # of Fields"
315 PRINT STRING$(79,95)
320 PRINT " Field #:- ";TAB(50);" Space left :- "
325 PRINT:PRINT
330 PRINT "4 = Field name:- ";TAB(40);"7 = Field Length:- "
335 PRINT "5 = Field Type:- ";TAB(40);"Field Starts at :- "
340 PRINT "6 = Min Value :- ";TAB(40);"8 = Max Value    :- "
```

```
341 PRINT BC$
345 RETURN
350 PRINT CS$;
351 PRINT CO$;
355 PRINT RV$;"DATABASE INPUT";ER$
360 PRINT:PRINT:PRINT:PRINT
365 PRINT "Filename   :- ";TAB(40)"Date Created   :- "
370 PRINT "# of Fields:- ";TAB(40)"Date of Update :- "
375 PRINT STRING$(79,95)
380 PRINT
385 PRINT "Rec # :- "
390 PRINT:PRINT
391 PRINT BC$
395 RETURN
400 X1=738:X2=4:X3=0:X4=0:GOSUB 85:F$(X)=X0$:GOSUB 80:PRINT F$(X)
    :RETURN
405 X1=818:X2=2:X3=0:X4=0:GOSUB 85:T$(X)=X0$:GOSUB 80:PRINT T$(X)
    :RETURN
410 X1=898:X2=10:X3=-9999999999#:X4=9999999999#:GOSUB 85:MI(X)=X0#
    :GOSUB 80:PRINT MI(X):RETURN
415 X1=778:X2=3:X3=1:X4=256:GOSUB 85:L(X)=X0#:GOSUB 80:PRINT L(X)
    :RETURN
420 X1=938:X2=10:X3=-9999999999#:X4=9999999999#:GOSUB 85:MA(X)=X0#
    :GOSUB 80: PRINT MA(X):RETURN
425 X1=335:X2=7:X3=0:X4=0:GOSUB 85:F$=X0$:GOSUB 80:PRINT F$:RETURN
430 X1=392:X2=2:X3=1:X4=127:GOSUB 85:F=X0#:GOSUB 80:PRINT F:RETURN
435 X3$="NOT ALLOWED":GOSUB 185:RETURN
440 X1=738:GOSUB 80:PRINT "        "
445 X1=818:GOSUB 80:PRINT "    "
450 X1=898:GOSUB 80:PRINT "          "
455 X1=778:GOSUB 80:PRINT "     "
460 X1=858:GOSUB 80:PRINT "     "
465 X1=938:GOSUB 80:PRINT "          "
470 RETURN
475 PRINT CS$:GOSUB 3160
476 IF DK$="" THEN DK$="SY0:D"
477 GOTO 500
480 GOSUB 3100:PRINT RV$DC$"'D Data Disk is on "ER$CH$
481 PRINT DC$")D1       SY0:"
    PRINT DC$"*D2       SY1:"
    PRINT DC$"+D3       SY2:"
483 PRINT DC$"6C";BC$;:DE$=INPUT$(1):PRINT CO$
484 IF VAL(DE$)<1 OR VAL(DE$)>2 THEN PRINT DC$"6C ":GOTO 483
485 TP=ASC(DE$)-8:TP$=CHR$(TP):PRINT DC$TP$"D"RV$DE$ER$DC$"6C";
486 IF VAL(DE$)=1 THEN DK$="SY0:D"
487 IF VAL(DE$)=2 THEN DK$="SY1:D"
488 IF VAL(DE$)=3 THEN DK$="SY2:D"
489 RETURN
495 PRINT CS$;E$+"x";CHR$(49);DC$;CHR$(56);CHR$(32);E$+"1":X1=0
    :GOSUB 80:SYSTEM
500 CLOSE:GOSUB 250
505 PRINT DC$"6C";BC$;:DE$=INPUT$(1):PRINTCO$
```

```
507 IF VAL(DE$)<1 OR VAL(DE$)>6 THEN PRINT DC$"6C ":GOTO 505
508 T1=ASC(DE$)-8:T1$=CHR$(T1):PRINT DC$T1$"D"RV$DE$ER$DC$"6C";
510 X0#=VAL(DE$)
513 GOSUB 40
515 ON X0# GOSUB 540,980,1705,2630,480,495
520 GOTO 475
540 DI$=DA$
545 GOSUB 295
550 X1=360:GOSUB 80:PRINT DA$
555 GOSUB 425
560 IF X0#=-1 THEN RETURN
565 GOSUB 430
570 IF X0#=-1 THEN 555
575 ON ERROR GOTO2345
580 ERASE F$,T$,MI,L,SA,MA
585 DIM F$(F),T$(F),MI(F),L(F),SA(F),MA(F)
590 SU=0
595 X=1
600 X1=491:GOSUB 80:PRINT X
605 GOSUB 400
610 GOSUB 405:IF T$(X)="A" THEN MI(X)=0:X1=898:GOSUB 80:PRINT MI(X)
612 IF T$(X)<>"A" THEN GOSUB 410
615 IF T$(X)="DI" THEN L(X)=2:X1=778:GOSUB 80:PRINT L(X)
616 IF T$(X)="DS" THEN L(X)=4:X1=778:GOSUB 80:PRINT L(X)
617 IF T$(X)="DD" THEN L(X)=8:X1=778:GOSUB 80:PRINT L(X)
618 IF T$(X)="A" THEN GOSUB 415
620 SA(X)=SU+1:X1=858:GOSUB 80:PRINT SA(X)
625 SU=SU+L(X)
630 X1=545:GOSUB 80:PRINT 255-SU:IF SU>255 THEN X3$="Out of Range"
    :GOSUB 185: GOTO 615
635 IF T$(X)="A" THEN MA(X)=0:X1=938:GOSUB 80:PRINT MA(X):GOTO 640
636 GOSUB 420
640 X1$="Line to Change ?":GOSUB 235:X2=1:X3=0:X4=8:GOSUB 85
645 IF X0#<1 THEN 675
650 CH=X0#
655 SU=SU-L(X)
660 ON CH GOSUB 425,435,430,400,610,410,415,420
665 SU=SU+L(X)
670 GOTO 640
675 GOSUB 440
680 X=X+1:IF X<F+1 THEN 600
685 PRINT CS$;:PRINT RV$;"Specials";ER$
690 PRINT:PRINT:PRINT:PRINT
692 GOSUB 3060
695 Y1=6
700 FOR Y=1 TO 9
705 SP$(Y)="":FOR Y%=1 TO F*5:SP$(Y)=SP$(Y)+" ":NEXT
710 X1=160:GOSUB 80:PRINT "Special #:-";Y
715 X1=400:GOSUB 80
720 PRINT "Target field:-":PRINT"Source field:-":PRINT"Action:-"
725 X1=415:GOSUB 2340:X2=4:X3=0:X4=0:GOSUB 85:IF X0#=-1 THEN 800
    ELSEMID$(SP$(Y),1,4)=X0$
```

```
726 GOSUB 735:IF X0=-1 THEN 725
730 X1=495:GOSUB 2340:X2=4:X3=0:X4=0:GOSUB 85:IF X0#=-1 THEN 790
    ELSE MID$(SP$(Y),Y1,4)=X0$
731 GOSUB 735:IF X0=-1 THEN 730
734 GOTO 755
735 FOR X5%=1 TO F
740 IF X0$=F$(X5%) THEN X0=0:RETURN
745 NEXT X5%
750 X3$="INVALID FIELD":GOSUB 185:X0=-1:RETURN
755 X1=575:GOSUB 2340:X2=1:X3=0:X4=0:GOSUB 85:MID$(SP$(Y),
    Y1+4,1)=X0$
760 IF X0$="+" OR X0$="-" OR X0$="*" OR X0$="/" THEN 770
765 X3$="INVALID ACTION":GOSUB 185:GOTO 755
770 Y1=Y1+5
775 X1$="MORE":GOSUB 235:X2=1:X3=0:X4=0:GOSUB 85:IF X0$="Y" OR X0$=
    "y" THEN 780 ELSE 790
780 X1=495:GOSUB 80:PRINT "    ":X1=575:GOSUB 80:PRINT " "
785 GOTO 730
790 Y1=6:NEXT Y
800 OPEN "O",1,F$
805 PRINT #1,F$;",";DI$;",";DA$;",";F
810     FOR X=1 TO F
815     PRINT #1,F$(X);",";T$(X);",";MI(X);L(X);SA(X);MA(X)
820     NEXT X
825     FOR Y=1 TO 9
830     PRINT #1,SP$(Y)
835     NEXT Y
840 CLOSE 1:RETURN
845 FOR Y%=1 TO 9
850 IF MID$(SP$(Y%),1,4)="    " THEN 865
855 IF MID$(SP$(Y%),1,4)=F$(X) THEN 870
860 NEXT Y%
865 SP=0:RETURN
870 Y1=6
875 TN=0
880 FOR L%=1 TO 5*F
885 IF MID$(SP$(Y%),Y1,1)=" " THEN 950
890 TP$=MID$(SP$(Y%),Y1,4):FOR X1%=1 TO F
895                         IF TP$=F$(X1%) THEN 905
900                         NEXT X1%
902 GOTO 950
905 IF RIGHT$(T$(X1%),1)="I" THEN NU=CVI(MID$(A$,SA(X1%),L(X1%)))
910 IF RIGHT$(T$(X1%),1)="S" THEN NU=CVS(MID$(A$,SA(X1%),L(X1%)))
915 IF RIGHT$(T$(X1%),1)="D" THEN NU=CVD(MID$(A$,SA(X1%),L(X1%)))
920 IF MID$(SP$(Y%),Y1+4,1)="+" THEN TN=TN+NU
925 IF MID$(SP$(Y%),Y1+4,1)="-" THEN TN=TN-NU
930 IF MID$(SP$(Y%),Y1+4,1)="*" THEN TN=TN*NU
935 IF MID$(SP$(Y%),Y1+4,1)="/" THEN TN=TN/NU
940 Y1=Y1+5
945 NEXT L%
950 SP=1:RETURN
955 FOR X=1 TO F
960 GOSUB 845
```

```
965 IF SP=1 THEN RETURN
970 NEXT X
975 Y5=0:RETURN
980 '
985 X1$="":A$=""
987 GOSUB 3105
990 PRINT S1$"% "STRING$(80," ")DC$"%?Data Records Section"ER$CH$
991 GOSUB 3100:PRINT DC$"& "E$"F"STRING$(80,"a")EG$
992 PRINT DC$")D1       Add a record to Database"
993 PRINT DC$"*D2       Change a record in Database"
994 PRINT DC$"+D3       Flag a record for Deletion"
995 PRINT DC$",D4       Repack records in Database"
996 PRINT DC$"6C";BC$;:DE$=INPUT$(1):PRINT CO$
997 IF VAL(DE$)<1 OR VAL(DE$)>4 THEN PRINT DC$"6C ":GOTO 996
998 CH=VAL(DE$)
1000 ON CH GOSUB 1015,1260,1465,1605
1005 CLOSE:GOSUB 795
1010 RETURN
1015 GOSUB 350
1020 X1=40:GOSUB 80:PRINT "ADD"
1025 GOTO 1105
1030 ON ERROR GOTO 2345
1035 X1=415:X2=7:X3=0:X4=0:GOSUB 85:IF LEN(X0$)=0 THEN RETURN
1040 F$=X0$
1045 OPEN "I",1,F$
1050 INPUT #1,F$,DI$,DB$,F
1055 X1=458:GOSUB 80:PRINT DI$:X1=538:GOSUB 80:PRINT DA$
1060 ERASE F$,T$,MI,L,SA,MA
1065 DIM F$(F),T$(F),MI(F),L(F),SA(F),MA(F)
1070     FOR X=1 TO F
1075     INPUT #1,F$(X),T$(X),MI(X),L(X),SA(X),MA(X)
1080     NEXT X
1085     FOR Y=1 TO 9
1090     INPUT #1,SP$(Y)
1095     NEXT Y
1096 GOSUB 3060
1100 CLOSE:RETURN
1105 GOSUB 1030
1110 IF LEN(X0$)=0 THEN RETURN
1115 OPEN "R",1,DK$+F$+".DAT"
1120 FIELD #1,255 AS B$
1125 A$=STRING$(255," ")
1130 SU=0
1135 FOR X=1 TO F
1140     FOR Y=1 TO L(X)
1145     X$=X$+" "
1150     NEXT Y
1155 R=LOF(1)+1
1160 X1=495:GOSUB 80:PRINT F
1165 X1=735:GOSUB 80:PRINT R
1170 X1=810:GOSUB 80:PRINT E$+"K"
1175 X1=810:GOSUB 80:PRINT F$(X):GOSUB 845:IF SP=0 THEN 1180 ELSE
     X0#=TN: GOTO 1180
```

```
1180 IF T$(X)="A" THEN X2=L(X) ELSE X2=10
1185 IF SP=1 THEN X1=X1+5:GOSUB 80:PRINT XO#:GOTO 1195
1190 X3=MI(X):X4=MA(X):X1=X1+5:GOSUB 85:X1$=XO$
1195 IF RIGHT$(T$(X),1)="I" THEN X1$=MKI$(XO#)
1200 IF RIGHT$(T$(X),1)="S" THEN X1$=MKS$(XO#)
1205 IF RIGHT$(T$(X),1)="D" THEN X1$=MKD$(XO#)
1210 FOR X9=1 TO L(X):X1$=X1$+" ":NEXT
1215 MID$(A$,SA(X),L(X))=X1$
1220 SU=SU+L(X)
1225 NEXT X
1230 A$=LEFT$(A$,SU)
1235 LSET B$=A$
1240 PUT #1,R:R=R+1
1245 X1$="MORE":GOSUB 235:INPUT XO$:IF LEFT$(XO$,1)="Y" OR LEFT$
     (XO$,1)="y" THEN 1130 ELSE 1255
1250 SU=0:GOTO 1165
1255 CLOSE 1:RETURN
1260 GOSUB 350
1265 A$="":X1$=""
1270 X1=40:GOSUB 80:PRINT "CHANGE"
1275 GOSUB 1030:IF XO$="" THEN CLOSE:RETURN
1280 OPEN "R",1,DK$+F$+".DAT"
1285 FIELD #1,255 AS B$
1290 X1=495:GOSUB 80:PRINT F
1295 X1=735:X2=3:X3=0:X4=LOF(1):GOSUB 85:R=XO#:IF R<1 THEN CLOSE:
     RETURN
1300 GET #1,R
1305 A$=B$
1310 SU=0
1315 '
1325 X1$="Field Descriptor ?":GOSUB 235:X2=4:X3=0:X4=0:GOSUB 85
1326 IF XO#=-1 THEN LSET B$=A$:PUT #1,R:CLOSE:GOTO 1295
1327 GOSUB 735:IF XO=-1 THEN 1325 ELSE X=X5%
1328 X1=810
1330 GOSUB 80:PRINT E$"1":GOSUB 80:PRINT X;F$(X)
1335 X1$=MID$(A$,SA(X),L(X))
1340 IF RIGHT$(T$(X),1)="I" THEN X9=CVI(X1$):GOTO 1360
1345 IF RIGHT$(T$(X),1)="S" THEN X9=CVS(X1$):GOTO 1360
1350 IF RIGHT$(T$(X),1)="D" THEN X9=CVD(X1$):GOTO 1360
1355 X2$=X1$:GOTO 1365
1360 X1=X1+8:GOSUB 80:PRINT X9:GOTO 1370
1365 X1=X1+8:GOSUB 80:PRINT X1$
1370 X1=X1-8
1375 '
1380 PRINT "New Value"
1390 Y5=1
1395 X1=X1+89
1405 IF T$(X)="A" THEN X2=L(X) ELSE X2=10
1410 X3=MI(X):X4=MA(X):GOSUB 85
1412 IF XO#=-1 THEN 1325
1415 IF T$(X)="A" THEN X1$=XO$
1420 IF RIGHT$(T$(X),1)="I" THEN X1$=MKI$(XO#)
1425 IF RIGHT$(T$(X),1)="S" THEN X1$=MKS$(XO#)
```

```
1430 IF RIGHT$(T$(X),1)="D" THEN X1$=MKD$(X0#)
1435 MID$(A$,SA(X),L(X))=STRING$(L(X)," ")
1440 MID$(A$,SA(X),L(X))=X1$
1445 IF Y5=0 THEN 1315
1450 IF Y5=1 THEN GOSUB 955
1455 IF SP=1 THEN Y5=0:X0#=TN:GOTO 1420
1460 LSET B$=A$:PUT #1,R:GOTO 1325
1465 '
1470 CLOSE
1475 GOSUB 350:A$="":X1$=""
1480 X1=40:GOSUB 80:PRINT "DELETE"
1485 GOSUB 1030
1490 IF LEN(X0$)=0 THEN RETURN
1495 OPEN "R",1,DK$+F$+".DAT"
1500 FIELD #1,255 AS B$
1505 X1=495:GOSUB 80:PRINT F
1510 X1=735:X2=3:X3=0:X4=LOF(1):GOSUB 85:R=X0#:IF R=-1 THEN RETURN
1512 X0$=""
1515 GET #1,R
1520 A$=B$:SU=0
1522 IF F>3 THEN F1=3 ELSE F1=F
1525 FOR X=1 TO F1
1530 X1=810:X1=(X1+(X-1)*80):GOSUB 80:PRINT E$+"K"
1535 GOSUB 80:PRINT X;F$(X)
1540 X1$=MID$(A$,SA(X),L(X))
1545 IF RIGHT$(T$(X),1)="I" THEN X9=CVI(X1$):GOTO 1565
1550 IF RIGHT$(T$(X),1)="S" THEN X9=CVS(X1$):GOTO 1565
1555 IF RIGHT$(T$(X),1)="D" THEN X9=CVD(X1$):GOTO 1565
1560 GOTO 1570
1565 X1=X1+8:GOSUB 80: PRINT X9: GOTO 1575
1570 X1=X1+8:GOSUB 80:PRINT X1$
1575 X1=X1-8
1580 NEXT X
1585 X1$="To DELETE, enter DELETE CODE":GOSUB 235:GOSUB 80:PRINT"?"
1590 D1$=INPUT$(3):IF D1$<>DL$ THEN X3$="INVALID CODE":GOSUB 185:
     RETURN
1595 A$="                                                              "
1600 LSET B$=A$:PUT #1,R:CLOSE:X3$="Record deleted":GOSUB 185:RETURN
1605 '
1610 X5=1
1615 CLOSE
1620 PRINT CS$;:X1$="Repack Routine - This routine repacks the
     Database" GOSUB 235
1625 PRINT:PRINT
1630 PRINT BC$:INPUT "FILE TO REPACK ";F$
1632 PRINT CO$;
1635 IF LEN(F$)=0 THEN RETURN
1640 ON ERROR GOTO 2345
1645 OPEN "I",1,DK$+F$+".DAT"
1650 CLOSE
1655 OPEN "R",1,DK$+F$+".DAT"
1660 FIELD #1,255 AS B$
1665 FOR Y%=1 TO LOF(1)
```

```
1670 GET #1,Y%:A$=B$:IF LEFT$(A$,20)=STRING$(20," ") THEN GOSUB 1680
1675 NEXT Y%
1679 CLOSE:RETURN
1680 FOR X%=Y% TO LOF(1)-1
1682 GET #1,X%+1:A$=B$:PUT #1,X%
1684 NEXT X%
1685 RETURN
1705 '
1706 TRUE=1:FALSE=0
1710 AN$="":OP$="":N$="":N=0
1715 PRINT CS$;:PRINTRV$;"Query";ER$;TAB(50);RV$;DA$;ER$:PRINT
1720 PRINT "Filename:-";TAB(40)"Date of last Update:-"
1721 PRINT BC$;
1725 X1=171:X2=7:X3=0:X4=0:GOSUB 85:F$=XO$:IF XO#=-1 THEN RETURN
1726 PRINT CO$;
1730 ON ERROR GOTO 2345
1735 CLOSE:OPEN "I",1,F$
1740 INPUT #1,F$,DI$,DB$,F
1745 ERASE F$,T$,MI,L,MA,SA,Q$
1750 DIM F$(F),T$(F),MI(F),L(F),MA(F),SA(F),Q$(3,F)
1755 FOR X=1 TO F
1760 INPUT #1,F$(X),T$(X),MI(X),L(X),SA(X),MA(X)
1765 NEXT X
1770 CLOSE
1772 GOSUB 3060
1775 X1=222:GOSUB 80:PRINT DB$
1780 OPEN "R",1,DK$+F$+".DAT"
1785 FIELD #1,255 AS B$
1790 Z=1
1795 PRINT:PRINT
1797 PRINT "Field Descriptor":PRINT "Operand":PRINT "Action":PRINT
     "AND/OR"
1798 PRINT BC$;
1799 FOR L4%=1 TO F
1800 X1=417:GOSUB 2340:X2=4:X3=0:X4=0:GOSUB 85:Q$(0,L4%)=XO$:IF
     XO#=-1 THEN 1715
1805 FOR X=1 TO F
1810 IF Q$(0,L4%)=F$(X) THEN 1825
1815 NEXT X
1820 X3$="Invalid Descriptor":GOSUB 185:GOTO 1800
1825 IF T$(X)="A" THEN X2=L(X) ELSE X2=10
1830 X1=497:GOSUB 2340:X3=MI(X):X4=MA(X):GOSUB 85:Q$(1,L4%)=XO$
1835 X1=577:GOSUB 2340:X2=2:X3=0:X4=0:GOSUB 85:Q$(2,L4%)=XO$
1836 AN$=Q$(2,L4%)
1840 IF AN$<>"=" AND AN$<>"<>" AND AN$<>"<" AND AN$<>">" AND AN$<>"
     <=" AND AN$<>">=" THEN X3$="OUT OF RANGE":GOSUB 185:GOTO 1835
1841 X1=657:GOSUB 2340:X2=3:X3=0:X4=0:GOSUB 85: Q$(3,L4%)=XO$
1842 IF XO$="" THEN 1845
1843 NEXT L4%
1845 IF AD=1 THEN 1865
1850 ON ERROR GOTO 2345
1855 ERASE R
1860 DIM R(LOF(1)+1)
```

```
1862 Z=1
1865 Y1=1
1870 GET #1,Y1
1875 A$=B$
1880 FLAG%=FALSE
1885 FOR L4%=1 TO F
1890 GOSUB 2000
1895 IF Q$(3,L4%)="AND" AND FLAG%=FALSE THEN 1955
1900 IF Q$(3,L4%)="OR" AND FLAG%=TRUE THEN 1955
1905 IF Q$(3,L4%)="" THEN 1955
1950 NEXT L4%
1955 IF FLAG%=TRUE THEN R(Z)=Y1:Z=Z+1
1960 Y1=Y1+1:IF Y1<=LOF(1) THEN 1870
1965 PRINT:PRINT"THERE ARE ";Z-1;" RECORDS THAT SATISFY THE QUERY"
1970 IF Z-1=0 THEN 1799
1975 X1$="Type 'P' to print records":GOSUB 235:X2=1:X3=0:X4=0:GOSUB
     85:IF X0#=-1 THEN RETURN ELSE GOTO 2115
1980 RETURN
2000 X0$=Q$(0,L4%):GOSUB 735
2001 N2$=RIGHT$(T$(X5%),1)
2003 N3$=Q$(1,L4%)
2005 N1$=MID$(A$,SA(X5%),L(X5%))
2006 IF T$(X5%)="A" THEN 2020
2007 IF N2$="I" THEN N1=CVI(N1$):N=VAL(N3$)
2008 IF N2$="S" THEN N1=CVS(N1$):N=VAL(N3$)
2009 IF N2$="D" THEN N1=CVD(N1$):N=VAL(N3$)
2010 AN$=Q$(2,L4%)
2011 IF AN$="=" AND N=N1 THEN 2019
2012 IF AN$="<" AND N1<N THEN 2019
2013 IF AN$=">" AND N1>N THEN 2019
2014 IF AN$="<>" AND N1<>N THEN 2019
2015 IF AN$="<=" AND N1<=N THEN 2019
2016 IF AN$=">=" AND N1>=N THEN 2019
2018 FLAG%=FALSE:RETURN
2019 FLAG%=TRUE:RETURN
2020 IF T$(X5%)="A" THEN N$=Q$(1,L4%):N1$=LEFT$(N1$,LEN(N$))
2025 AN$=Q$(2,L4%)
2030 IF AN$="=" AND N$=N1$ THEN FLAG%=TRUE:RETURN
2035 IF AN$="<" AND N1$<N$ THEN FLAG%=TRUE:RETURN
2040 IF AN$=">" AND N1$>N$ THEN FLAG%=TRUE:RETURN
2045 IF AN$="<>" AND N1$<>N$ THEN FLAG%=TRUE:RETURN
2050 IF AN$="<=" AND N1$<=N$ THEN FLAG%=TRUE:RETURN
2055 IF AN$=">=" AND N1$>=N$ THEN FLAG%=TRUE:RETURN
2060 FLAG%=FALSE:RETURN
2115 '
2120 X1$="1 = Screen, 2 = Printer 3 = Sort 4 = Disk ":GOSUB 235
2125 X2=1:X3=1:X4=4:GOSUB 85:CH=X0#:IF X0#=-1 THEN RETURN
2126 IF CH=4 THEN X1$="Enter Filename to be saved Under":GOSUB 235:
     X2=7:X3=0:X4=0:GOSUB 85:IF X0#=-1 THEN 2120
2127 IF CH=4 THEN F1$=X0$:F1$=DK$+F1$+".REC":WI=80:GOTO 2150
2130 IF CH=3 THEN GOSUB 2405:GOTO 2120
2135 IF CH=1 THEN F1$="TT:" ELSE F1$="AT:"
```

```
2140 IF CH=1 THEN PRINT CS$;
2144 IF CH=1 THEN WI=80:GOTO 2150
2145 X1$="Page Width ?":GOSUB 235:X2=3:X3=1:X4=250:GOSUB 85:WI=XO#:
     IF XO#=-1 THEN 2120
2150 X1$="1=FORMAT REPORT, 2=PAGE REPORT":GOSUB 235:X2=1:X3=1:X4=2:
     GOSUB 85:C1=XO#:IF C1=2 THEN 2160
2152 IF XO#=-1 THEN 2145
2155 GOSUB 2445
2157 IF XO#=-1 THEN 2150
2160 OPEN "O",2,F1$:PG=1
2162 IF CH=2 THEN PRINT #2,CHR$(18):IF WI>80 THEN PRINT #2,CHR$(15)
2165 IF CH=2 AND C1=1 THEN OUT 252,12
2175 IF CH=1 THEN PRINT CS$
2180 PRINT #2,"File: ";F$;TAB(40)"Date: ";DA$
2185 PRINT #2,"Last Update: ";DB$
2190 IF WI<1 THEN WI=80:PRINT #2,STRING$(WI,95)
2195 PRINT #2,"RECORDS REQUESTED:"
2200  PRINT #2,:PRINT #2,:GOSUB 2800
2205 FOR Y=1 TO Z-1
2210 IF C1=2 THEN 2245
2215 GET #1,R(Y):A$=B$
2220 GOSUB 2570:LI=LI+1:GOSUB 2785
2225 NEXT Y
2230 IF TO=1 THEN PRINT #2,ELSE GOTO 2305
2235 PRINT #2,:PRINT #2,STRING$(WI,95):GOSUB 3020
2240 GOTO 2305
2245 FOR Y=1 TO Z-1
2250 GET #1,R(Y):A$=B$
2255 PRINT #2,"REC #:-";R(Y)
2260 FOR X=1 TO F
2265 IF T$(X)="A" THEN PRINT #2,F$(X),MID$(A$,SA(X),L(X))
2270 IF RIGHT$(T$(X),1)="I" THEN N=CVI(MID$(A$,SA(X),L(X))):PRINT
     #2,F $(X),N
2275 IF RIGHT$(T$(X),1)="S" THEN N=CVS(MID$(A$,SA(X),L(X))):PRINT
     #2,F $(X),N
2280 IF RIGHT$(T$(X),1)="D" THEN N=CVD(MID$(A$,SA(X),L(X))):PRINT
     #2,F $(X),N
2285 NEXT X
2290 PRINT #2,:PRINT #2,
2295 IF CH=2 THEN 2300
2296 IF CH<>2 AND CH<>4 THEN CLOSE 2:OPEN "O",2,F1$:INPUT XO$
2300 NEXT
2305 PRINT #2,:CLOSE #2
2307 PRINT
2309 IF CH=4 THEN PRINT CS$
2310 INPUT "PRINTOUT COMPLETE - TYPE 'RETURN' TO CONTINUE";XO$
2312 PRINT CS$
2315 X1$="A= PRINT AGAIN, P=NEW HEADINGS, R=RESORT, E=EXIT":GOSUB 235
2320 X2=1:X3=0:X4=0:GOSUB 85:IF XO$="" THEN RETURN
2325 IF XO$="A" THEN 2160
2330 IF XO$="P" THEN 2135
2335 IF XO$="R" THEN 2115 ELSE RETURN
2340 GOSUB 80:PRINT E$+"K":RETURN
```

```
2345 IF ERR=53 AND ERL=1045 THEN X3$="No Such File":GOSUB 185:
     RESUME 1035
2347 IF ERR=5 AND ERL=2562 THEN RESUME 2563
2350 IF ERR=5 AND ERL=580 THEN RESUME 585
2355 IF ERR=5 AND ERL=1855 THEN RESUME 1860
2360 IF ERR=5 AND ERL=2480 THEN RESUME 2485
2365 IF ERR=53 AND ERL=1645 THEN X3$="NO SUCH FILE":GOSUB 185:
     RESUME 1630
2370 IF ERR=53 AND ERL=1735 THEN X3$="NO SUCH FILE":GOSUB 185:
     RESUME 1725
2375 IF ERR=5 AND ERL=1910 THEN RESUME 1920
2380 IF ERR=5 AND ERL=1060 THEN RESUME 1065
2385 IF ERR=5 AND ERL=1745 THEN RESUME   1750
2390 IF ERR=10 AND ERL=1860 THEN RESUME 1865
2395 ON ERROR GOTO 0
2400 '
2405 X1$="Field to sort on":GOSUB 235:X2=4:X3=0:X4=0:GOSUB 85:K$=
     X0$:IF X0#=-1T THEN ERASE TS$:RETURN
2410 GOSUB 735:IF X0=-1 THEN 2405 ELSE Y%=X5%
2430 X1$="1=Highest at top, 2=Lowest at top":GOSUB 235:X2=1:X3=1
     :X4=2: GOSUB 85:I IF X0#=-1   THEN 2405
2432 IF S2=0 THEN S2=1:GOTO 2435
2433 GOSUB 3430:GOTO 2440
2435 GOSUB 2830
2440 GOTO 2405
2445 ON ERROR GOTO 2345
2446 ERASE F1$
2447 DIM F1$(3,F)
2450 PRINT CS$;:PRINT RV$;"REPORT FORMATING";ER$
2452 CLOSE #3:X1$=REPORT FORMAT FILENAME TO READ ?":GOSUB 235:X2=9:
     X3= 0:X4=0 GOSUB 85:IF X0#=-1 THEN GOTO 2456 ELSE GOSUB 3350:
     GOTO 2560
2455 PRINT:PRINT:PRINT
2456 GOSUB 3060
2460 PRINT "Report Heading"
2465 X1=337:X2=40:X3=0:X4=0:GOSUB 85:RH$=X0$:IF X0#=-1 THEN RETURN
2470 X6=480
2490 F1=0:LI=0:PG=1
2492 X1=400:GOSUB 80:PRINT"FIELD   SUBHEADING   TAB >    4! FORMAT"
2493 PRINT STRING$(80,95)
2495 FOR X%=1 TO F
2505 X1=X6+(80*X%):X2=4:X3=0:X4=0:GOSUB 85:F1$(0,X%)=X0$:IF X0#=
     -1 THEN 2560
2510 GOSUB 735:IF X0=-1 THEN 2505 ELSE Y4%=X5%
2530 X1=X1+10:X2=12:X3=0:X4=0:GOSUB 85:F1$(1,X%)=X0$
2535 X1=X1+31:X2=3:X3=5:X4=WI:GOSUB 85:F1$(2,X%)=X0$
2540 IF T$(Y4%)="A" THEN 2550
2545 X1=X1+12:X2=12:X3=0:X4=0:GOSUB 85:F1$(3,X%)=X0$
2550 F1=F1+1
2555 NEXT X%
2560 PRINT:INPUT " TOTALS    (Y/N) ";X0$:IF X0$="Y" OR X0$="y"
     THEN T0=1 ELSE T0=0
```

```
2561 ON ERROR GOTO 2345
2562 ERASE T9
2563 DIM T9(F1)
2564 X1$="REPORT FILE NAME TO SAVE ?":GOSUB 235:X2=9:X3=0:X4=0:
     GOSUB 85: IF X0#<>-1 THEN GOSUB 3365
2565 X0#=0:X0$="":RETURN
2570 PRINT #2,:PRINT #2,R(Y);
2572 FOR Y%=1 TO F1
2575 IF F1$(0,Y%)="" THEN RETURN
2580 FOR X=1 TO F
2585 IF F1$(0,Y%)=F$(X) THEN 2600
2590 NEXT X
2595 RETURN
2600 '
2601 IF T$(X)="A" THEN PRINT #2,TAB(VAL(F1$(2,Y%)));MID$(A$,SA(X),
     L(X));
2602 IF F1$(3,Y%)<>"" THEN GOSUB 3000:GOTO 2620
2605 IF RIGHT$(T$(X),1)="I" THEN N=CVI(MID$(A$,SA(X),L(X))):
     PRINT #2,TAB(VAL(F1$(2,Y%)));N;:T9(Y%)=T9(Y%)+N
2610 IF RIGHT$(T$(X),1)="S" THEN N=CVS(MID$(A$,SA(X),L(X))):
     PRINT #2,TAB(VAL(F1$(2,Y%)));N;:T9(Y%)=T9(Y%)+N
2615 IF RIGHT$(T$(X),1)="D" THEN N=CVD(MID$(A$,SA(X),L(X))):
     PRINT #2,TAB(VAL(F1$(2,Y%)));N;:T9(Y%)=T9(Y%)+N
2620 NEXT Y%
2625 RETURN
2630 '
2635 PRINT CS$;RV$;"REVEIW";ER$;TAB(60);RV$;DA$;ER$
2640 PRINT:PRINT:PRINT:PRINT
2645 PRINT " Filename     :- ";TAB(40)"Date Created    :-":PRINT
     TAB(40)" Date of Update :-"
2650 PRINTSTRING$(80,"-"):PRINT:GOSUB 330
2655 X1=415:X2=7:X3=0:X4=0:GOSUB 85:F$=X0$:IF X0#=-1 THEN RETURN
2660 CLOSE:ON ERROR GOTO 2345:GOSUB 1045
2665 FOR X=1 TO F
2666 PRINT CO$
2670 X1=738:GOSUB 80:PRINT F$(X)
2675 X1=818:GOSUB 80:PRINT T$(X)
2680 X1=898:GOSUB 80:PRINT MI(X)
2685 X1=778:GOSUB 80:PRINT L(X)
2690 X1=938:GOSUB 80:PRINT MA(X)
2692 PRINT BC$
2695 PRINT:PRINT:PRINT"NEXT (Y/N)":INPUT NE$:IF NE$="Y" OR NE$="y"
     THEN 2700 ELSE 2705
2700 NEXT
2705 RETURN
2785 IF LI<50 THEN RETURN
2790 PRINT#2,:IF CH<>4 THEN CLOSE 2:OPEN "O",2,F1$
2795 OUT 252,12:PRINT #2,:PRINT #2,
2800 PRINT #2,TAB((WI-LEN(RH$))/2);RH$;TAB(WI-10);"PAGE ";PG
2805 PRINT #2,:PRINT #2,
2807 PRINT #2,"REC";
2810 FOR X8%=1 TO F1
```

```
2815 PRINT #2,TAB(VAL(F1$(2,X8%)));F1$(1,X8%);
2820 NEXT
2825 PRINT #2,:PRINT #2,STRING$(WI,95):LI=1:PG=PG+1:RETURN
2830 DIM TS$(Z-1)
2835 FOR Y=1 TO Z-1
2840 GOSUB 3500:TS$(Y)=T$
2850 NEXT Y
2855 N%=Z-1:M%=N%
2860 M%=INT(M%/2)
2865 IF M%=0 THEN RETURN
2870 J%=1:K%=N%-M%
2875 I%=J%
2880 L%=I%+M%
2885 IF XO#=1 AND T$(Y%)="A" AND TS$(I%)>=TS$(L%) OR
     XO#=1 AND T$(Y%)<>"A" AND VAL(TS$(I%)>=VAL(TS$(L%)) THEN 2920
2890 IF XO#=2 AND T$(Y%)="A" AND TS$(I%)<=TS$(L%) OR
     XO#=2 AND T$(Y%)<>"A" AND VAL(TS$(I%)<=VAL(TS$(L%)) THEN 2920
2895 SWAP TS$(I%),TS$(L%)
2900 SWAP R(I%),R(L%)
2905 I%=I%-M%
2910 IF I%<1 THEN 2920
2915 GOTO 2880
2920 J%=J%+1
2925 IF J%>K% THEN 2860
2930 GOTO 2875
2935 PRINT CS$:PRINT RV$;"COPYWRITE 1980 by"
2940 PRINT "Greg GREENE, 207-885 Craigflower RD"
2945 PRINT "Victoria B.C. Canada";ER$
2950 PRINT :PRINT :PRINT"ser # 81-1-1"
2955 PRINT:PRINT"Program Must be rerun now"
2960 END
3000 IF RIGHT$(T$(X),1)="I" THEN N=CVI(MID$(A$,SA(X),L(X))):PRINT #2,
     TAB(VAL(F1$(2,Y%))) USING F1$(3,Y%);N;:T9(Y%)=T9(Y%)+N
3005 IF RIGHT$(T$(X),1)="S" THEN N=CVS(MID$(A$,SA(X),L(X))):PRINT #2,
     TAB(VAL(F1$(2,Y%))) USING F1$(3,Y%);N;:T9(Y%)=T9(Y%)+N
3010 IF RIGHT$(T$(X),1)="D" THEN N=CVD(MID$(A$,SA(X),L(X))):PRINT #2,
     TAB(V1L(F1$(2,Y%))) USING F1$(3,Y%);N;:T9(Y%)=T9(Y%)+N
3015 RETURN
3020 FOR X8%=1 TO F1
3025 IF T9(X8%)=0 THEN PRINT #2,TAB(VAL(F1$(2,X8%)));T9(X8%);
     :GOTO 3050
3030 PRINT #2,TAB(VAL(F1$(2,X8%)))USING F1$(3,X8%);T9(X8%);
3050 NEXT X8%
3055 PRINT #2,:PRINT #2,STRING$(WI,95):RETURN
3060 PRINT E$+"j";
3065 X1=1600:GOSUB 80
3067 PRINT "FIELD DESCRIPTORS"
3070 FOR X7%=1 TO F
3075 PRINT F$(X7%);"-";L(X7%);" ";
3080 NEXT
3090 PRINT E$+"k";
3095 RETURN
```

```
3100 PRINT DC$")C"E$"1"
3101 PRINT DC$"*C"E$"1"
3102 PRINT DC$"+C"E$"1"
3103 PRINT DC$",C"E$"1":PRINT DC$"-D"E$"1":PRINT DC$".C"E$"1"
3104 RETURN
3105 PRINT CS$S1$" 8 Greg Greene & Associates Database"ER$CH$
3110 PRINT E$"y4";
3120 PRINT DC$"$ "GM$STRING$(80,"a")EG$CH$
3125 PRINT GM$DC$"% "STRING$(80," ")EG$
3130 PRINT DC$"& "GM$STRING$(80,"a")EG$
3135 PRINT S1$"'D Menu "ER$CH$
3140 PRINT DC$"4 ";GM$STRING$(80,"a")EG$
3145 PRINT S1$"5 Please make the Selection "
3150 PRINT S1$"6 You Want --------------> "ER$
3155 RETURN
3160 PRINT J$E$+"x"CHR$(49);DC$"8 "E$"1"K$:RETURN
3350 OPEN "I",3,X0$+".RPT"
3352 INPUT #3,RH$,F1
3354 FOR L1%=0 TO 3
3356    FOR L2%=1 TO F
3358             INPUT #3,F1$(L1%,L2%)
3360    NEXT L2%
3362 NEXT L1%
3364 CLOSE #3:RETURN
3365 OPEN "O",3,X0$+".RPT"
3366 PRINT #3,RH$;",";F1
3368 FOR L1%=0 TO 3
3370    FOR L2%=1 TO F
3372             PRINT #3,F1$(L1%,L2%)
3374    NEXT L2%
3376 NEXT L1%
3378 CLOSE #3:RETURN
3430 ' SECONDARY SORT
3435 FOR Y=1 TO Z-2
3440    IF TS$(Y)=TS$(Y+1) THEN GOSUB 3525
3445 NEXT Y
3450 IF SW=1 THEN SW=0:GOTO 3435
3455 RETURN
3500 GET #1,R(Y):A$=B$
3503 IF T$(Y%)="A" THEN T$=MID$(A$,SA(Y%),L(Y%))
3505 IF T$(Y%)="DI" THEN T$=STR$(CVI(MID$(A$,SA(Y%),L(Y%))))
3510 IF T$(Y%)="DS" THEN T$=STR$(CVS(MID$(A$,SA(Y%),L(Y%))))
3515 IF T$(Y%)="DD" THEN T$=STR$(CVD(MID$(A$,SA(Y%),L(Y%))))
3520 RETURN
3525 GOSUB 3500:T1$=T$:Y=Y+1:GOSUB 3500:T2$=T$:Y=Y-1
3530 IF XO#=1 AND T$(Y%)="A" AND T1$>=T2$ OR XO#=1 AND T$(Y%)<>"A" AND
     VAL(T1$)>=VAL(T2$) THEN RETURN
3535 IF XO#=2 AND T$(Y%)="A" AND T1$<=T2$ OR XO#=2 AND T$(Y%)<>"A" AND
     VAL(T1$)<=VAL(T2$) THEN RETURN
3540 SWAP TS$(Y),TS$(Y+1):SWAP R(Y),R(Y+1):SW=1:RETURN
```

Appendix B
Flowcharts of the Database Manager Program

The flowcharts shown in this section are provided to help you get a better understanding of the logic in the program. They will also be of great value if you are translating to a different system. While every effort has been made to stick to convention in the drawings, I have, occasionally resorted to placing convenience ahead of it! The primary purpose of any flowchart technique is to convey to the user the flow of logic used in designing the program. In a conventional chart, all connections to off sheet charts are done with a letter or number notation that bears no resemblance to the line numbers of the program. I have chosen however to tie the connections to actual line numbers and subroutines that exist in the listing. I do this so that the novice can find his way a little easier.

I believe that with the source listings, the English flowcharts, and the drawings, no one should have any problem in grasping how the program works. In fact, I suspect that many of you will see several ways to improve both the coding and the logic. In order to change it, you first need to understand the code I have written, and that's one of the purposes of this book! For those of you who either don't wish, or don't feel up to changing things, the program works as is.

The symbols I have used are shown in Fig. B-1. The program flowcharts follow.

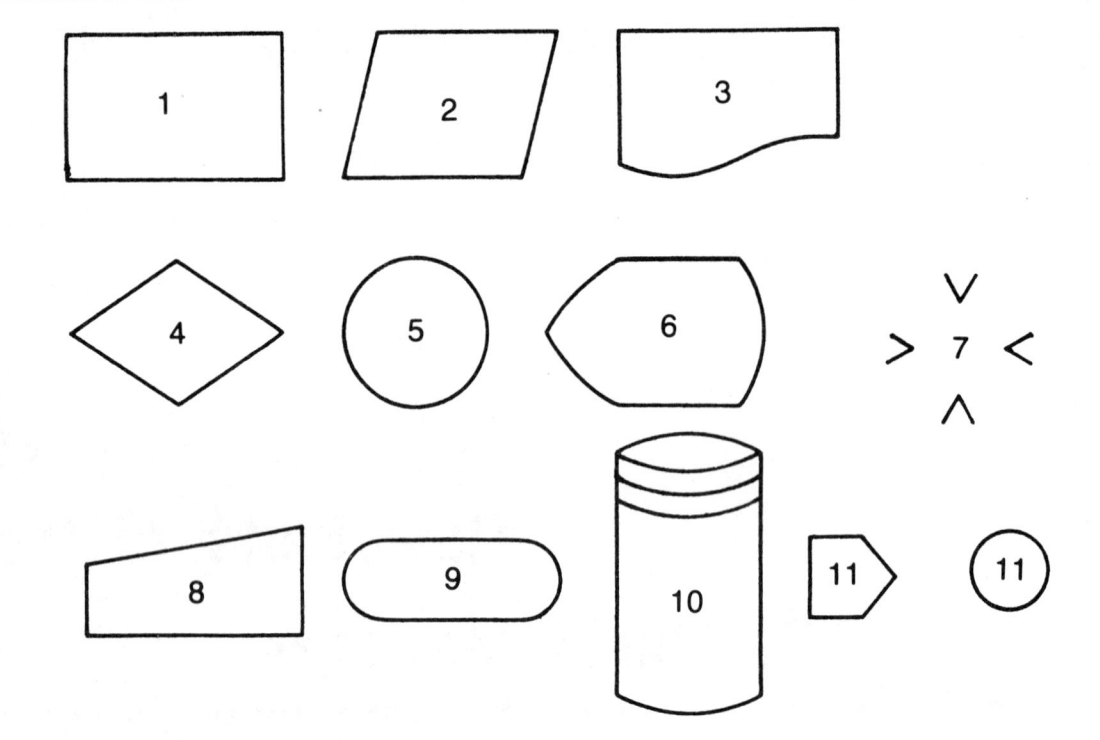

1. A program routine.
2. An I/O routine.
3. A document (Printed page).
4. A decision box, with the yes decision branching to the right, and the no decision exiting out the bottom.
5. A GOSUB with the starting line of the routine in the circle.
6. A screen display or action.
7. The direction of program logic if not left to right or top to bottom.
8. An input from the keyboard.
9. A subroutine return statement or program start or end.
10. A disk based file.
11. Connectors to join a chart with a chart on the next page or a chart on the same page where drawing line would confuse the reader.

Fig. B-1. Flowchart symbols.

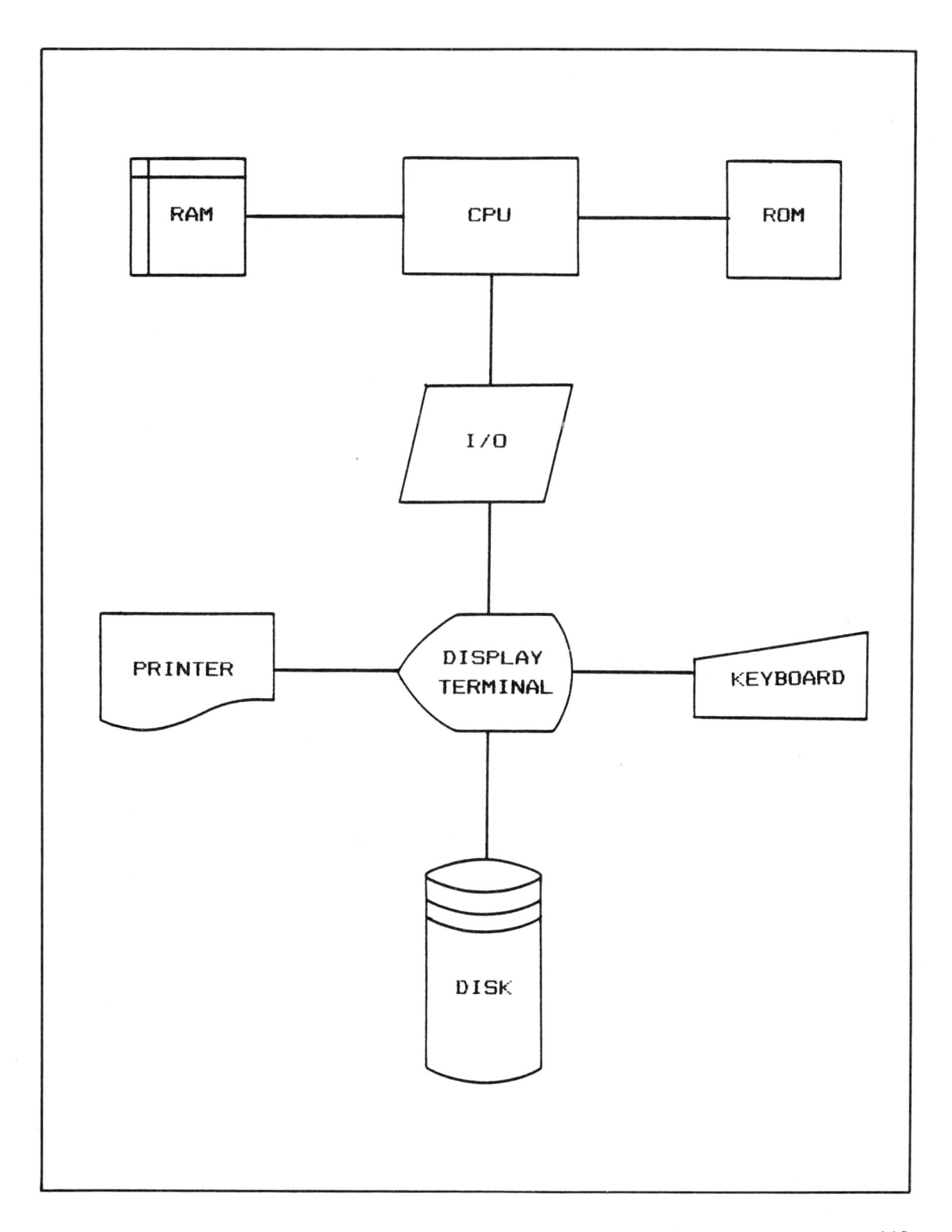

```
┌─────────────────────────────────────────────────┐
│                                                 │
│   ┌─────┐      ┌─────────┐      ┌─────┐         │
│   │ RAM │──────│   CPU   │──────│ ROM │         │
│   └─────┘      └─────────┘      └─────┘         │
│                     │                           │
│                     │                           │
│                   ┌───┐                         │
│                   │I/O│                         │
│                   └───┘                         │
│                     │                           │
│                     │                           │
│   ┌────────┐    ┌─────────┐    ┌──────────┐     │
│   │PRINTER │────│ DISPLAY │────│ KEYBOARD │     │
│   │        │    │TERMINAL │    │          │     │
│   └────────┘    └─────────┘    └──────────┘     │
│                     │                           │
│                     │                           │
│                   ┌────┐                        │
│                   │DISK│                        │
│                   └────┘                        │
│                                                 │
└─────────────────────────────────────────────────┘
```

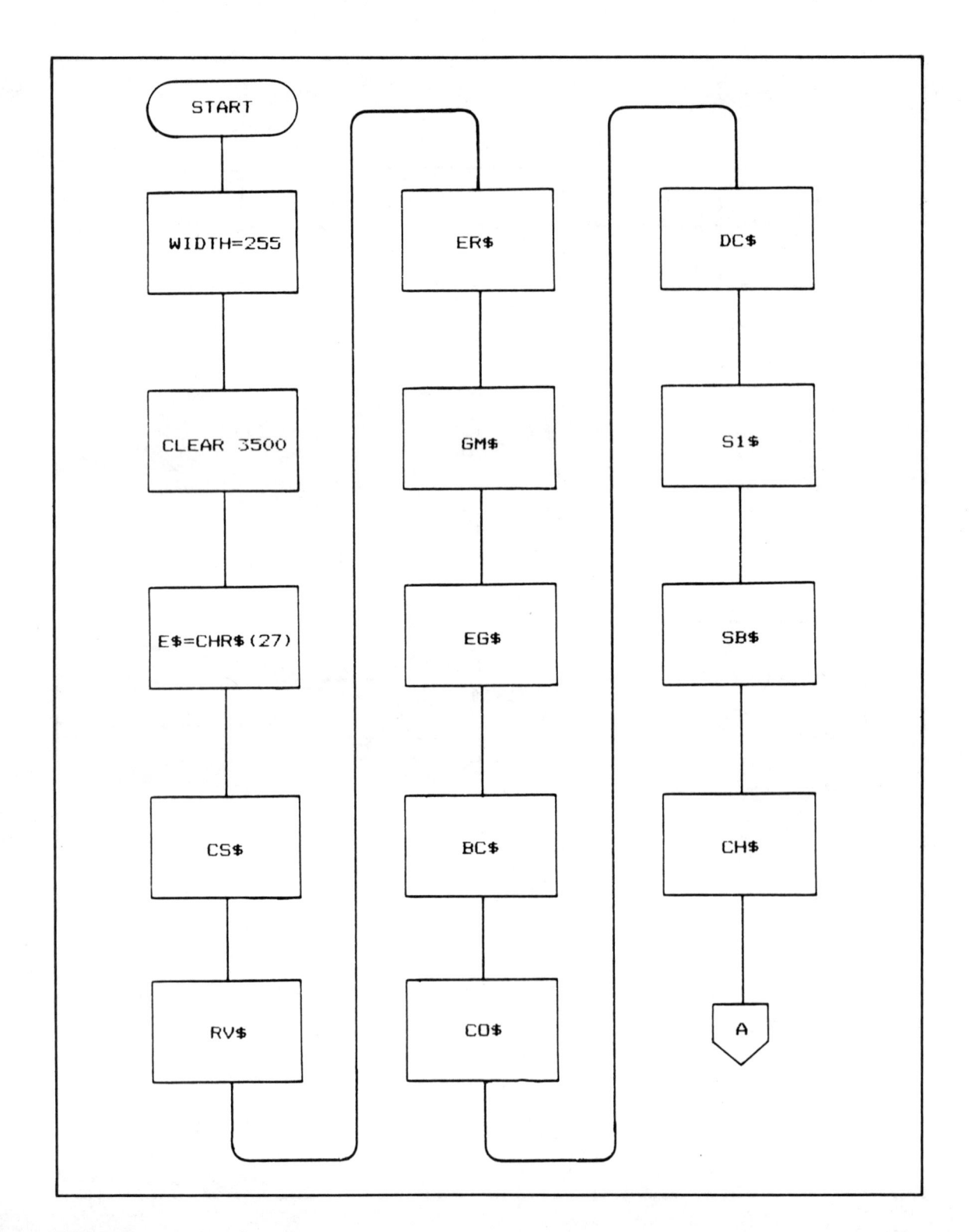

```
                START
                  │
                  ▼
            ┌───────────┐      ┌───────┐      ┌───────┐
            │ WIDTH=255 │      │  ER$  │      │  DC$  │
            └───────────┘      └───────┘      └───────┘
                  │                │              │
                  ▼                ▼              ▼
            ┌───────────┐      ┌───────┐      ┌───────┐
            │ CLEAR 3500│      │  GM$  │      │  S1$  │
            └───────────┘      └───────┘      └───────┘
                  │                │              │
                  ▼                ▼              ▼
            ┌───────────┐      ┌───────┐      ┌───────┐
            │E$=CHR$(27)│      │  EG$  │      │  SB$  │
            └───────────┘      └───────┘      └───────┘
                  │                │              │
                  ▼                ▼              ▼
            ┌───────────┐      ┌───────┐      ┌───────┐
            │    CS$    │      │  BC$  │      │  CH$  │
            └───────────┘      └───────┘      └───────┘
                  │                │              │
                  ▼                ▼              ▼
            ┌───────────┐      ┌───────┐         ╱A╲
            │    RV$    │      │  CO$  │         ‾‾‾
            └───────────┘      └───────┘
```

```
   ┌──┐      ┌─────────┐      ┌─────────┐
   │40│──────│  MENU   │──────│ RETURN  │
   └──┘      │ PROMPT  │      └─────────┘
             └─────────┘
```

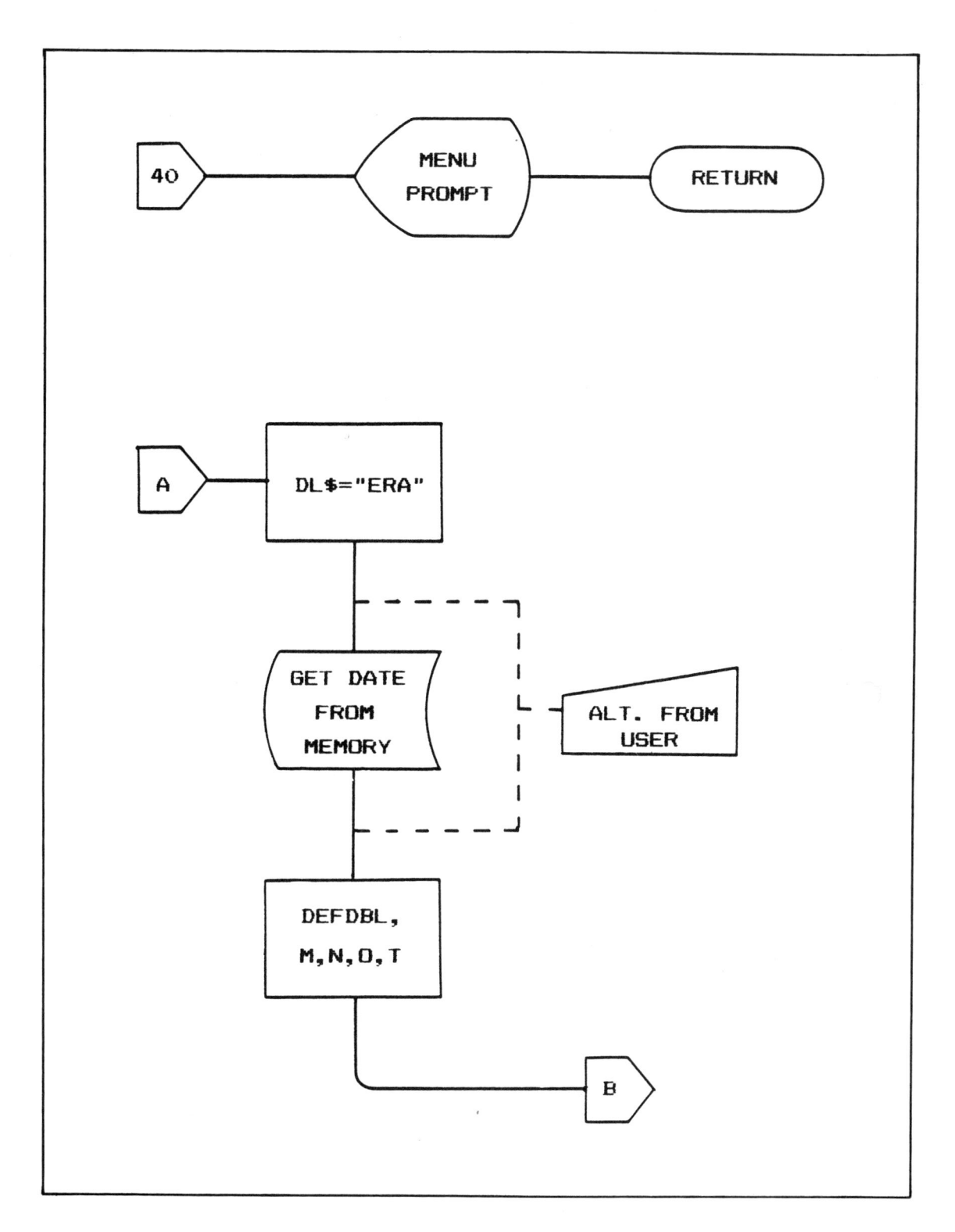

```
   ┌──┐      ┌─────────┐
   │ A│──────│DL$="ERA"│
   └──┘      └─────────┘
                  │
                  ┊
             ┌─────────┐        ┌──────────┐
             │GET DATE │        │ ALT. FROM│
             │  FROM   │┄┄┄┄┄┄┄│   USER   │
             │ MEMORY  │        └──────────┘
             └─────────┘
                  │
             ┌─────────┐
             │ DEFDBL, │
             │ M,N,O,T │
             └─────────┘
                  │
                  └──────┐
                      ┌──┐
                      │ B│
                      └──┘
```

```
┌─────┐   ┌─────────┐   ┌──────────┐   ┌──────────┐
│  80 ├──►│ ROW/COL ├──►│   SET    ├──►│  RETURN  │
└─────┘   └─────────┘   │  CURSOR  │   └──────────┘
                        └──────────┘
```

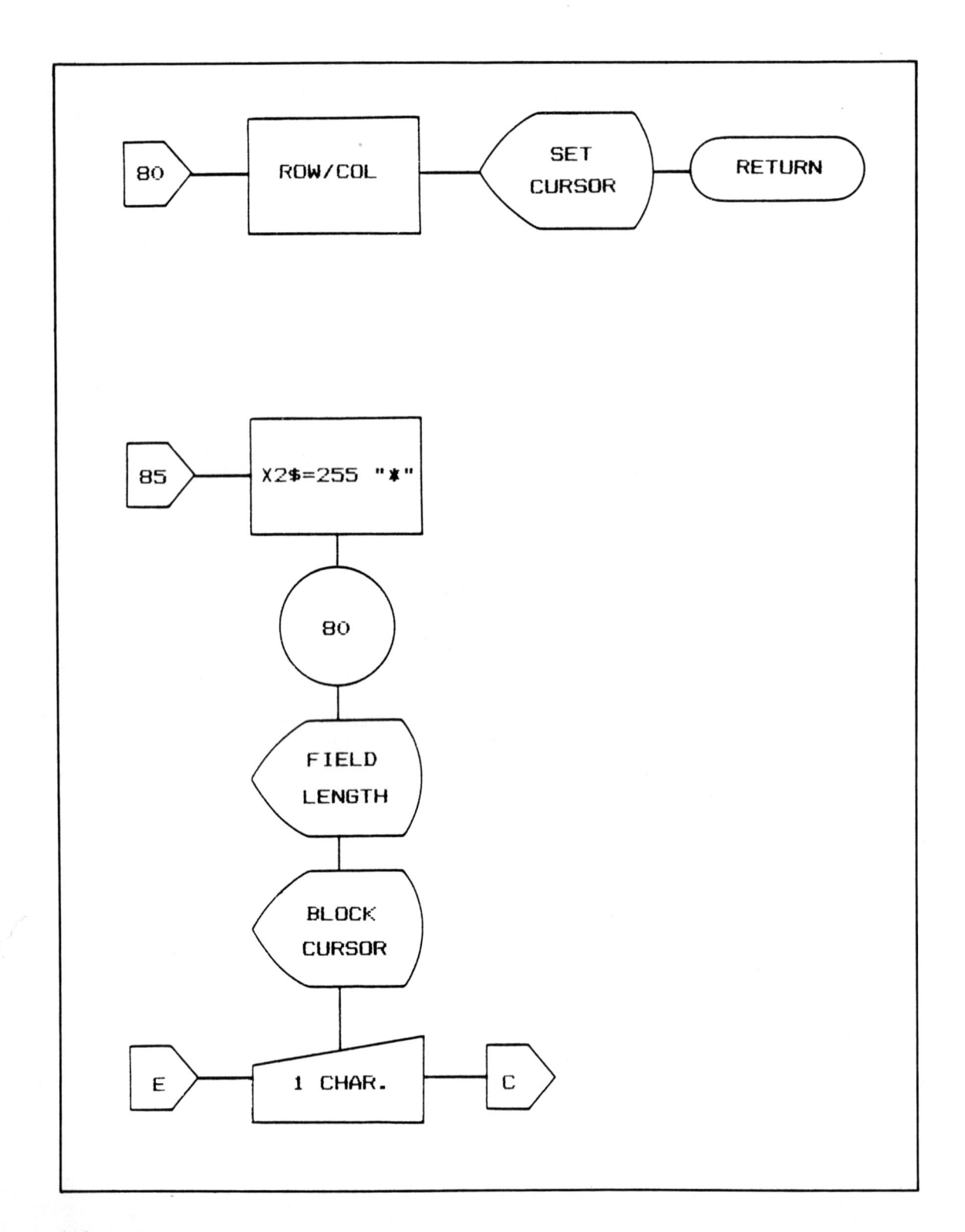

```
┌─────┐   ┌──────────────┐
│  85 ├──►│ X2$=255 "*"  │
└─────┘   └──────┬───────┘
                 │
              ( 80 )
                 │
           ┌─────┴─────┐
           │   FIELD   │
           │   LENGTH  │
           └─────┬─────┘
                 │
           ┌─────┴─────┐
           │   BLOCK   │
           │  CURSOR   │
           └─────┬─────┘
                 │
   ┌───┐   ┌─────┴─────┐   ┌───┐
   │ E ├──►│  1 CHAR.  ├──►│ C │
   └───┘   └───────────┘   └───┘
```

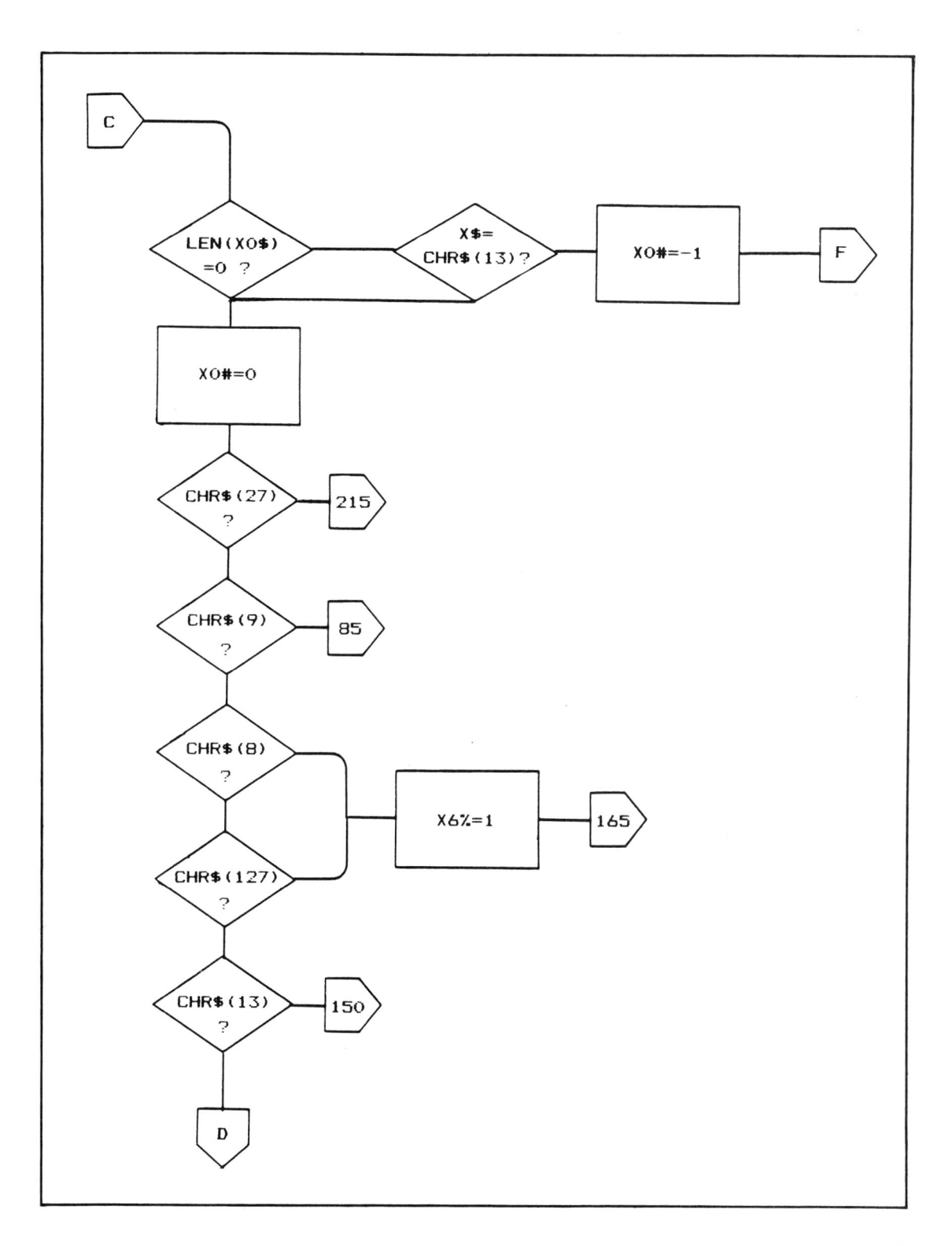

```
┌─C
│
▼
◇ LEN(X0$)=0 ? ──── ◇ X$=CHR$(13)? ──── □ X0#=-1 ──── ▷ F
│
▼
□ X0#=0
│
▼
◇ CHR$(27)? ──── ▷ 215
│
▼
◇ CHR$(9)? ──── ▷ 85
│
▼
◇ CHR$(8)? ────┐
│              │
▼              ▼
◇ CHR$(127)? ─ □ X6%=1 ──── ▷ 165
│
▼
◇ CHR$(13)? ──── ▷ 150
│
▼
▷ D
```

117

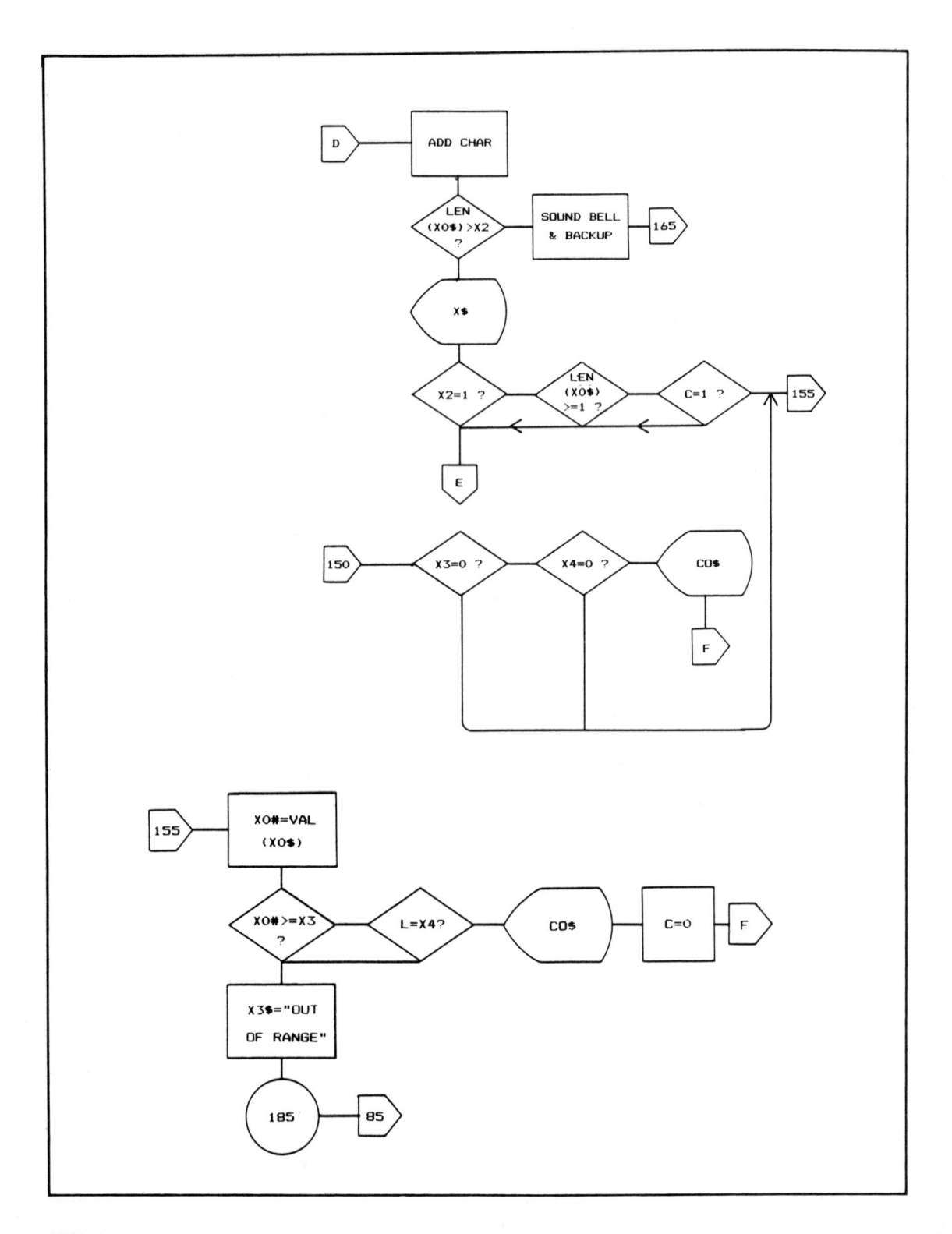

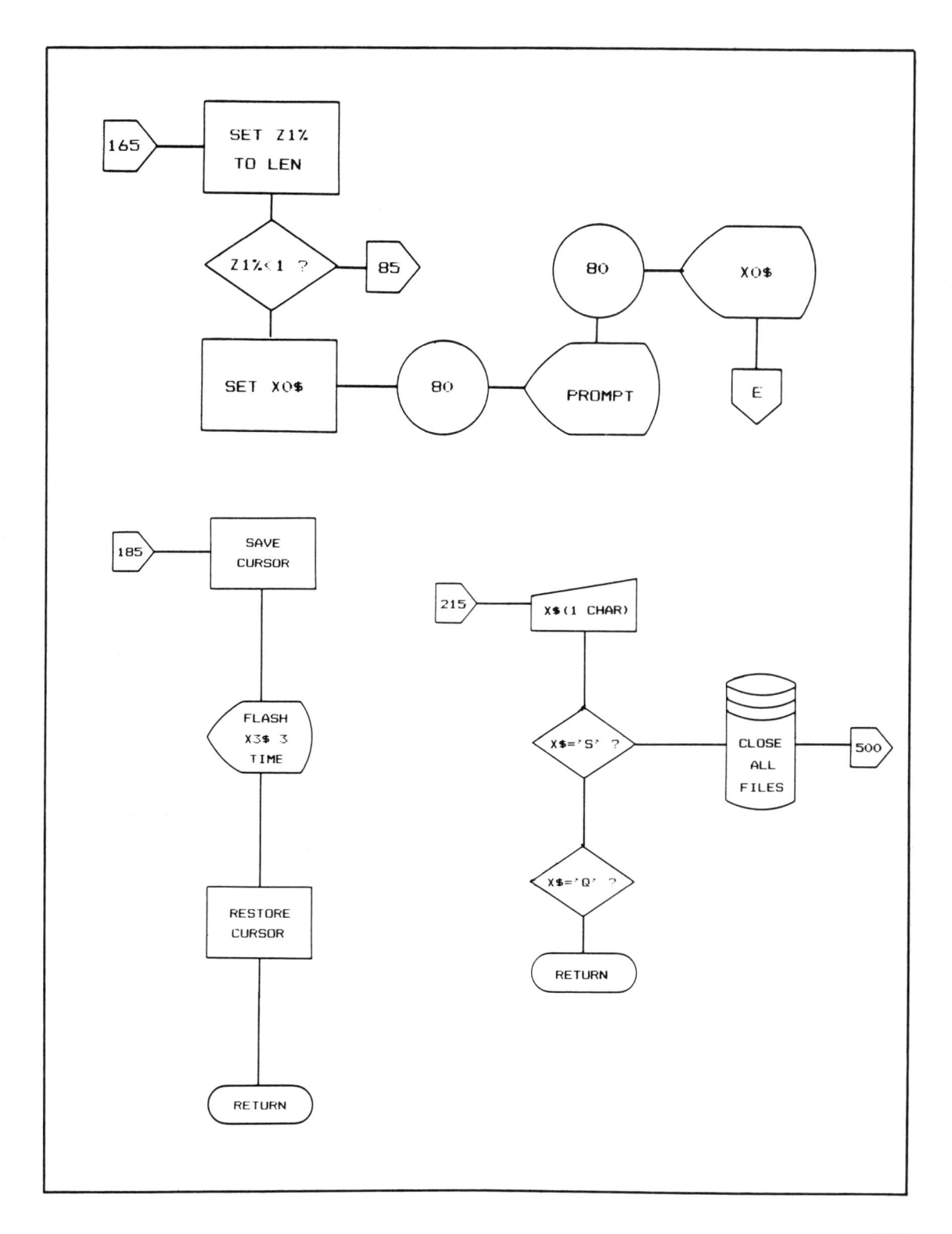

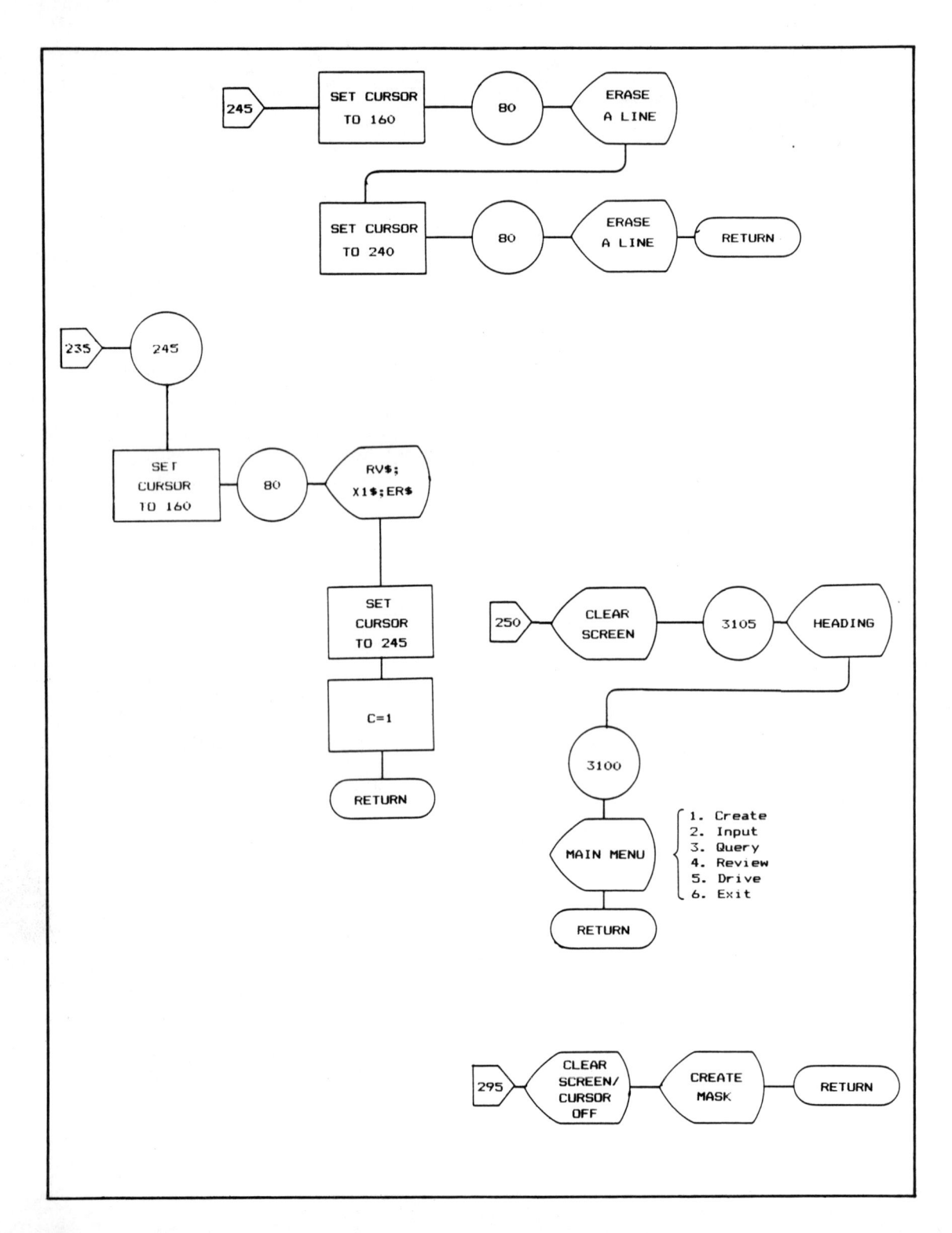

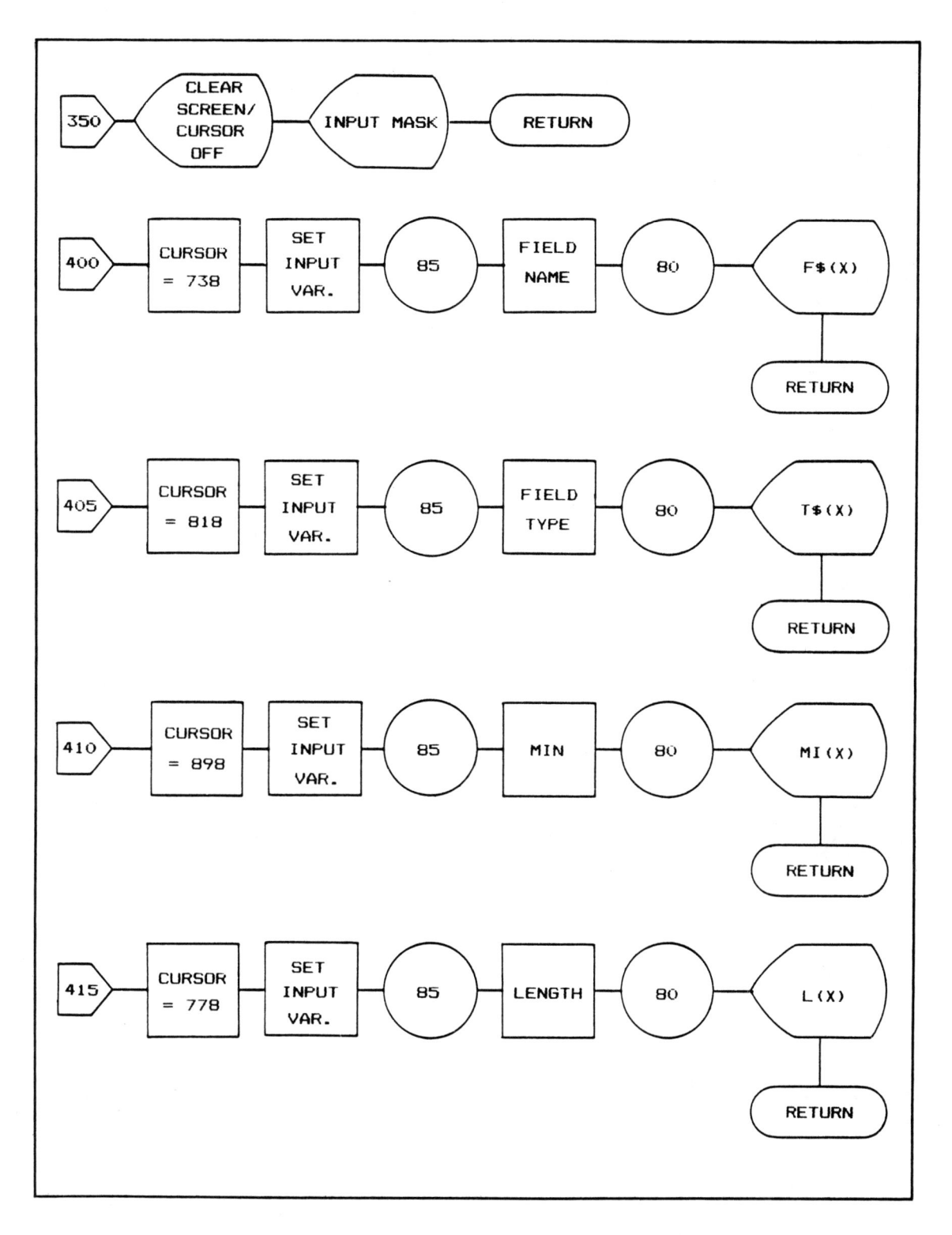

```
350 → CLEAR SCREEN/ CURSOR OFF → INPUT MASK → RETURN

400 → CURSOR = 738 → SET INPUT VAR. → 85 → FIELD NAME → 80 → F$(X) → RETURN

405 → CURSOR = 818 → SET INPUT VAR. → 85 → FIELD TYPE → 80 → T$(X) → RETURN

410 → CURSOR = 898 → SET INPUT VAR. → 85 → MIN → 80 → MI(X) → RETURN

415 → CURSOR = 778 → SET INPUT VAR. → 85 → LENGTH → 80 → L(X) → RETURN
```

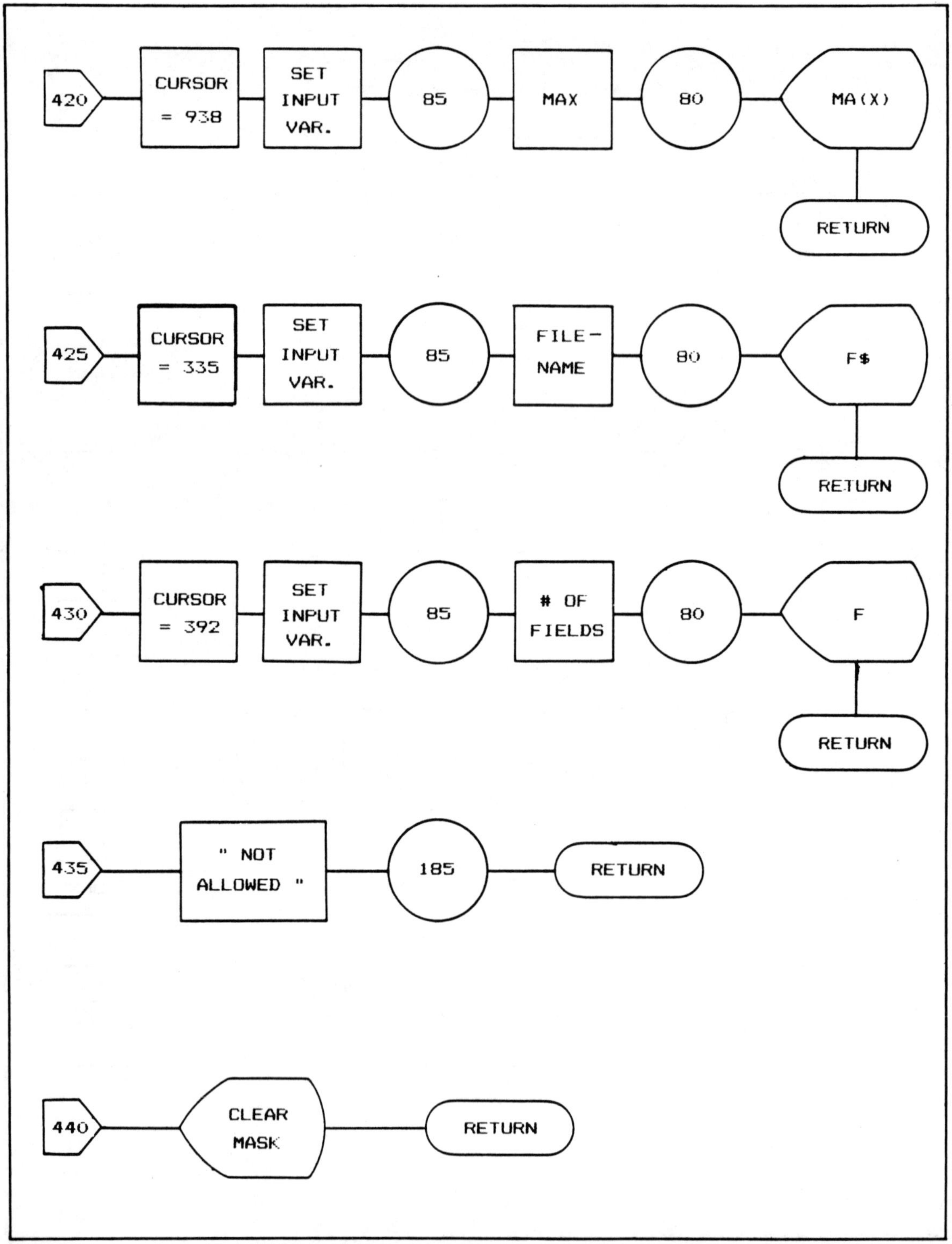
420
CURSOR = 938
SET INPUT VAR.
85
MAX
80
MA(X)
RETURN
425
CURSOR = 335
SET INPUT VAR.
85
FILE-NAME
80
F$
RETURN
430
CURSOR = 392
SET INPUT VAR.
85
OF FIELDS
80
F
RETURN
435
" NOT ALLOWED "
185
RETURN
440
CLEAR MASK
RETURN

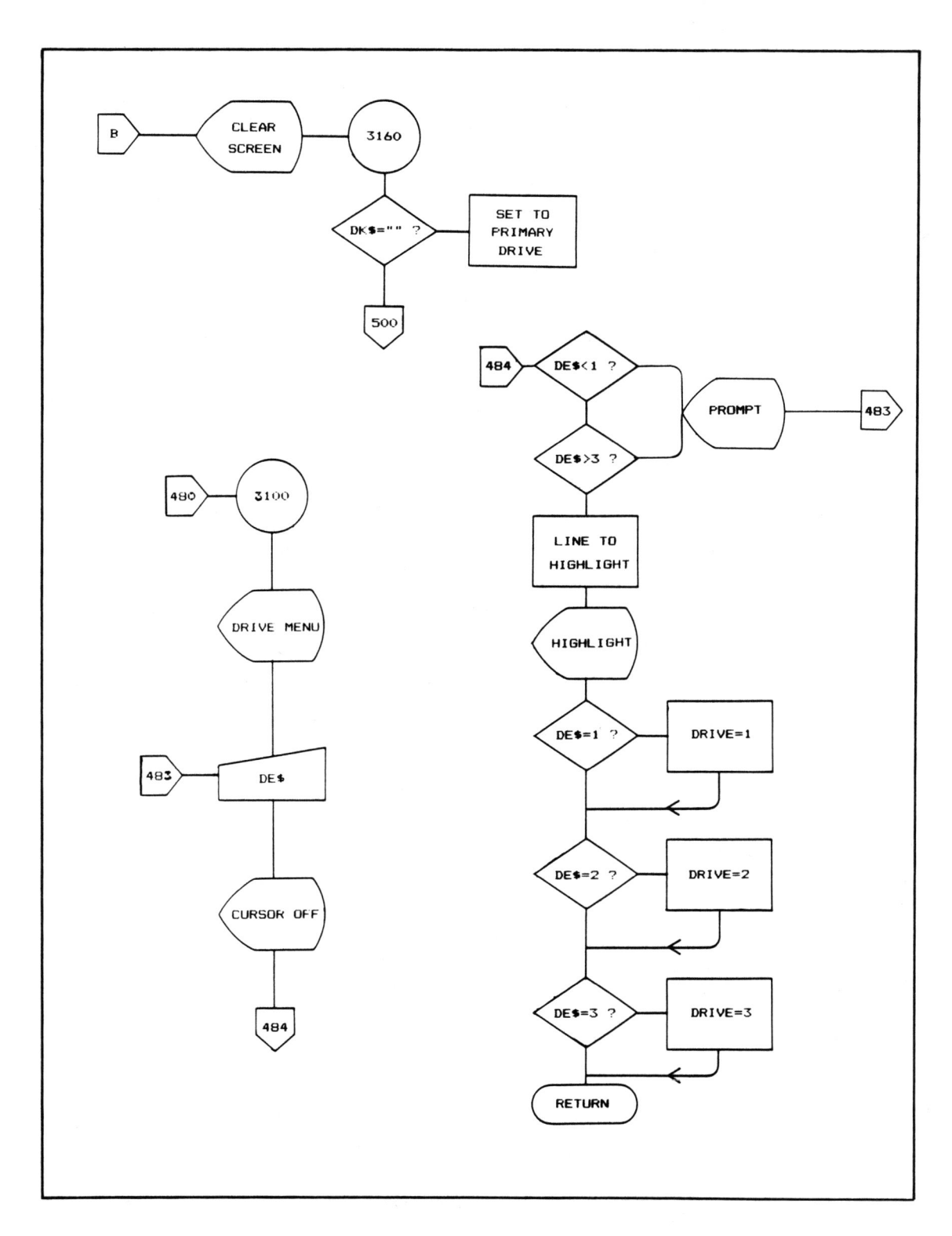

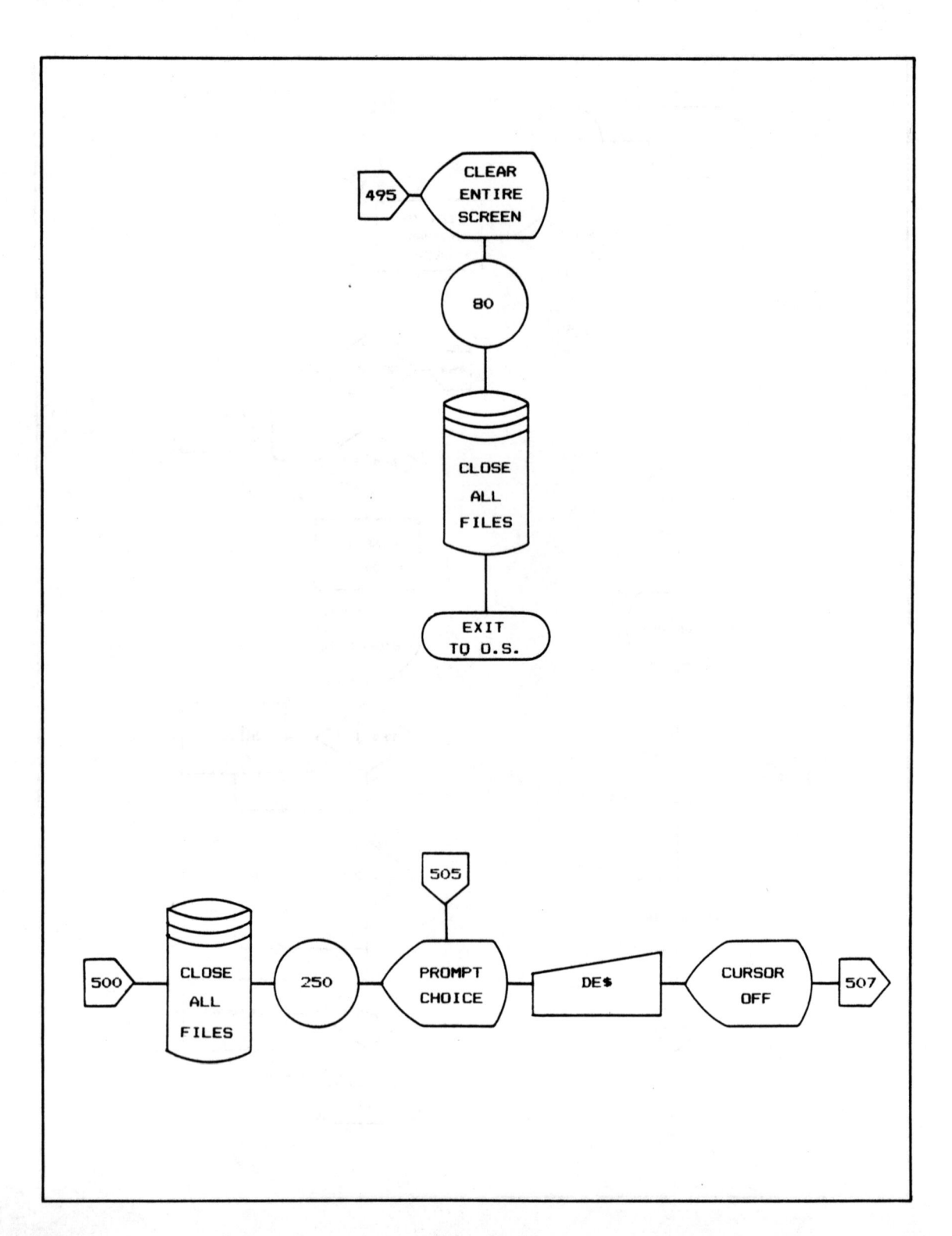

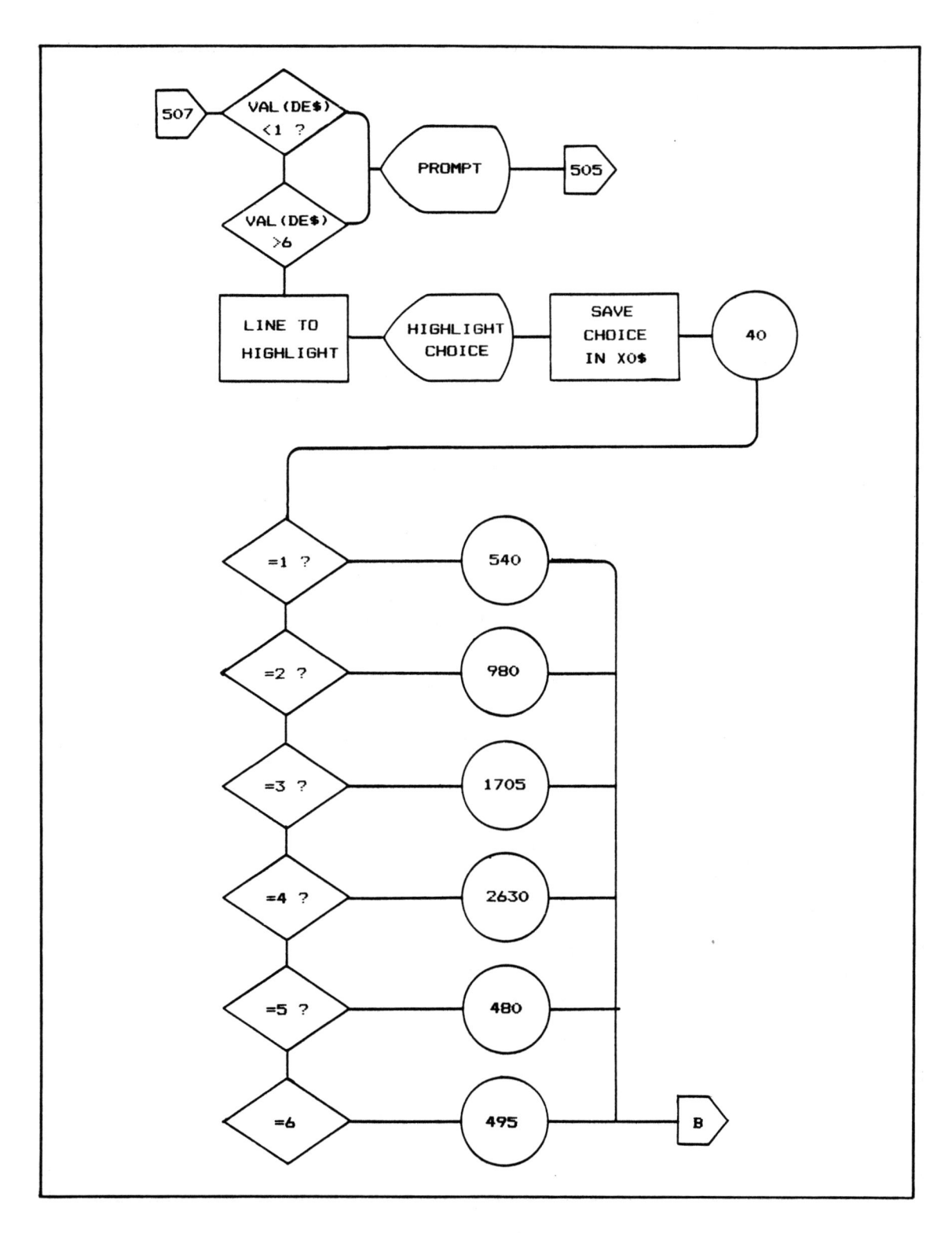

```
                    ┌─ VAL(DE$) <1 ? ─ yes ─► PROMPT ──► 505
  507 ──► 
                    └─ VAL(DE$) >6 ? ─ yes ─┘
                           │ no
                           ▼
                    LINE TO HIGHLIGHT ──► HIGHLIGHT CHOICE ──► SAVE CHOICE IN X0$ ──► ( 40 )
```

- =1 ? → (540)
- =2 ? → (980)
- =3 ? → (1705)
- =4 ? → (2630)
- =5 ? → (480)
- =6 → (495) → B

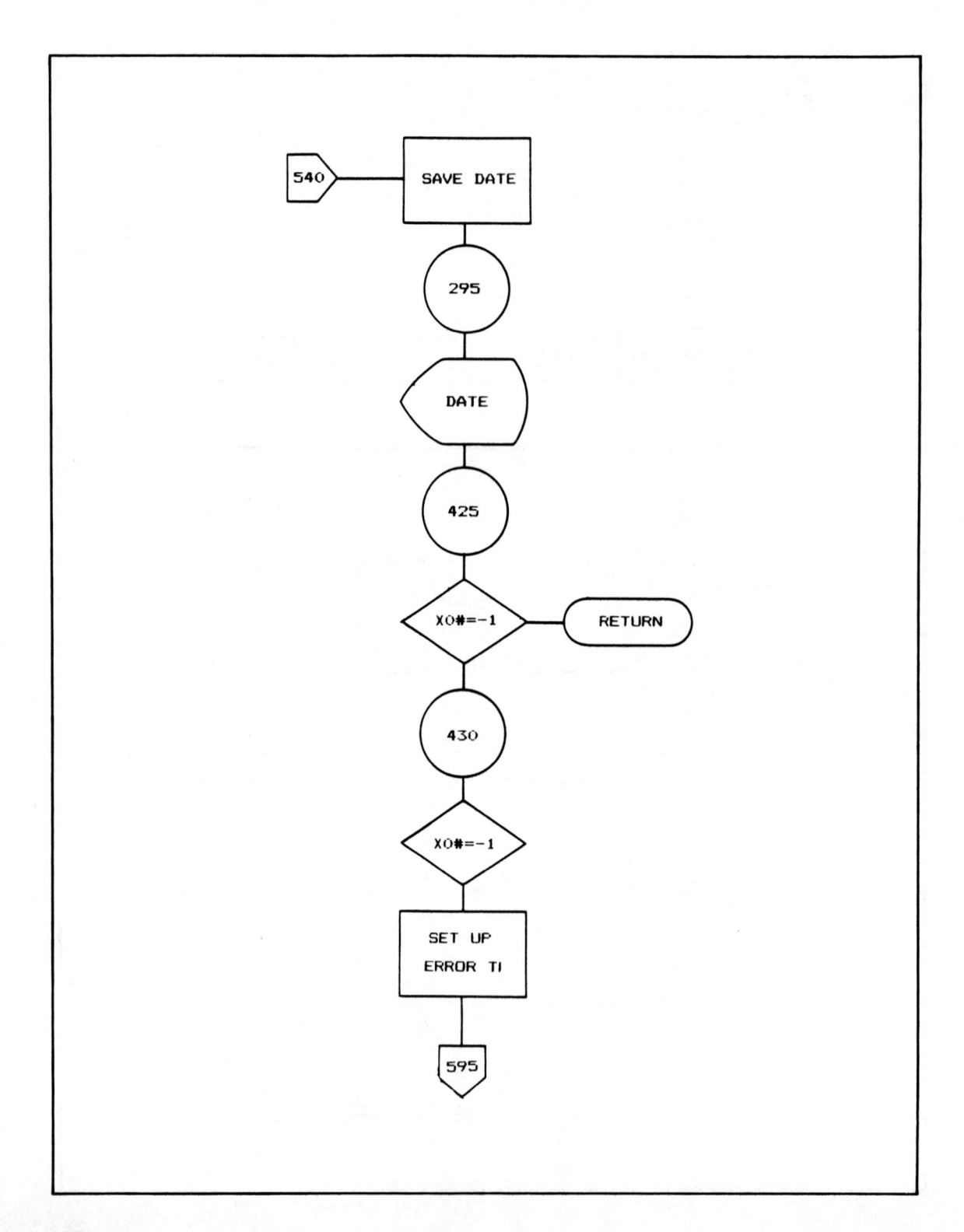

```
     ┌─────┐   ┌──────────────┐
     │ 540 ├───┤  SAVE DATE   │
     └─────┘   └──────┬───────┘
                      │
                    ( 295 )
                      │
                   ╱ DATE ╲
                      │
                    ( 425 )
                      │
                   ╱ X0#=-1 ╲──────( RETURN )
                   ╲         ╱
                      │
                    ( 430 )
                      │
                   ╱ X0#=-1 ╲
                   ╲         ╱
                      │
                ┌─────────────┐
                │   SET UP    │
                │  ERROR TI   │
                └──────┬──────┘
                       │
                    ╲ 595 ╱
```

126

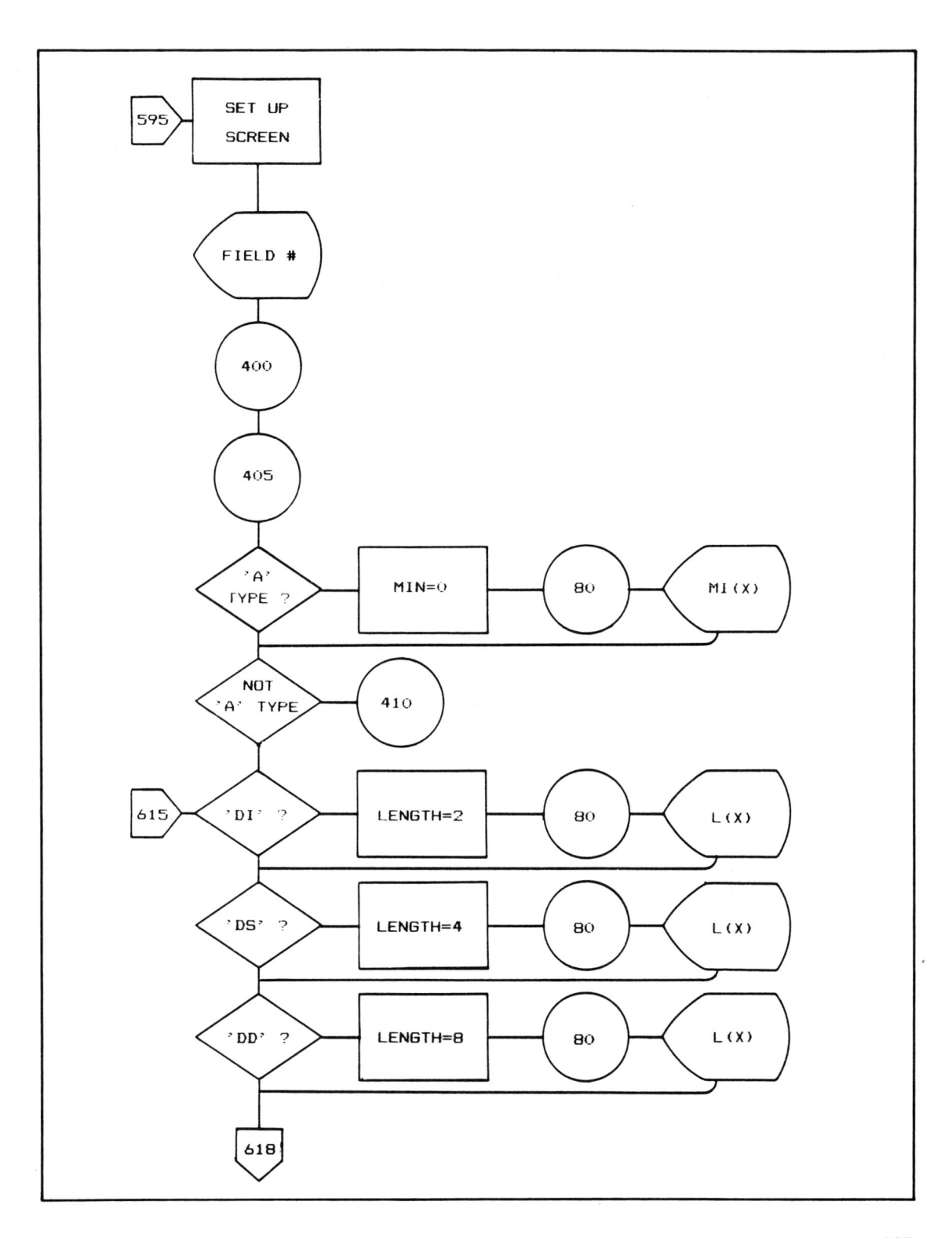

```
[595] SET UP SCREEN
   │
   ⬡ FIELD #
   │
   ◯ 400
   │
   ◯ 405
   │
   ◇ 'A' TYPE ? ──── [MIN=0] ──── ◯ 80 ──── ⬢ MI(X)
   │
   ◇ NOT 'A' TYPE ──── ◯ 410
   │
[615] ◇ 'DI' ? ──── [LENGTH=2] ──── ◯ 80 ──── ⬢ L(X)
   │
   ◇ 'DS' ? ──── [LENGTH=4] ──── ◯ 80 ──── ⬢ L(X)
   │
   ◇ 'DD' ? ──── [LENGTH=8] ──── ◯ 80 ──── ⬢ L(X)
   │
   [618]
```

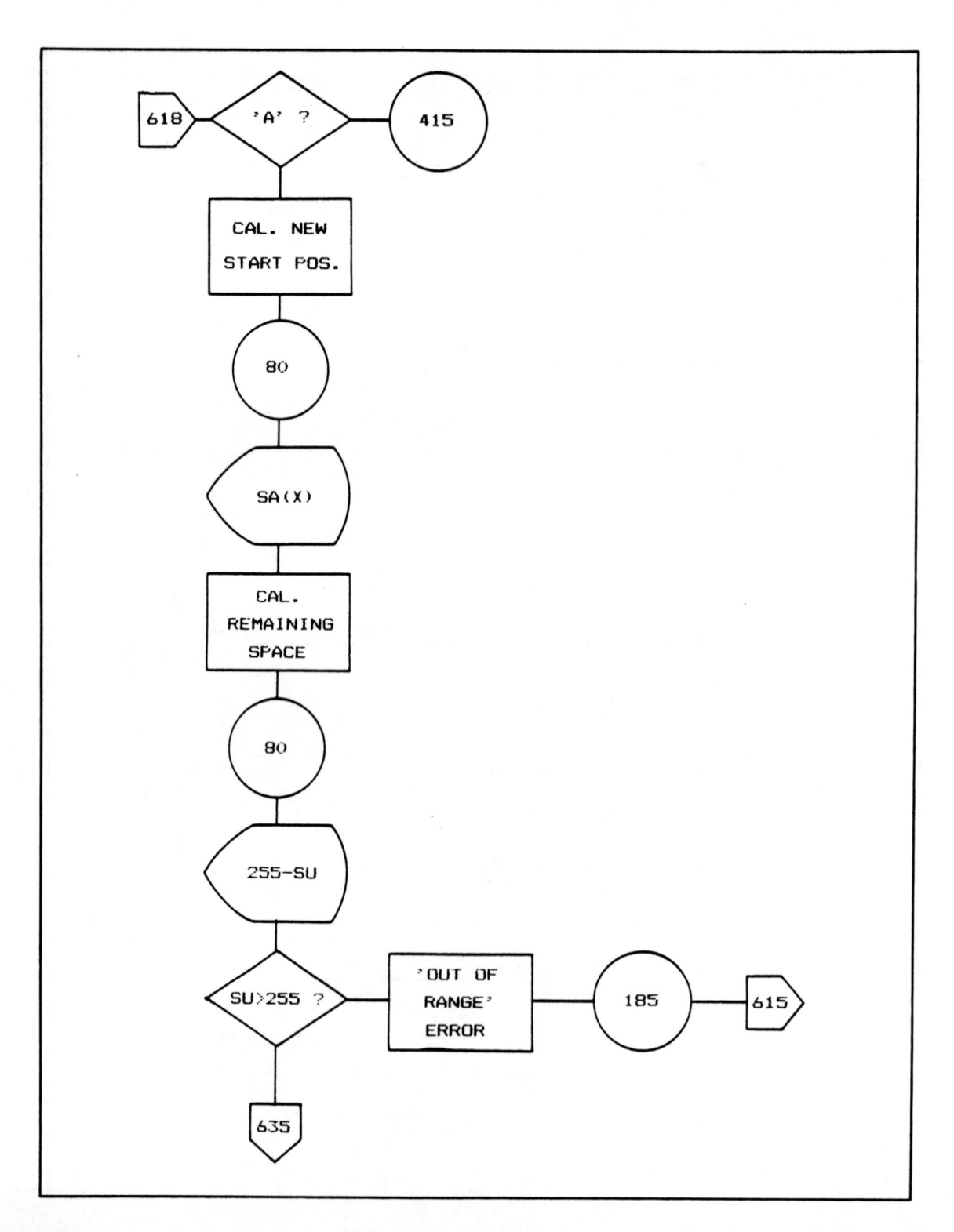

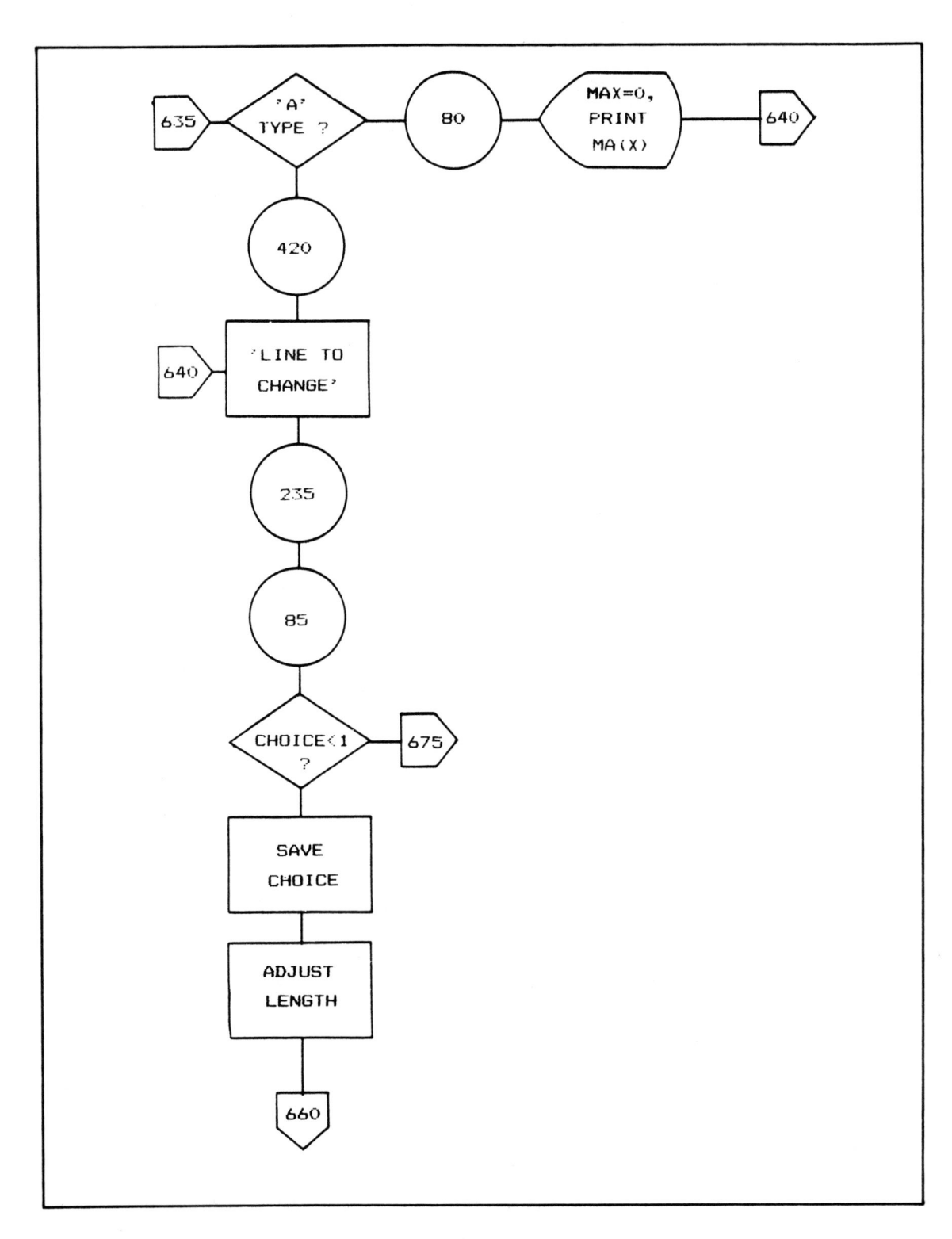

```
┌─────┐   ╱╲         ╭──╮   ╱─────────╲   ┌─────┐
│ 635 │──╱'A'╲──────( 80 )─(  MAX=0,   )──│ 640 │
└─────┘  ╲TYPE╱      ╰──╯  (  PRINT    )  └─────┘
          ╲?╱                ╲  MA(X) ╱
           │
         ╭───╮
        ( 420 )
         ╰───╯
           │
┌─────┐ ┌────────┐
│ 640 │─│'LINE TO│
└─────┘ │ CHANGE'│
        └────────┘
            │
         ╭───╮
        ( 235 )
         ╰───╯
            │
         ╭───╮
        (  85 )
         ╰───╯
            │
          ╱╲
         ╱CHOICE<1╲──┐ 675 ┐
         ╲   ?    ╱  └─────┘
          ╲╱
           │
       ┌───────┐
       │ SAVE  │
       │CHOICE │
       └───────┘
           │
       ┌───────┐
       │ADJUST │
       │LENGTH │
       └───────┘
           │
        ┌─────┐
        │ 660 │
        └─────┘
```

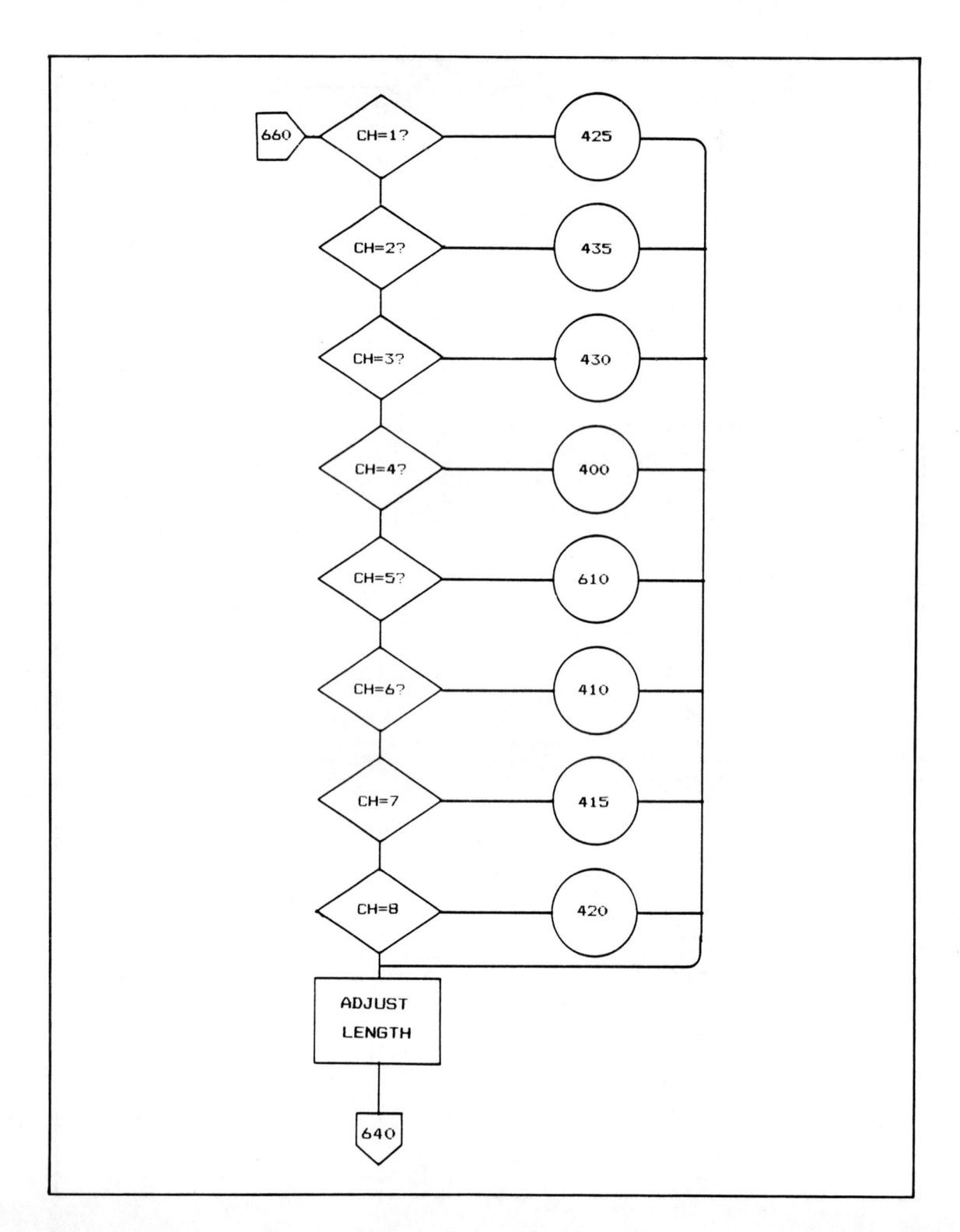

```
         ┌─────┐ ◇ CH=1? ─────── ( 425 )─┐
         │ 660 │    │                     │
         └─────┘ ◇ CH=2? ─────── ( 435 )─┤
                    │                     │
                 ◇ CH=3? ─────── ( 430 )─┤
                    │                     │
                 ◇ CH=4? ─────── ( 400 )─┤
                    │                     │
                 ◇ CH=5? ─────── ( 610 )─┤
                    │                     │
                 ◇ CH=6? ─────── ( 410 )─┤
                    │                     │
                 ◇ CH=7  ─────── ( 415 )─┤
                    │                     │
                 ◇ CH=8  ─────── ( 420 )─┤
                    │                     │
                    ▼◄────────────────────┘
              ┌───────────┐
              │  ADJUST   │
              │  LENGTH   │
              └───────────┘
                    │
                 ┌─────┐
                 │ 640 │
                 └─────┘
```

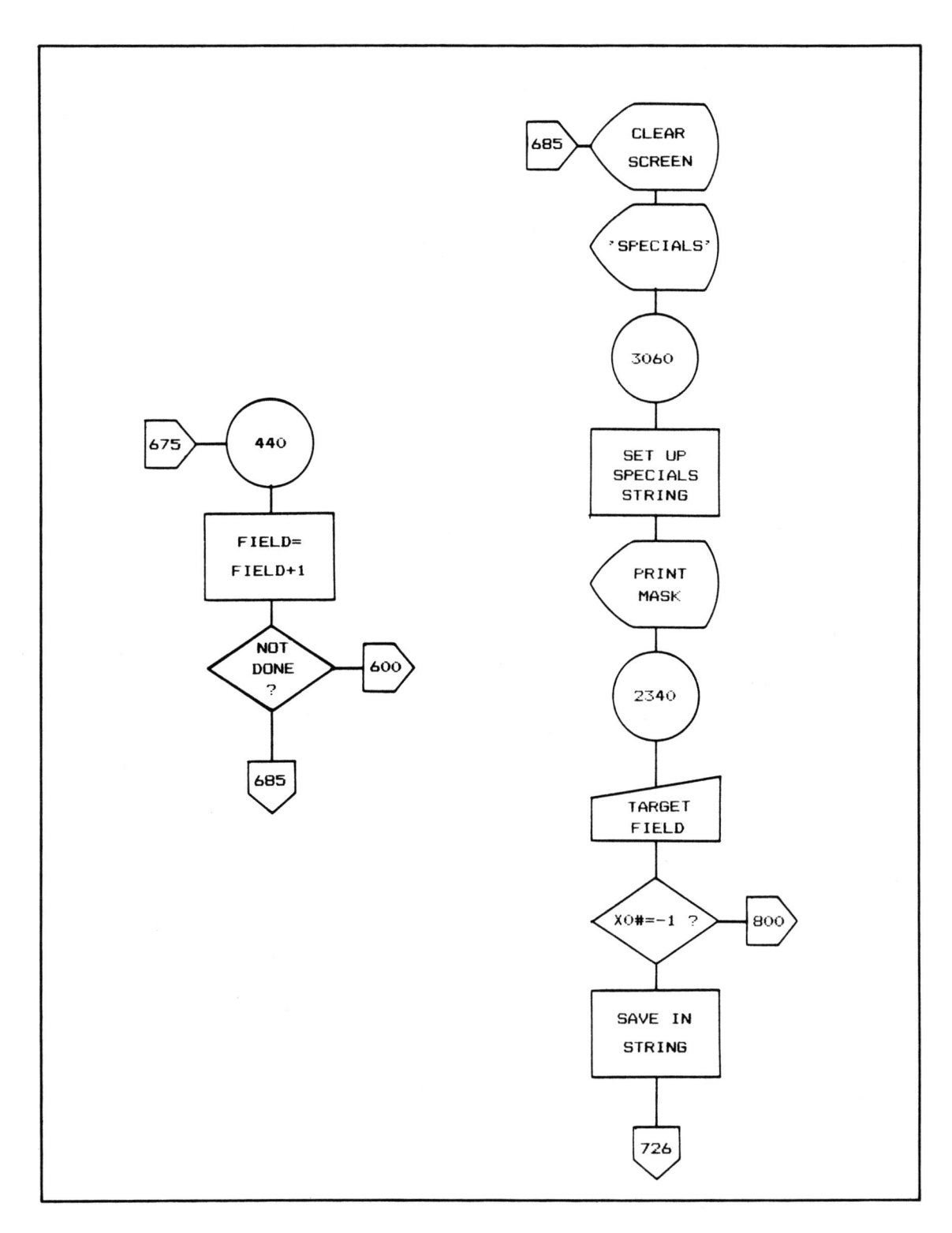

```
                                    ┌─────┐
                               685 ─┤CLEAR │
                                    │SCREEN│
                                    └──┬───┘
                                       │
                                  ╱'SPECIALS'╲
                                       │
                                     (3060)
                                       │
                                  ┌─────────┐
                                  │ SET UP  │
                                  │SPECIALS │
                                  │ STRING  │
                                  └────┬────┘
                                       │
                                    ╱PRINT╲
                                    ╲MASK ╱
                                       │
                                     (2340)
                                       │
                                  ╱TARGET ╲
                                  ╲ FIELD ╱
                                       │
        ┌─────┐                        ◇
   675─┤ 440 │                    ◇XO#=-1 ?◇──┤800│
        └──┬──┘                        ◇
           │                           │
      ┌─────────┐                 ┌─────────┐
      │ FIELD=  │                 │ SAVE IN │
      │ FIELD+1 │                 │ STRING  │
      └────┬────┘                 └────┬────┘
           │                           │
         ◇NOT◇                        │726│
         ◇DONE◇──┤600│
         ◇ ? ◇
           │
         │685│
```

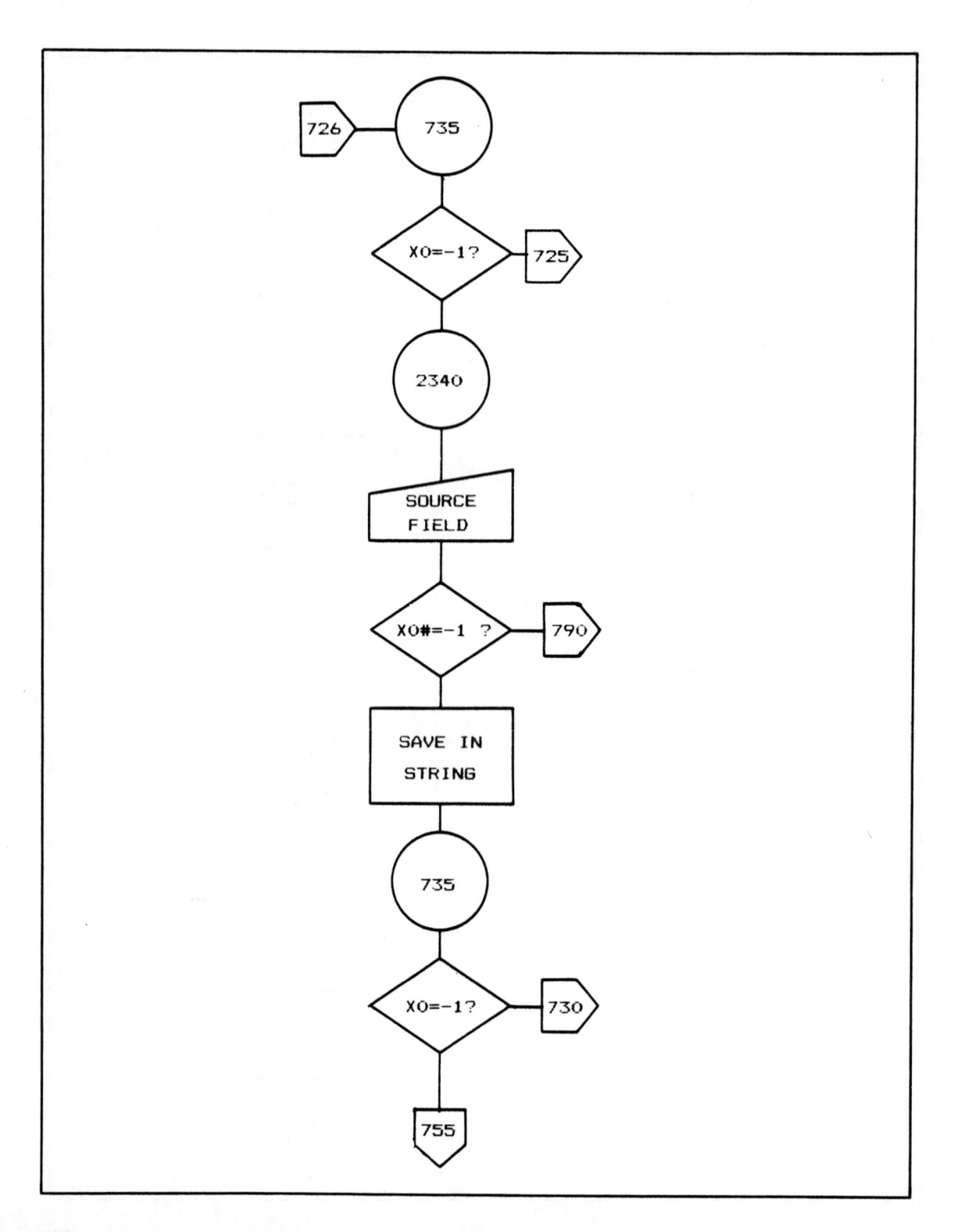

```
        ┌───┐  ╱‾‾‾╲
        │726├─┤ 735 │
        └───┘  ╲___╱
                 │
                ╱ ╲
               ╱   ╲    ┌───┐
              ╱XO=-1╲───┤725│
              ╲  ?  ╱   └───┘
               ╲   ╱
                ╲ ╱
                 │
               ╱‾‾‾╲
              │2340 │
               ╲___╱
                 │
         ┌───────────┐
         │  SOURCE   │
         │  FIELD    │
         └───────────┘
                 │
                ╱ ╲
               ╱   ╲    ┌───┐
              ╱XO#=-1╲──┤790│
              ╲  ?  ╱   └───┘
               ╲   ╱
                ╲ ╱
                 │
         ┌───────────┐
         │  SAVE IN  │
         │  STRING   │
         └───────────┘
                 │
               ╱‾‾‾╲
              │ 735 │
               ╲___╱
                 │
                ╱ ╲
               ╱   ╲    ┌───┐
              ╱XO=-1╲───┤730│
              ╲  ?  ╱   └───┘
               ╲   ╱
                ╲ ╱
                 │
               ┌───┐
               │755│
               └───┘
```

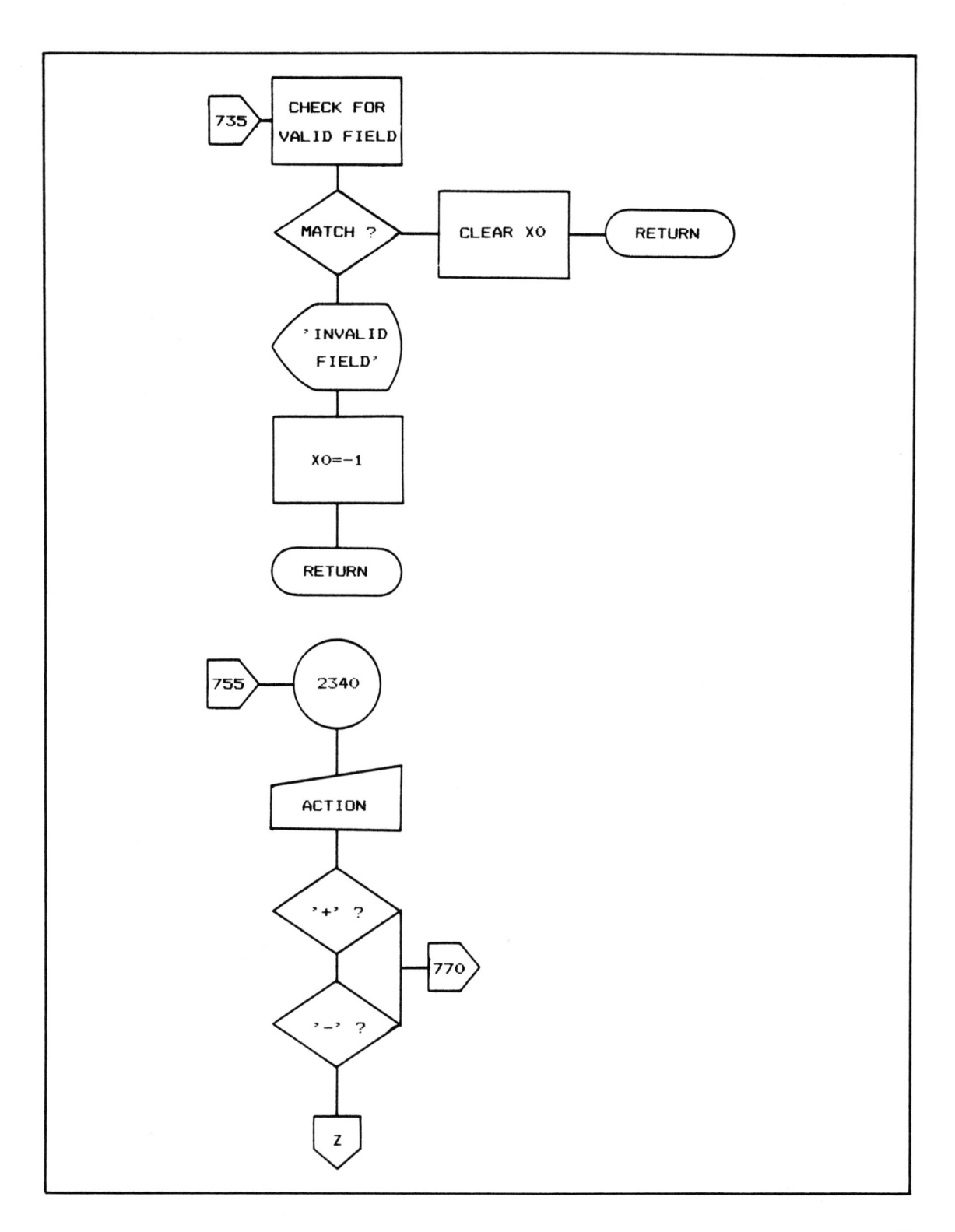

```
     ┌──────────────┐
 735 │ CHECK FOR    │
─────┤ VALID FIELD  │
     └──────┬───────┘
            │
         ╱MATCH?╲──────→ [CLEAR X0] ──→ ( RETURN )
         ╲      ╱
            │
       'INVALID
        FIELD'
            │
         X0=-1
            │
        ( RETURN )


 755 ─── ( 2340 )
            │
         [ACTION]
            │
          ╱'+'?╲──────→ 770
          ╲    ╱
            │
          ╱'-'?╲
          ╲    ╱
            │
            Z
```

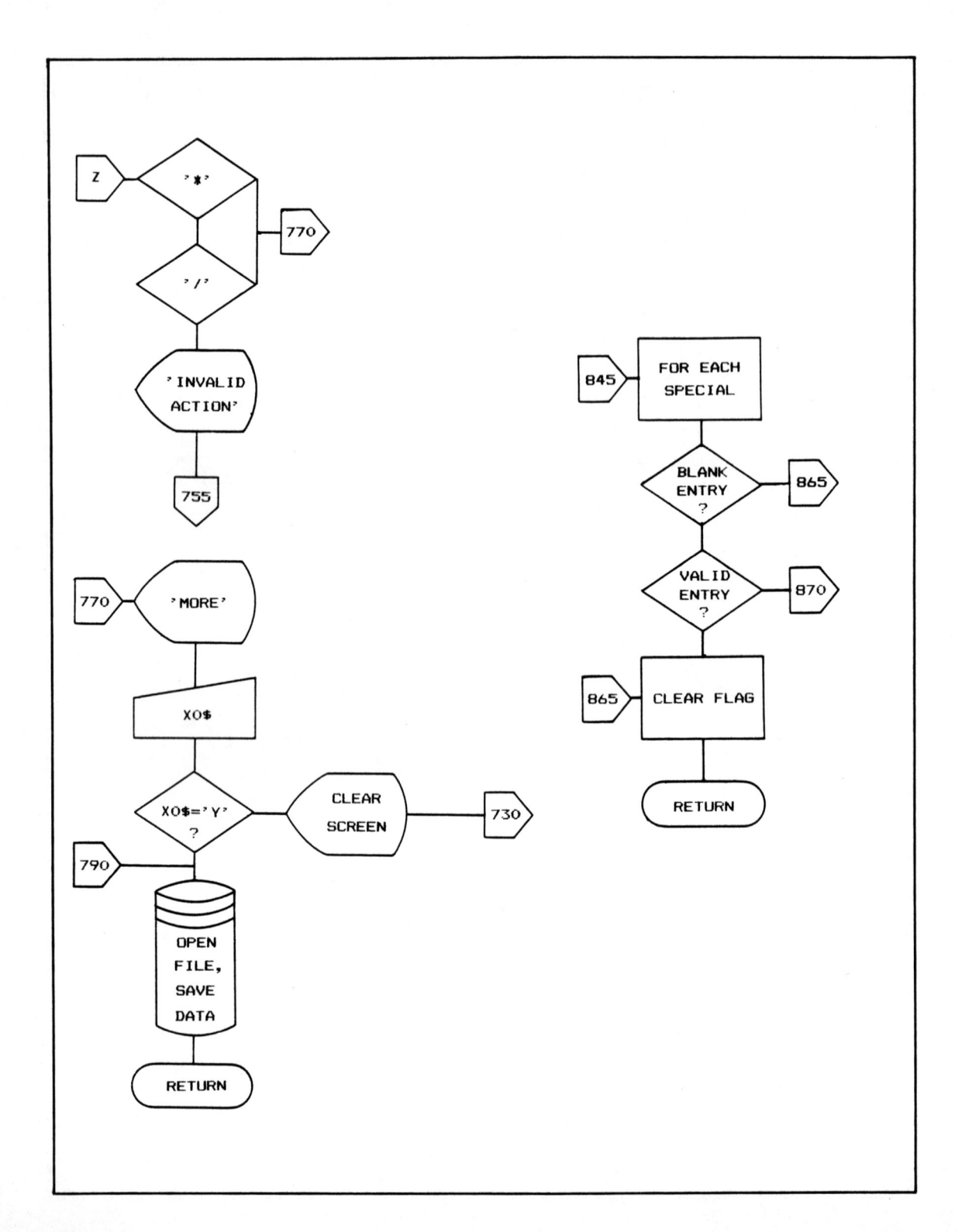

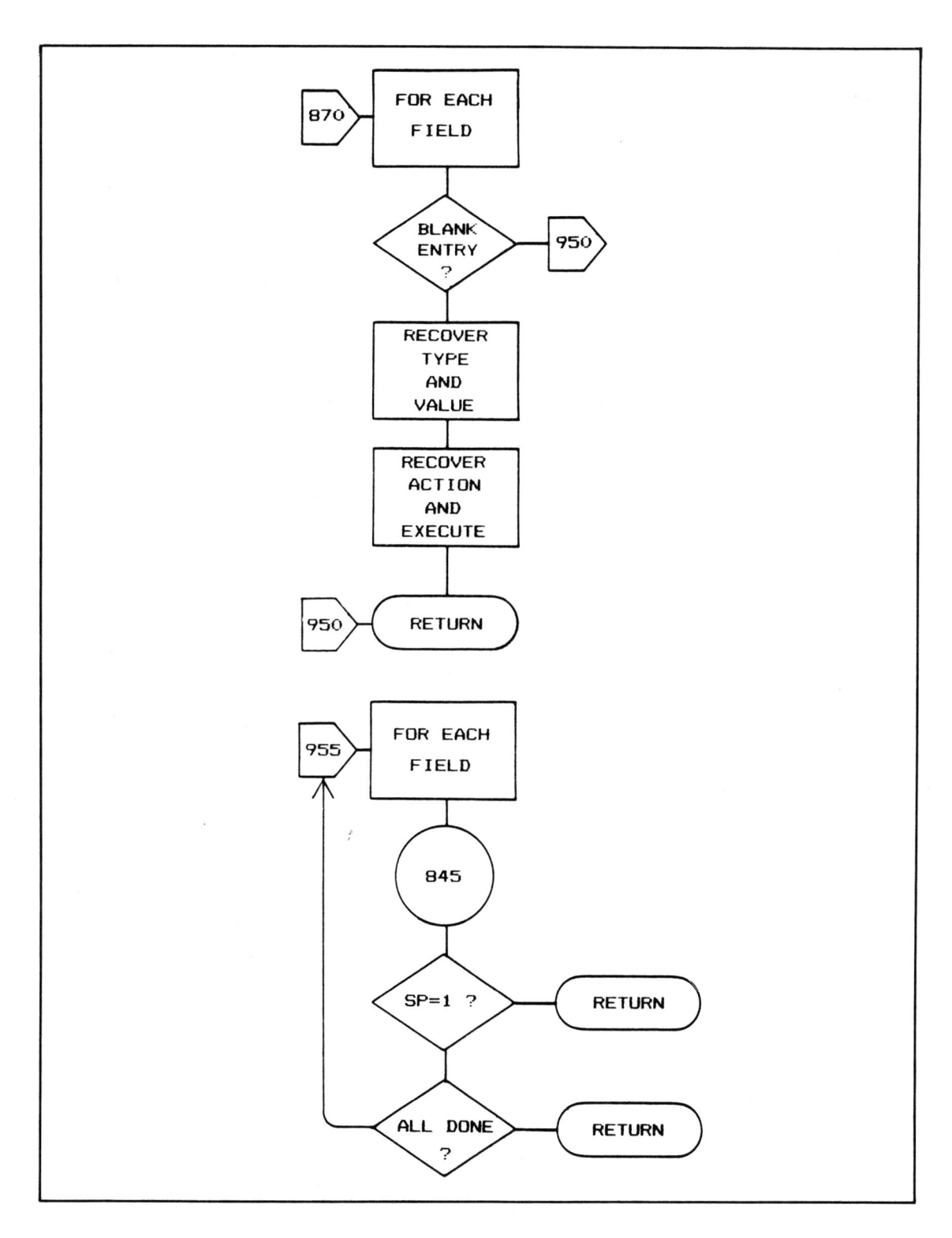

```
┌─────┐  ┌──────────┐
│ 870 │──│ FOR EACH │
└─────┘  │  FIELD   │
         └────┬─────┘
              │
           ╱─────╲
          ╱ BLANK ╲   ┌─────┐
          ╲ ENTRY ╱───│ 950 │
           ╲  ?  ╱    └─────┘
            ╲─╱
             │
      ┌──────────┐
      │ RECOVER  │
      │   TYPE   │
      │   AND    │
      │  VALUE   │
      └────┬─────┘
      ┌──────────┐
      │ RECOVER  │
      │  ACTION  │
      │   AND    │
      │ EXECUTE  │
      └────┬─────┘
┌─────┐   ╭──────────╮
│ 950 │───│  RETURN  │
└─────┘   ╰──────────╯


┌─────┐  ┌──────────┐
│ 955 │──│ FOR EACH │
└─────┘  │  FIELD   │
   ▲     └────┬─────┘
   │          │
   │        ╱───╲
   │       ( 845 )
   │        ╲───╱
   │          │
   │       ╱──────╲    ╭──────────╮
   │      ╱ SP=1 ? ╲───│  RETURN  │
   │      ╲        ╱   ╰──────────╯
   │       ╲──────╱
   │          │
   │       ╱──────╲    ╭──────────╮
   └──────╱ ALL DONE╲──│  RETURN  │
          ╲    ?   ╱   ╰──────────╯
           ╲──────╱
```

136

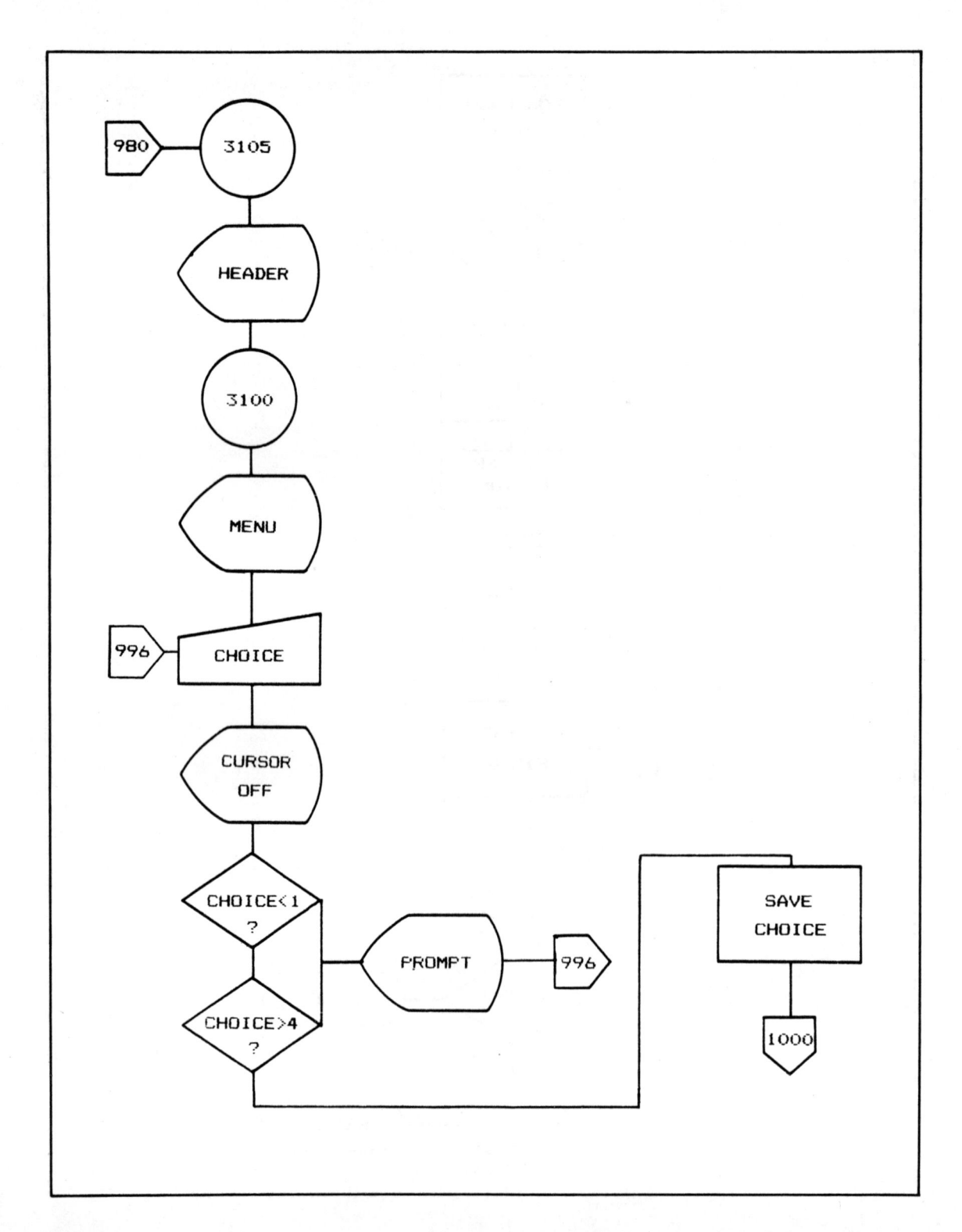

137

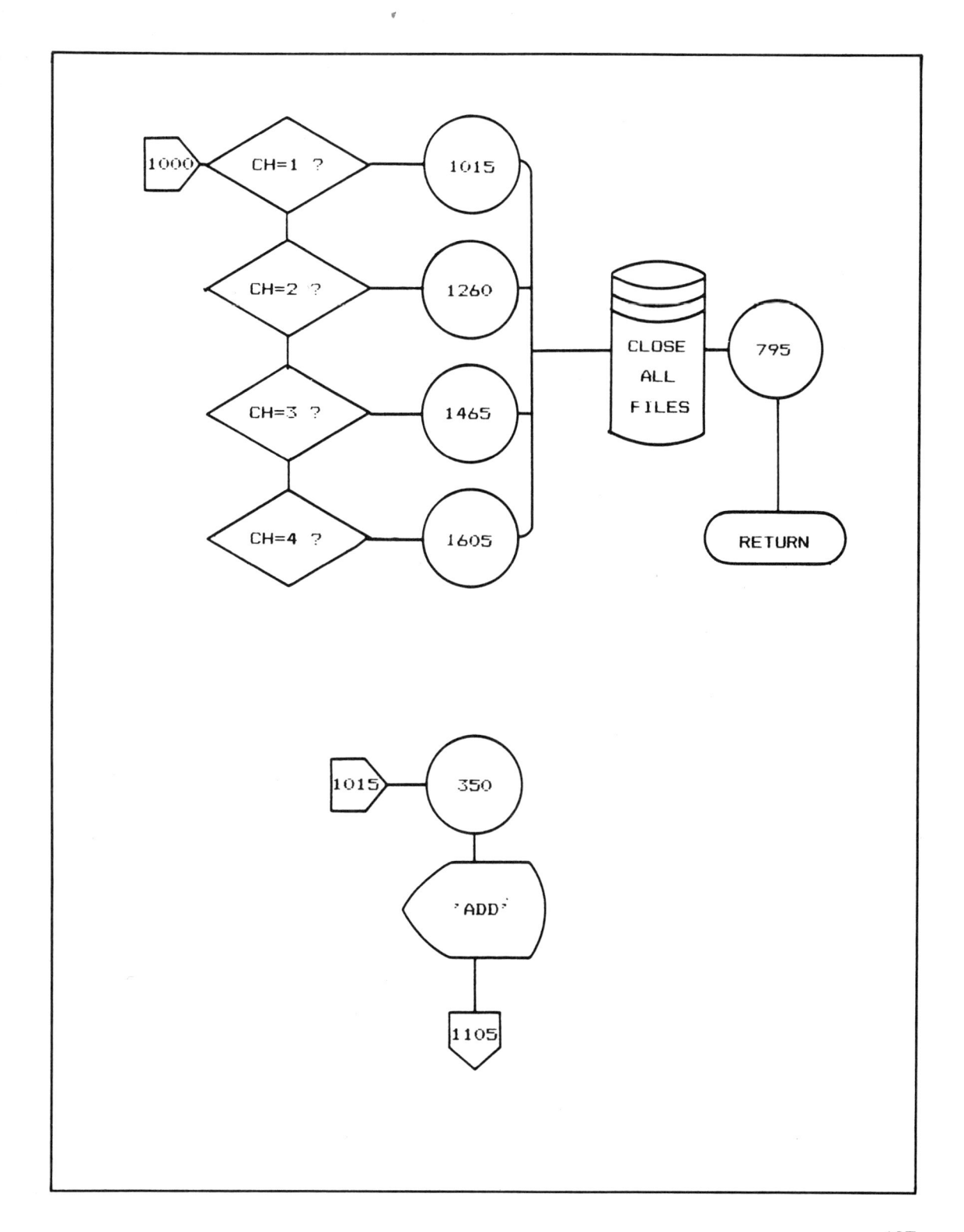

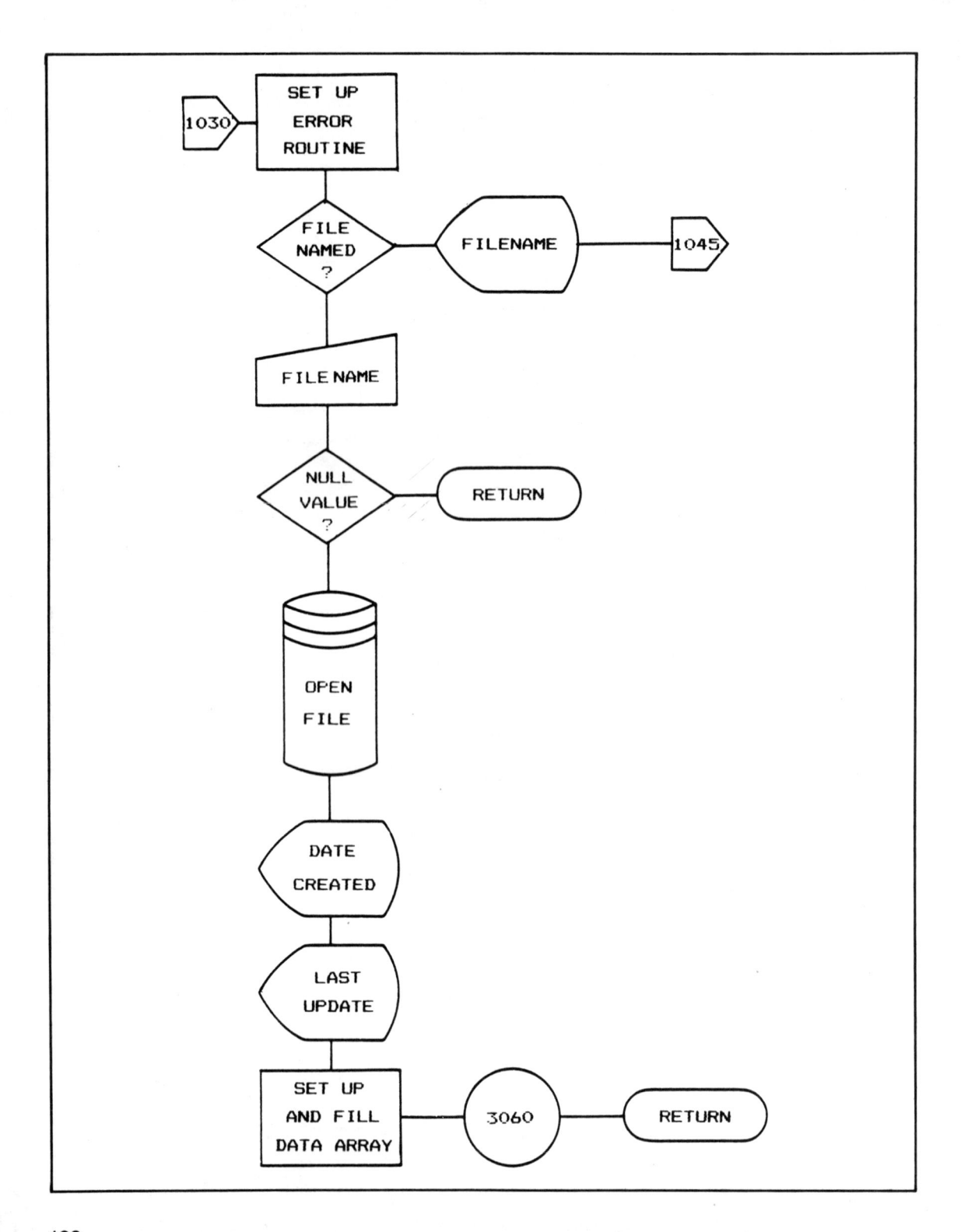

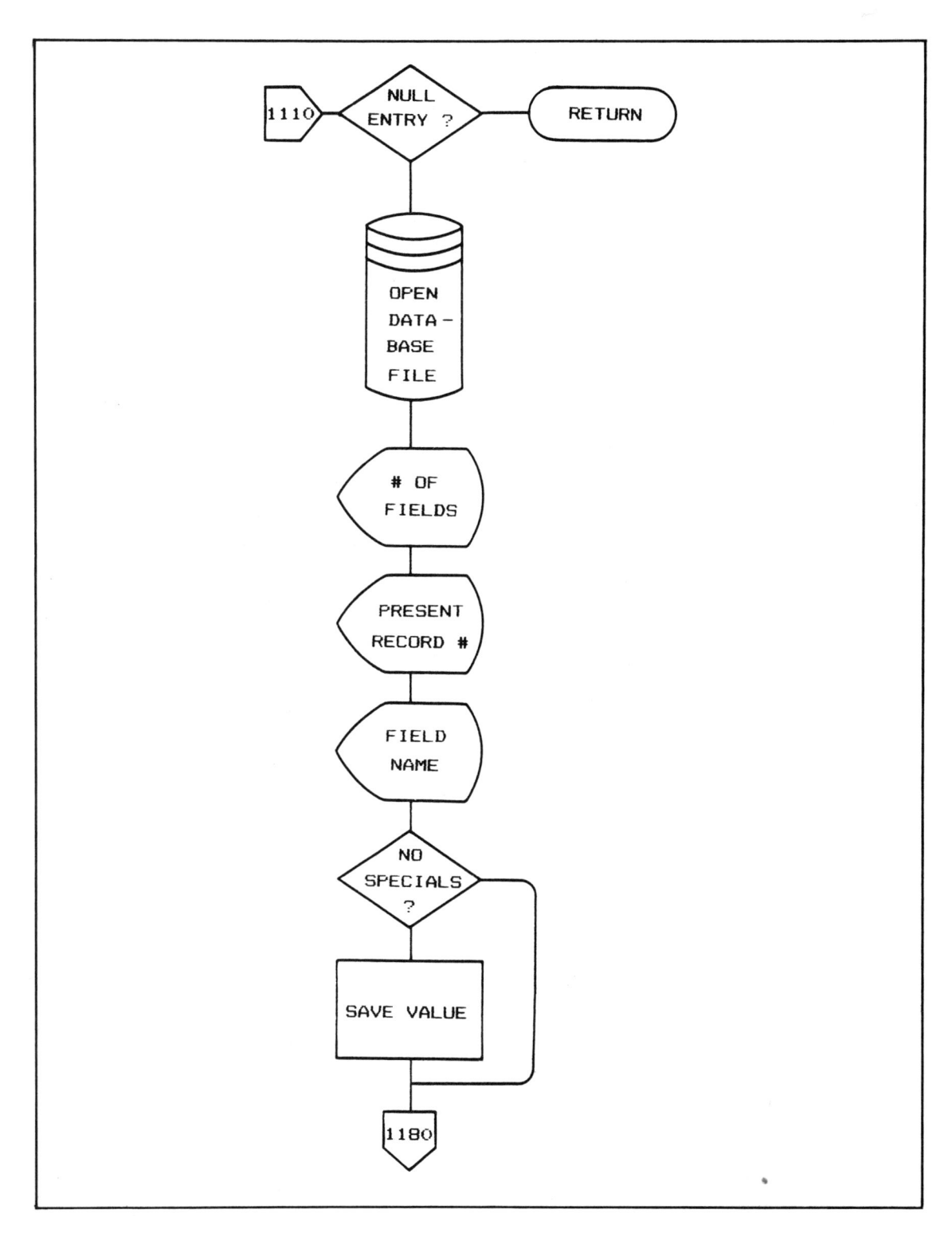

```
        ┌─────────┐
  ┌1110┐ │  NULL   │   ┌─────────┐
  └────┤ │ ENTRY ? ├───┤ RETURN  │
        └────┬────┘   └─────────┘
             │
        ╔════╧════╗
        ║  OPEN   ║
        ║ DATA -  ║
        ║  BASE   ║
        ║  FILE   ║
        ╚════╤════╝
             │
        ┌────┴────┐
        │  # OF   │
        │ FIELDS  │
        └────┬────┘
             │
        ┌────┴────┐
        │ PRESENT │
        │RECORD # │
        └────┬────┘
             │
        ┌────┴────┐
        │  FIELD  │
        │  NAME   │
        └────┬────┘
             │
        ┌────┴────┐
        │   NO    │
        │ SPECIALS├──┐
        │   ?     │  │
        └────┬────┘  │
             │       │
        ┌────┴────┐  │
        │  SAVE   │  │
        │  VALUE  │  │
        └────┬────┘  │
             │◄──────┘
          ┌1180┐
          └────┘
```

140

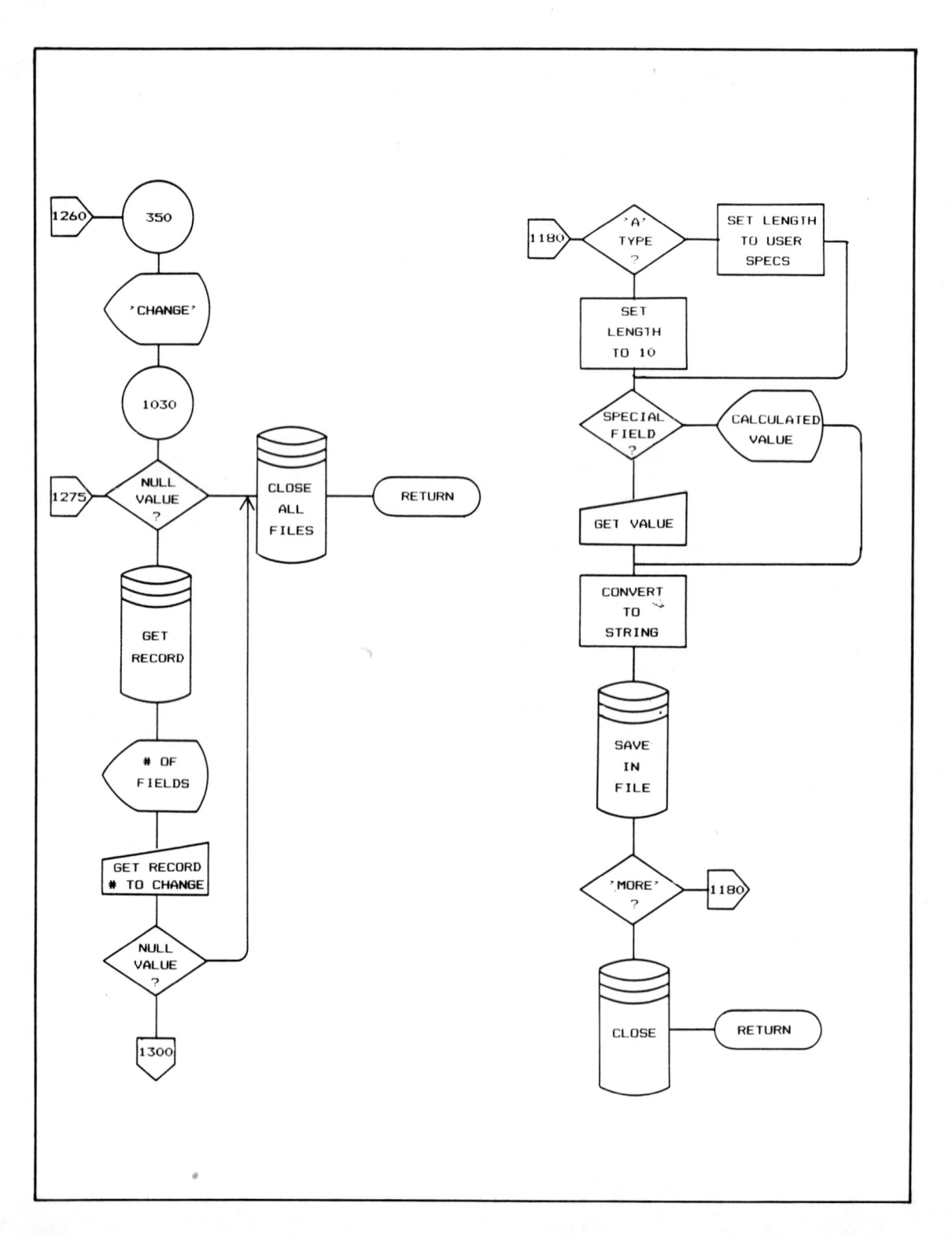

141

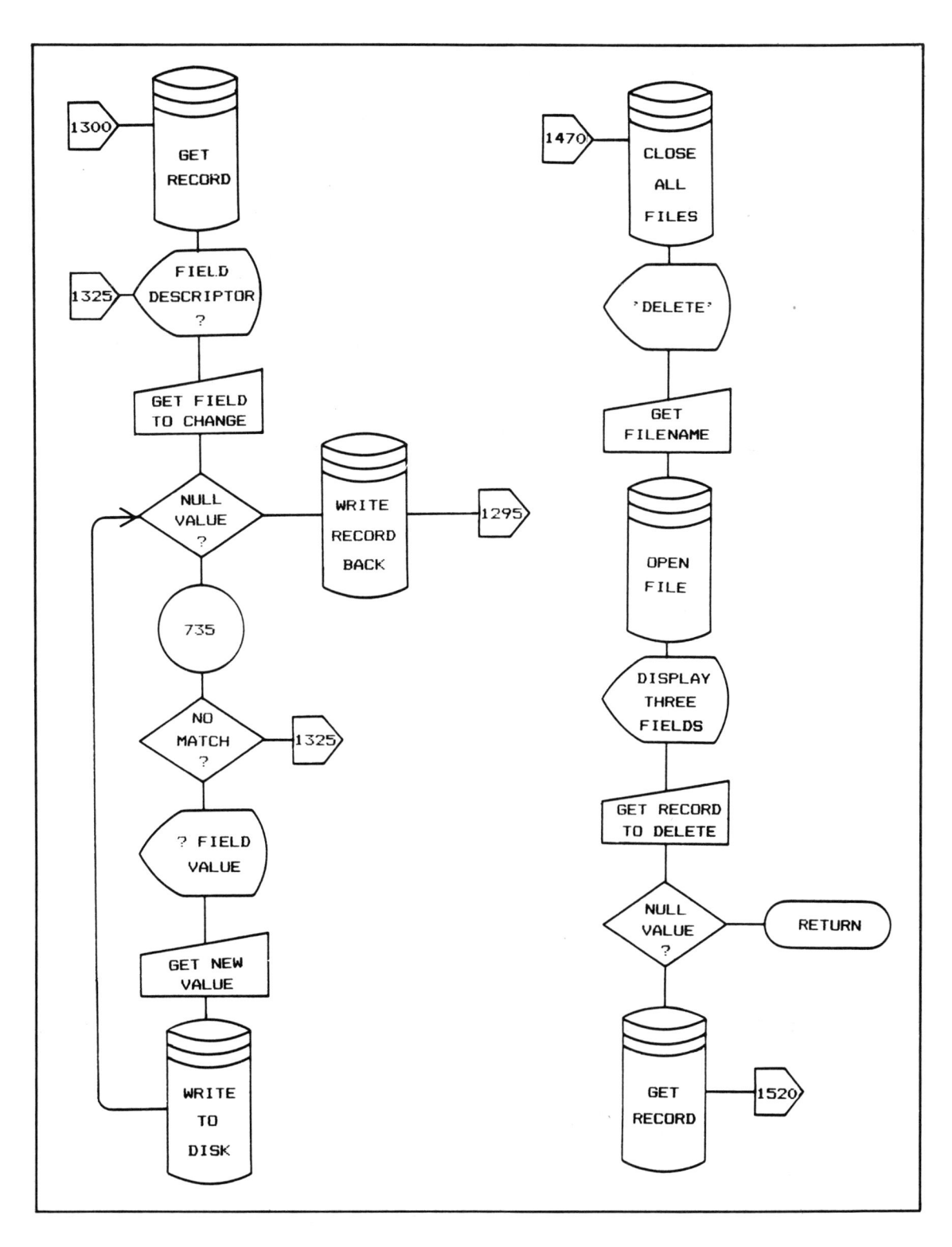

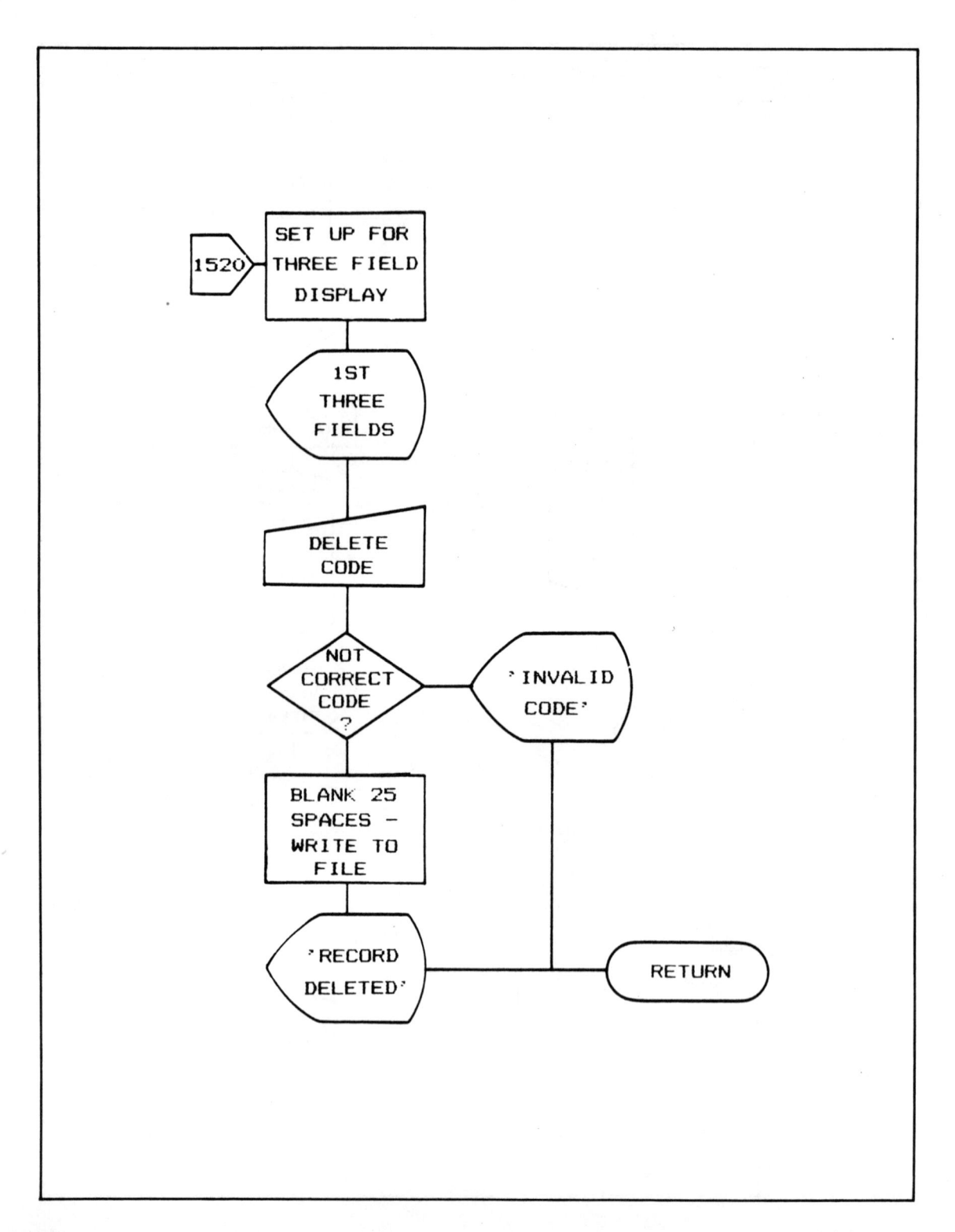

```
     ┌─────────────┐
     │ SET UP FOR  │
(1520)│ THREE FIELD │
     │   DISPLAY   │
     └──────┬──────┘
            │
         ┌──┴──┐
         │ 1ST │
         │THREE│
         │FIELDS│
         └──┬──┘
            │
        ┌───┴────┐
        │ DELETE │
        │  CODE  │
        └───┬────┘
            │
          ╱   ╲
        ╱  NOT  ╲          ┌──────────┐
       ╱ CORRECT ╲─────────│ 'INVALID │
       ╲  CODE   ╱         │  CODE'   │
        ╲   ?   ╱          └─────┬────┘
          ╲   ╱                  │
            │                    │
    ┌───────┴───────┐            │
    │   BLANK 25    │            │
    │   SPACES -    │            │
    │   WRITE TO    │            │
    │     FILE      │            │
    └───────┬───────┘            │
            │                    │
     ┌──────┴──────┐      ┌──────┴──────┐
     │  'RECORD    │──────│   RETURN    │
     │  DELETED'   │      │             │
     └─────────────┘      └─────────────┘
```

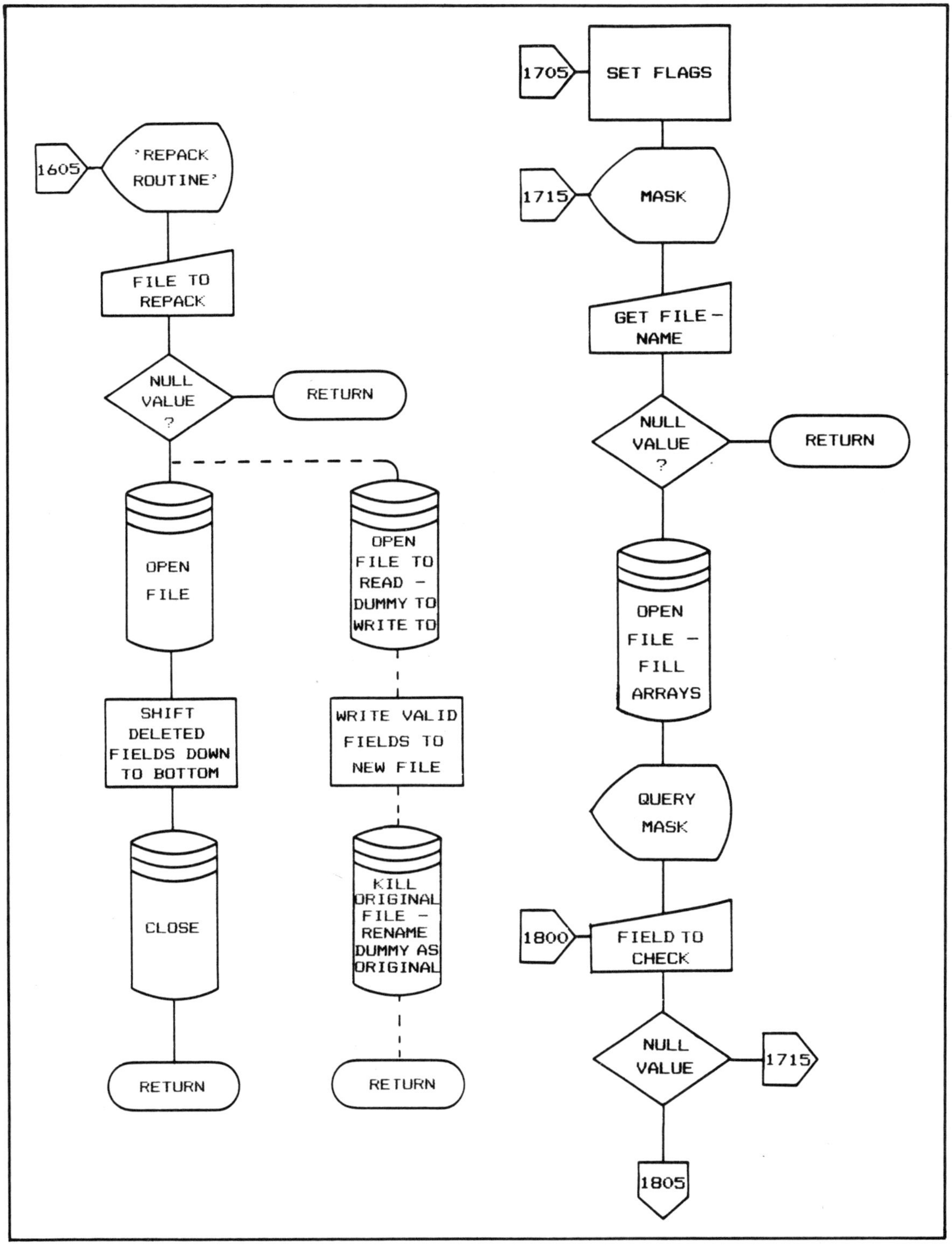
1605
'REPACK ROUTINE'
FILE TO REPACK
NULL VALUE ?
RETURN
OPEN FILE
SHIFT DELETED FIELDS DOWN TO BOTTOM
CLOSE
RETURN
OPEN FILE TO READ - DUMMY TO WRITE TO
WRITE VALID FIELDS TO NEW FILE
KILL ORIGINAL FILE - RENAME DUMMY AS ORIGINAL
RETURN
1705
SET FLAGS
1715
MASK
GET FILE-NAME
NULL VALUE ?
RETURN
OPEN FILE - FILL ARRAYS
QUERY MASK
1800
FIELD TO CHECK
NULL VALUE
1715
1805

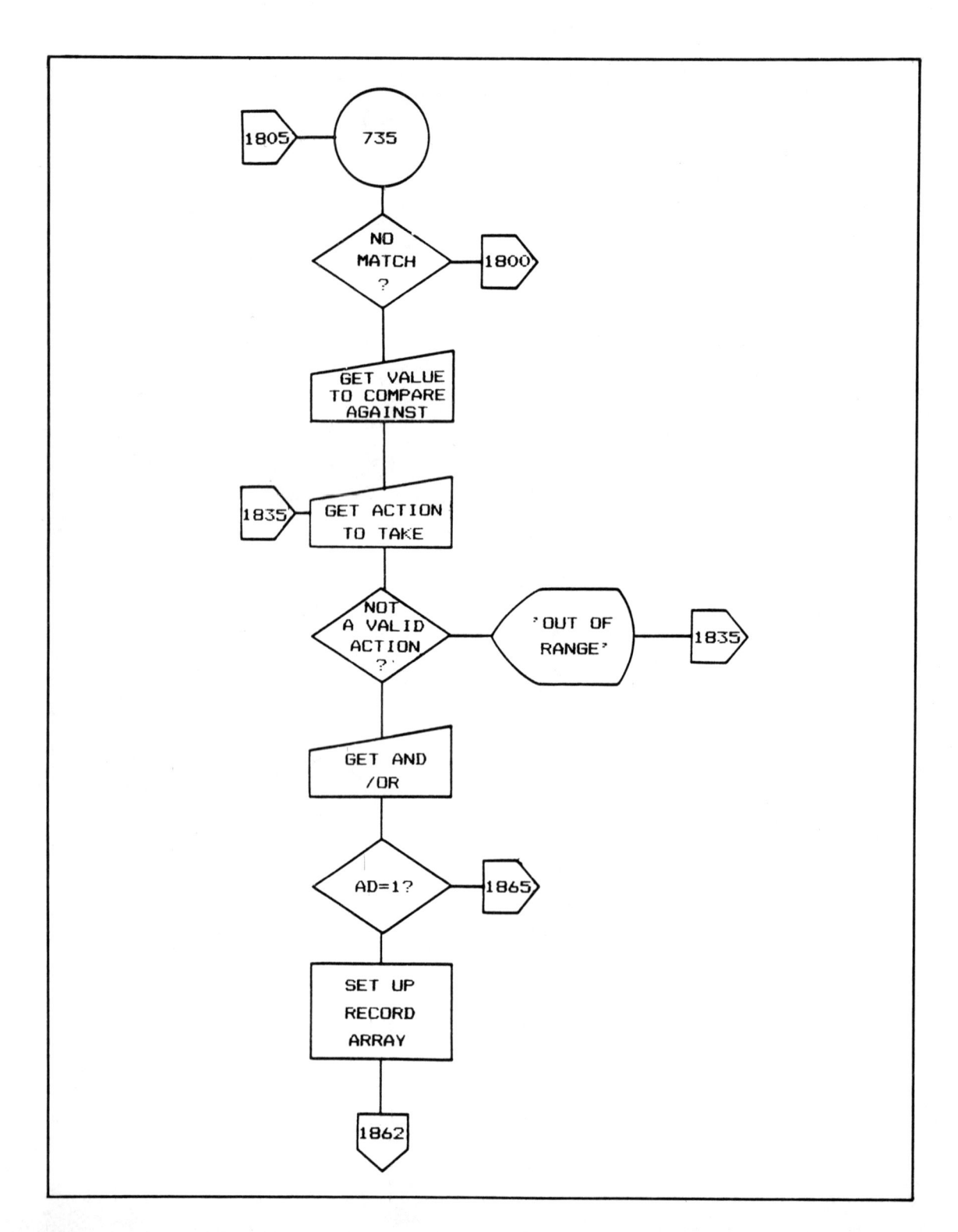

```
                    ┌─────┐    ╭─────╮
                    │1805 ├────┤ 735 │
                    └─────┘    ╰──┬──╯
                                  │
                               ╱ NO ╲
                              ╱MATCH ╲────┐1800┐
                              ╲  ?   ╱    └────┘
                               ╲    ╱
                                 │
                          ┌──────┴──────┐
                          │ GET VALUE   │
                          │ TO COMPARE  │
                          │  AGAINST    │
                          └──────┬──────┘
                                 │
              ┌─────┐    ┌───────┴──────┐
              │1835 ├────┤  GET ACTION  │
              └─────┘    │   TO TAKE    │
                         └───────┬──────┘
                                 │
                              ╱ NOT ╲
                             ╱A VALID╲        ╭─────────╮
                             ╲ ACTION╱────────┤ 'OUT OF ├────┐1835┐
                              ╲  ?  ╱         │  RANGE' │    └────┘
                                 │            ╰─────────╯
                          ┌──────┴──────┐
                          │  GET AND    │
                          │    /OR      │
                          └──────┬──────┘
                                 │
                              ╱     ╲
                             ╱ AD=1? ╲────┐1865┐
                              ╲     ╱     └────┘
                                 │
                          ┌──────┴──────┐
                          │   SET UP    │
                          │   RECORD    │
                          │   ARRAY     │
                          └──────┬──────┘
                                 │
                              ┌──┴──┐
                              │1862 │
                              └─────┘
```

144

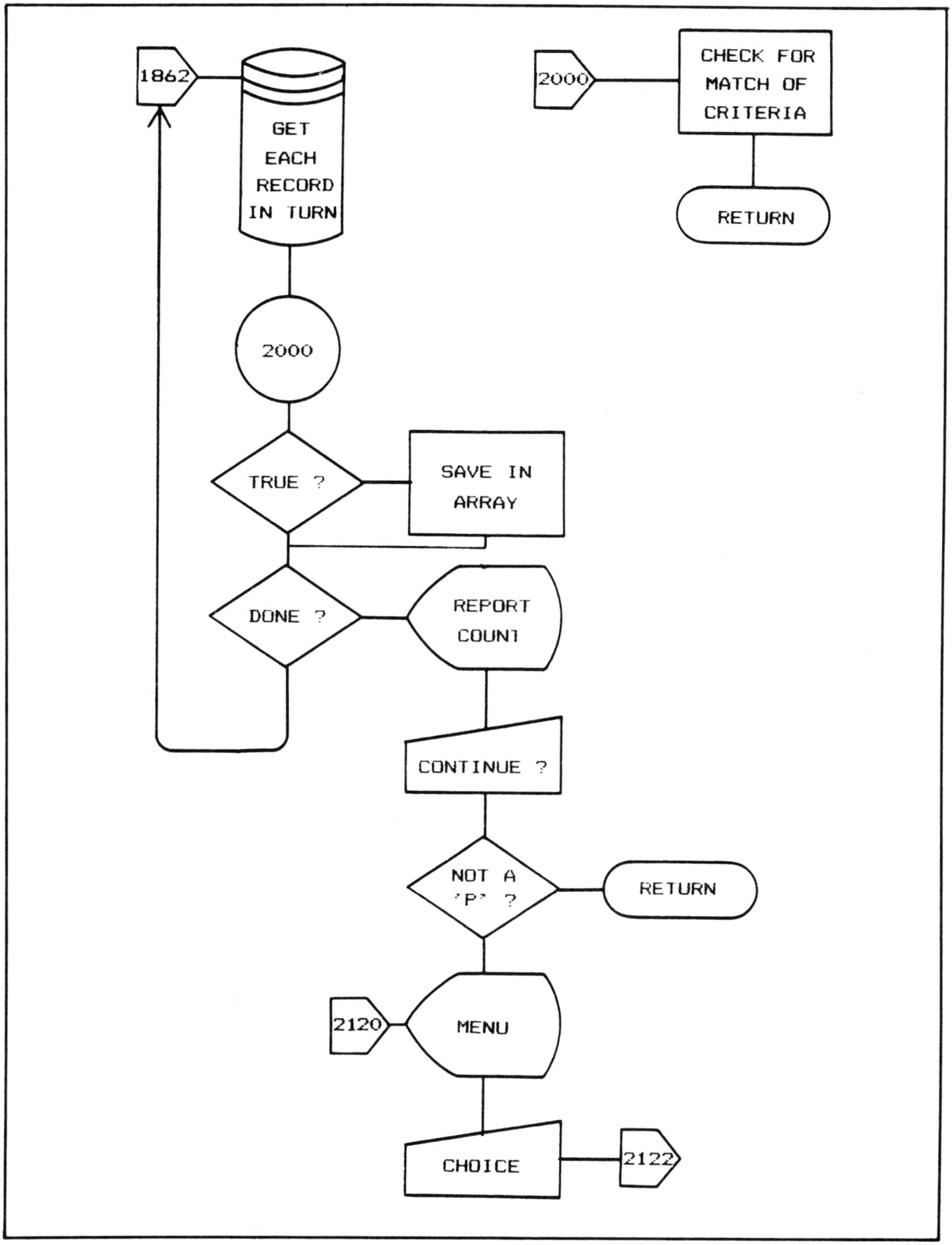
1862
GET
EACH
RECORD
IN TURN
2000
TRUE ?
SAVE IN
ARRAY
DONE ?
REPORT
COUNT
CONTINUE ?
NOT A
'P' ?
RETURN
2120
MENU
CHOICE
2122
2000
CHECK FOR
MATCH OF
CRITERIA
RETURN

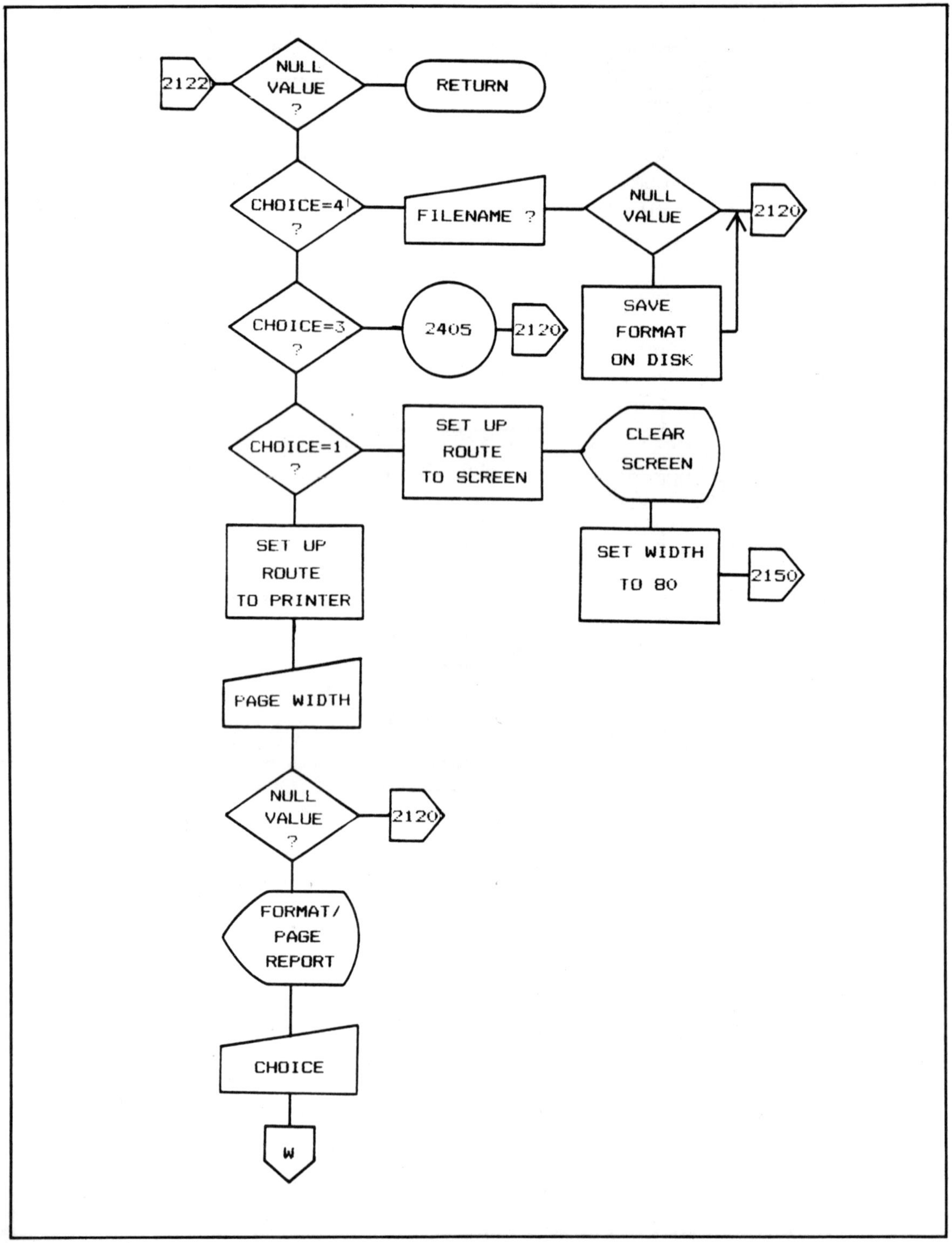
2122
NULL VALUE ?
RETURN
CHOICE=4 ?
FILENAME ?
NULL VALUE
2120
SAVE FORMAT ON DISK
CHOICE=3 ?
2405
2120
CHOICE=1 ?
SET UP ROUTE TO SCREEN
CLEAR SCREEN
SET WIDTH TO 80
2150
SET UP ROUTE TO PRINTER
PAGE WIDTH
NULL VALUE ?
2120
FORMAT/ PAGE REPORT
CHOICE
W

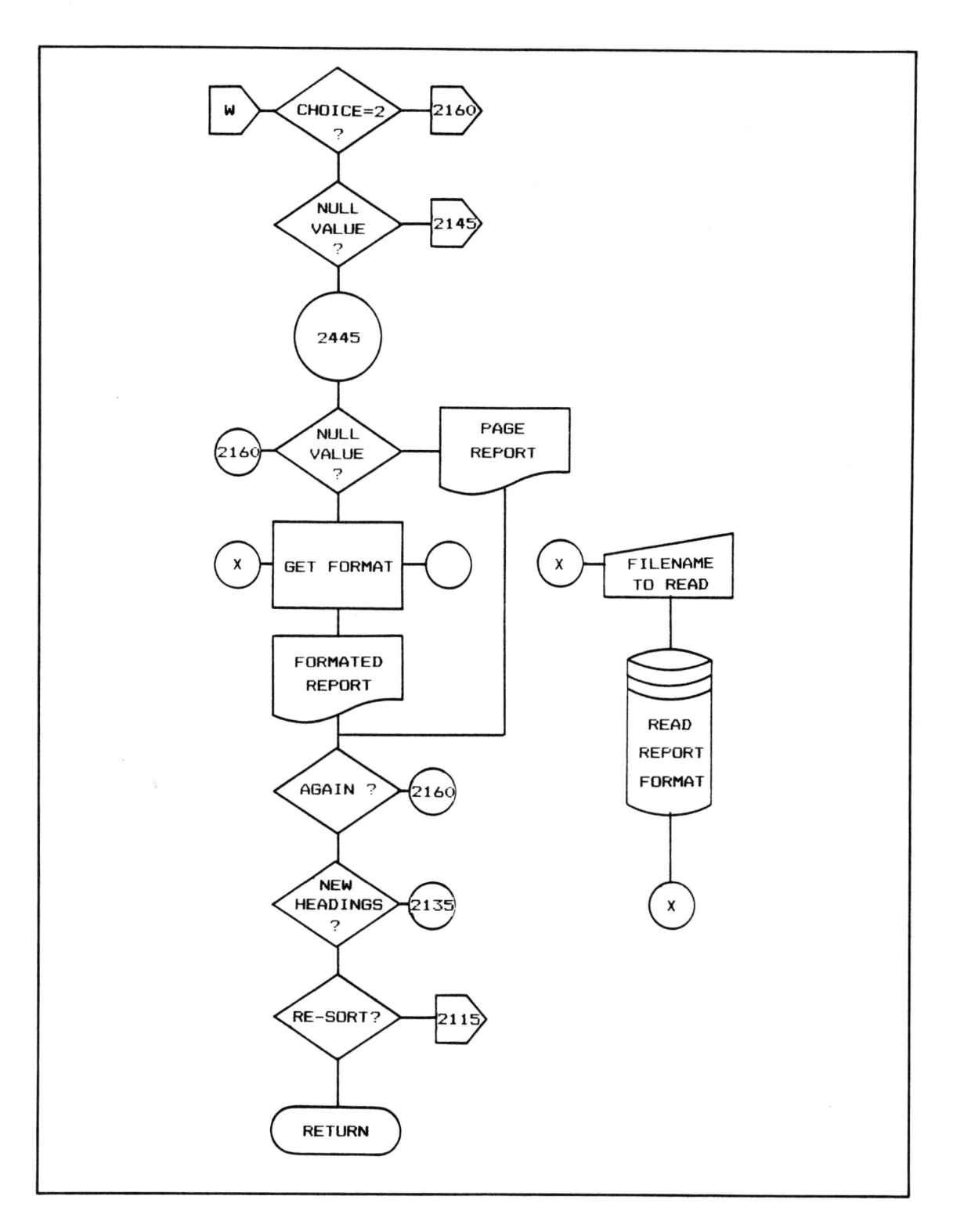

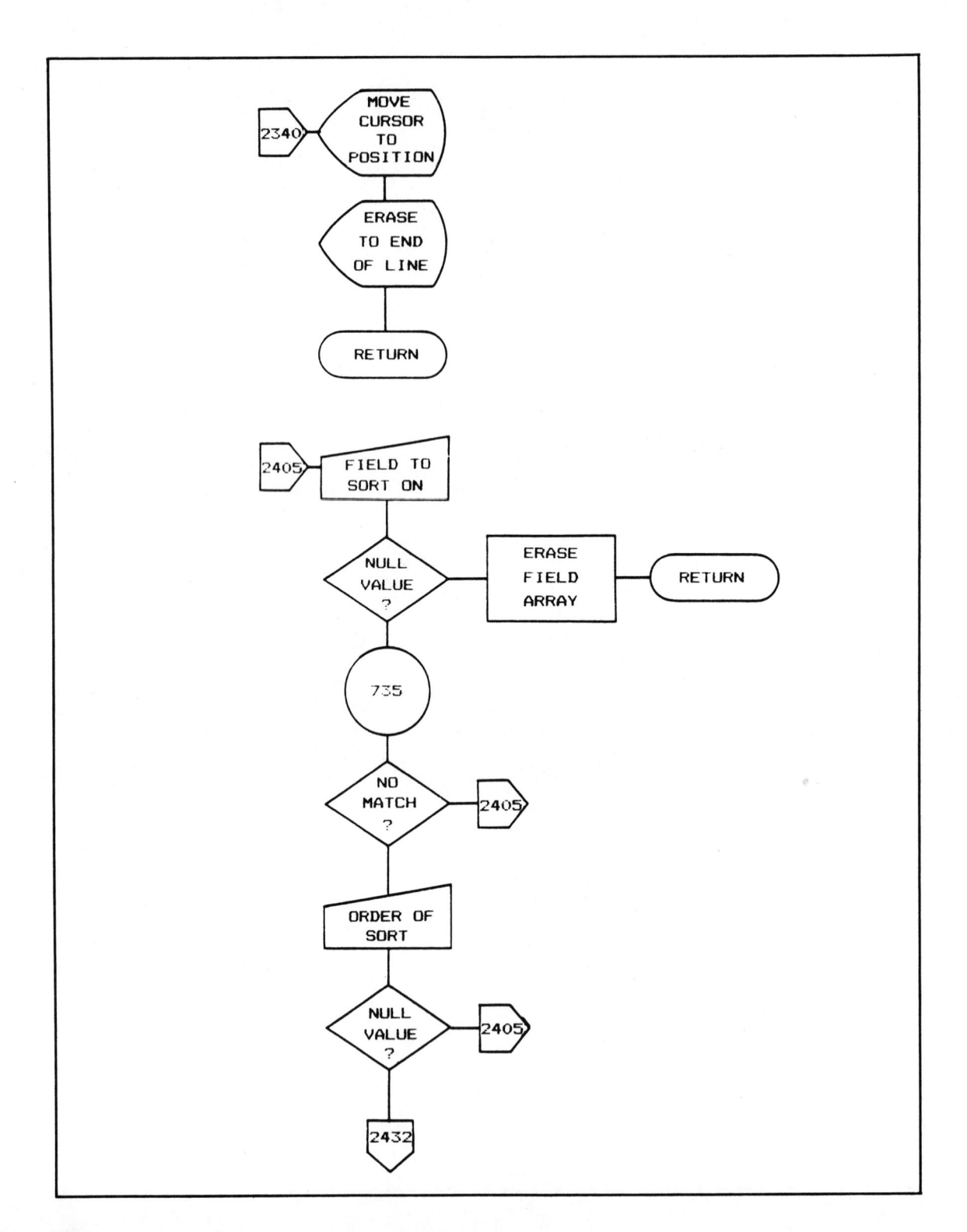

```
   ┌─────┐    MOVE
   │2340 ├───CURSOR
   └─────┘     TO
            POSITION
               │
            ERASE
            TO END
            OF LINE
               │
            RETURN


   ┌─────┐   FIELD TO
   │2405 ├───SORT ON
   └─────┘      │
              NULL         ERASE
              VALUE ─────  FIELD  ─── RETURN
               ?           ARRAY
               │
              (735)
               │
               NO        ┌─────┐
             MATCH ──────│2405 │
               ?         └─────┘
               │
            ORDER OF
             SORT
               │
              NULL       ┌─────┐
              VALUE ─────│2405 │
               ?         └─────┘
               │
            ┌─────┐
            │2432 │
            └─────┘
```

```
┌2432┐  ◇ S2=0 ? ─── □ S2=1 ─── ○ 2830
          │
          └── ○ 3430 ─────────── ┌2405┐
```

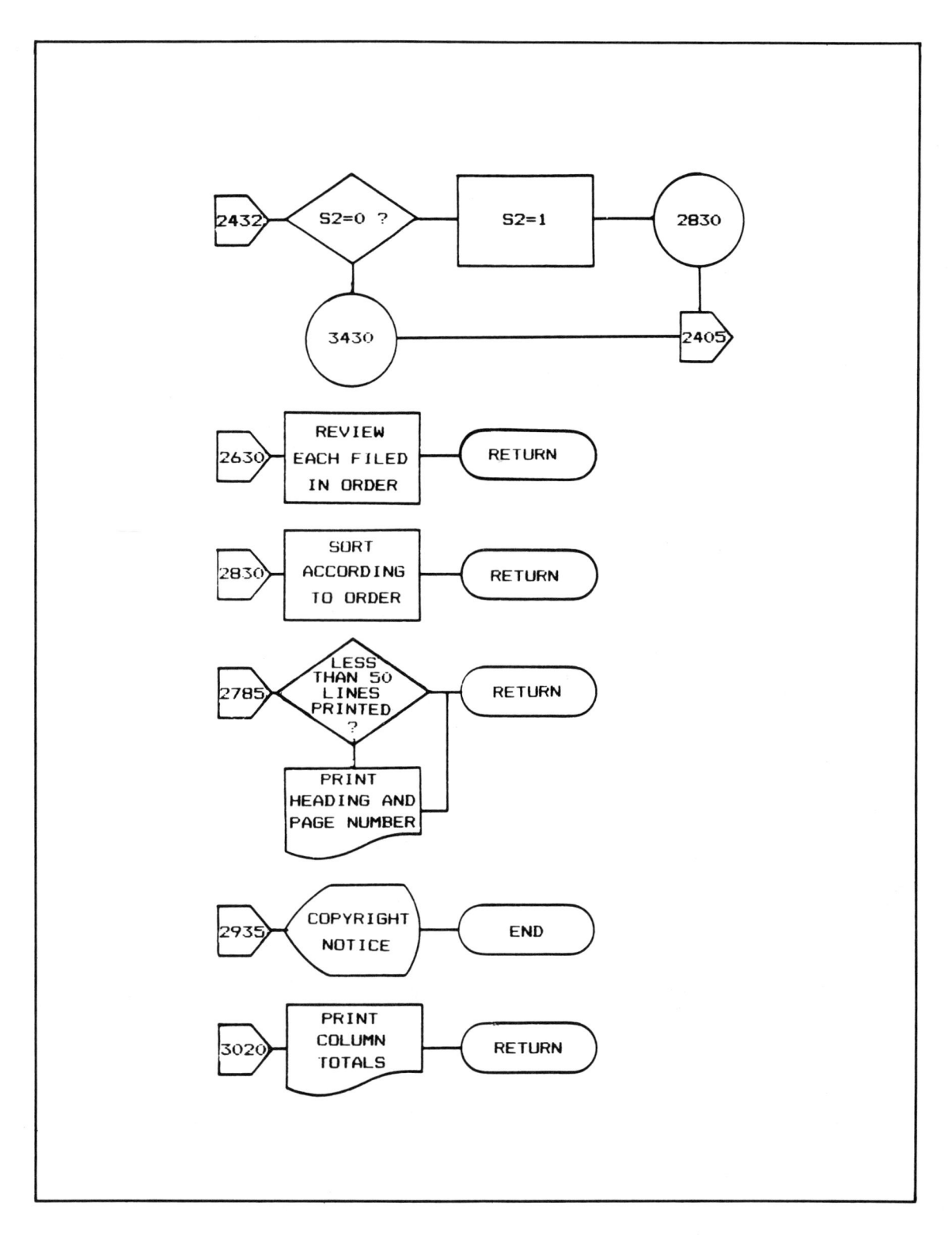

```
┌2630┐ □ REVIEW EACH FILED IN ORDER ── ( RETURN )
```

```
┌2830┐ □ SORT ACCORDING TO ORDER ── ( RETURN )
```

```
┌2785┐ ◇ LESS THAN 50 LINES PRINTED ? ── ( RETURN )
            │
            PRINT HEADING AND PAGE NUMBER
```

```
┌2935┐ COPYRIGHT NOTICE ── ( END )
```

```
┌3020┐ PRINT COLUMN TOTALS ── ( RETURN )
```

Appendix C

User's Manual for the Database Manager Program

DBS is an interactive program for use on the Heath/Zenith H/Z-89, 90 computer series. It expects the following hardware configuration

1.) HEATH/ZENITH H/Z-89, Z-90 SERIES
2.) 64K RAM
3.) HDOS VERS 2
4.) One or more disk drives
5.) Printer

DBS can be used to keep track of almost any type of data. It is set up so that you can instruct the program as to which data to use, where to put it, and what range limitations exist. In order to do this, you must be familiar with the terminology and definitions the program expects so that both you and the program speak the same language.

DEFINITIONS

The following are some definitions that you will need to be familiar with.

Field. A field is a particular piece of information. For example if you were using DBS to keep track of names and addresses in a mailing list, one field would be the name of the person concerned. Another field would be his address and another, the zip code. You can see that the word *field* represents the smallest piece of information you want the program to look after for you.

Record. A record is a collection of fields that make up all the information you wish to have concerning a specific entry. For instance, using the example above, the entire name, address, and all other information concerning one individual would constitute a single record.

File. A file is a collection of records. Using the same example again, all of the records concerning your mailing list would constitute a file.

To review using the mailing list example, a data record is structured like this:

Decredenza, Alphonso
123 Any Street
Victoria
B.C.
V8T 4M4

The name Decredenza, Alphonso would be a

FIELD. All the fields together would be a RECORD. All the records make up a FILE.

Of course DBS will allow you to store any type of data in the fields to make up your own set of records and files. Thus you can use DBS to keep track of a mailing list, an inventory, checks, accounting information, the information in your filing cabinet, or . . . but the list can go on and on! Let's take a look at some of the definitions relating to setting up fields of your choice.

Field Descriptor. A field descriptor is a four character word that tells the program what to call a particular field so that it can keep it separated from the others. This group of characters will be a unique set so that both you and the program can tell what kind of data is related to this field. For example, in the mailing program above, the first field might have the field descriptor, NAME applied to it. This is a logical choice as it will tell you what is in the field. The next field might have the descriptor ADD1, which means address line one. There will be times when the field descriptor may be cryptic and its meaning not very clear; especially if the data is being read by someone familiar with the program. Don't worry, DBS will allow you to format a report with 12 character headings to better describe the information in each field.

Field Type. Now that you have told the program what to call the field that you wish to store some data in, you must now instruct it as to the type of data it is to place there. There are four possible data types. The first, and probably most common, is the type of data represented by letters, numbers, and punctuation. For example, the address field has both letters and numbers. This type of data is said to be *alphanumeric*. You tell the program that you wish to store alphanumeric data by typing in the letter A when asked for the field type. If you wish to store numerical information, you have a choice of three types. The first type is called an *integer*. An integer is a number that ranges from −32767 to +32767. No decimal points are allowed. An integer is stored on the disk in a two byte space. Thus, if you need a number that falls into the integer's range, then you can tell the computer to store the data as an integer by typing DI, which stands for

*D*igital *I*nteger data, when asked for the data type. An example of an integer number would be the number of people in a family. This number should never have a decimal, and should never exceed 32,767! If you suspect that the value you are going to store will have a decimal point in it and be less than six digits long, you can use *single precision* numbers, which are stored on the disk in a four byte space. This is adequate for most quantities as it is accurate to six significant figures. This data type is specified by entering **DS** when prompted by the program. If you are storing information about money, it is recommended that you use the third type of data notation, **DD**. This stands for *D*igital *D*ouble precision and in this program will allow you to store numbers up to 10 digits long.

Minimum Value. DBS will allow you to set a minimum value for the data being entered when the data is numerical in nature. That is, you can specify that the program not accept any numerical data into a specific field if it is less than a certain value. If an entry that is less than the specified value is entered, it will be rejected and an Out-of-range error message displayed.

Maximum Value. DBS will also allow you to set a maximum value for the data being entered when the data is numerical in nature. As in the example above, if the entry is higher than the value set, an error message is displayed and the entry is rejected. This will help you avoid erroneous entries. No range setting is allowed for alphanumeric data because it is not needed.

Field Length. You must set the length of any alphanumeric fields. In effect, you are telling the program how much space to use for the values expected in this field. It is important to realize that you must allow for the worst case. That is, you must make allowances for the longest entry you can reasonably expect to use. Once data is entered, there isn't any way to return and adjust the field lengths. The field lengths are automatically set if the information is a numeric quantity. This length is determined by the data specification you entered when asked for the field type. If you specified DI, the length is 2 bytes; if you specified DS, the length is 4; if you specified DD, the length is 8. In an alphanumeric field you set the length by allowing one byte for each letter and each space in the expected data values.

Field Starts at. This is a calculation that DBS makes for you. It lets you know where in a record the data for a particular field begins.

These, then, are the definitions and terminology that DBS uses. As you work with the program, you will find yourself becoming more and more familiar with them.

PROGRAM FEATURES

DBS has many features that will allow you to use it easily and assist you in getting the information into the file with a minimum of errors.

Record Length. Each record may have up to 127 fields in it, but the total space used by all of the fields combined must not exceed 255 bytes. If a record uses less than 255 bytes, the program will use all the space and fill the unused portion with blanks. This means that later we can add more fields to the record.

User-Chosen Range Settings. This feature allows you to insure that obviously wrong values are not entered. Entries outside the range that you set will not be accepted; an out-of-range error will occur, and you will be given the opportunity to reenter the information. You can also set length limits for alphanumeric data; this will allow you to prevent the entry of a 7 character word when only six characters are allowed.

Formatted Printing. You can set up special report formats. In these you can replace the four-character field descriptor headings with 12 character report headings. You can format all the numerical columns so that they line up and have dollar signs. You can specify where on the print line each field goes and in what order. Once you set up a particular report format, you can save it for later use. You can have numerical columns added from top to bottom, and if the report exceeds fifty lines, a new page is generated and the headings and page numbers printed.

Page Reports. This will allow you to make a complete print out of all the information relating to a particular record. All field descriptors and related information are printed.

Special Fields. This will allow you to set up a target field that will receive the values of preceding fields. In this way you can have totals, subtotals, averages, etc. All calculations are done by the program at the time the data is entered or modified, if the entry or modification will affect one or more of the target fields.

Selected Queries. This part of the program allows you to select records for printing or viewing by having the value of any or all fields checked. The operators used are the $=$, $<>$, $>$, $<$, $>=$, $<=$, and even $, which is a symbol for the instring function. Thus you can check a field by entering the field descriptor, an operand to provide the program with a value to check against, and one of the relational operators. You can also use the *and* or *or* functions to check for different sets of conditions in different fields. In this manner you can retrieve all the records in which the name field begins with the letter A and the age field contains a 30.

Field Sorting. Once you have retrieved the records, you can sort based on the values in any field, in either ascending or descending order. The program will adjust for either numeric or alphanumeric values. A secondary sort can be specified whereby those records that are equal in value in the first sort are sorted according to a second set of criteria.

File Transfer. When a data file grows too large to be handled easily on one disk, you can select a group of records to be transferred to another disk. In this way the files can become more selective in nature and more easily handled.

USING THE PROGRAM

To show you how to use the program, let's create a sports competition file, enter some data and retrieve, sort, and print it.

First we need to know what kind of data and how much we will be asking the program to look after for us. Remember those definitions we went over earlier? Now is the time we can put them to use. Consider the chart in Fig. C-1.

The asterisks are prompts to let you know how much room is available for your entry. Note that the field descriptor entry field has four characters. You may enter up to four characters, but not more. Minimum and maximum values are set to accept up to 10 characters; that is a 10 digit number. Of course if you have specified an integer or single precision number as the data type, you will not use all the spaces.

Before you start entering data into the system, you will have to decide what attributes you will want in the program. For practice you can use the program to set up a database that will keep track of both alphanumeric and numeric information, and let you try out the special fields.

In the database you will want to keep track of the following things: the competitors number, his name, his score for the first event, his score for the second event, and of course the total score in the competition. The chart in Fig. C-1 shows how these things fit. First you will want a field for the competitors number. Start by giving the field a distinctive name. Use COMP. Next you have to tell the program what kind of data is to be stored in this field. Since you plan to have no more than 200 people competing, you can use an integer format, 50 enter DI. Since this is a numerical data set, you can tell the program to use a minimum value of 0 and a maximum value of 200. This will prevent the entry of a competitor with a number less than 0 or higher than 200. The field length of two is automatically calculated by the program.

Next you will have to use another four character letter group for the field descriptor to name the next field, which will hold the competitor's name. You can use NAME. This data is alphanumeric in nature so use the data type A. Since you cannot set a minimum or maximum value for an alphanumeric data field, the program sets both of these fields to 0. You must set the length of the field. Set it to 15, which should allow you to enter the name and initial of any competitor. In the next three fields, use the field descriptor MCH1, MCH2, and TOTL. Since the competitor can only earn a score of 300 in either match, you can use the DI data type again and set the minimum and maximum values accordingly. Note that the TOTL field will be used to keep the combined score in, so its maximum value should be set to 600. Look at the filled in chart shown in Fig. C-2.

Running the Program

Now that you have the chart prepared, you can turn on the computer. First load in your printer driver! The program expects to see the driver named AT:, so if your driver is named something

Field #	1	2	3	4	5
Field Descriptor	****	****	****	****	****
Data Type	**	**	**	**	**
Min Val	*******	*********	*********	*********	*******
Field Length	***	***	***	***	***
Max Val	*******	*********	*********	*********	*******

Fig. C-1. Data preparation chart.

```
-------------------------------------------------------------------
 Field # :      1   :     2    :     3    :     4    :     5
-------------------------------------------------------------------
 Field
 Descriptor   COMP      NAME        MCH1       MCH2       TOTL

 Data
 Type         DI        A           DI         DI         DI

 Min
 Value        0         0           0          0          0

 Field
 Length       2         15          2          2          2

 Max
 Value        200       0           300        300        600
-------------------------------------------------------------------
```

Fig. C-2. Filled-in data preparation chart.

else, rename it to **AT:**. Then put the disk into drive 0 and press the reset button. Load BASIC using the following command structure.

When the program begins to run, it takes a few seconds to set up the memory space in the system. Then it displays a menu and asks you to select a function. The first selection you should make is to tell the program where you wish the data files kept. If you are using a multidrive system, simply type in the drive number.

After returning to the menu, select the create function so that you can transfer the information from the chart you just made into the computer. You will note that you do not have to enter a carriage return by striking the enter key when answering questions that can be answered with one keystroke. You will also note that the asterisks extend one position farther to the right than the actual length of the input. This is normal, and you will still enter the correct number of characters. You may also note that the characters you type in seem to appear in random order as you type. However, they will be processed and straightened out so that they will be printed as you typed them. This is all done by the input processing routine. Sometimes it will not be able to display characters as fast as you can type them but it will remember what you typed and catch up!

Creating the Parameters File

You are now in the section of the program that will set up the file that will tell the program all about the data it will be working with. The first thing that the program needs to know is what to call the program itself. Since this example will be used to keep scores, call the file Scores. Next you will need to tell the computer how many fields it can expect to see in the data base. For this program you need five fields. Now a chart will appear asking for information from the chart that you prepared. Just fill in the data as requested. Note how the program skips over some questions in response to the answers you give. If you make a mistake in entering the data, don't worry. You can enter the line number of the erroneous data when you are done with each field, and the program will give you a chance to correct it.

After all the field data has been entered, the program will automatically go to the specials section. This is the section of the program that will allow you to set up special fields that will receive the data from one or more other fields. In this program the TOTL field is such a field. The program uses the data from MCH1 and the data from MCH2 to compute the total score for each competitor. The TOTL field is the target field because it is where the total is to go. The first source field is the MCH1 field, so enter it as the source field. Since you want the program to add the data, you use the + sign as the action symbol. Other action symbols are the − sign for subtraction, the / for division, and the * for multiplication. When you have entered the + sign, the program will ask if you wish to enter more; answer with a Y. You want to enter the field descriptor of our second source field. This is MCH2, so enter that and type a + for the action again. Now when asked for more, type N. You will then be asked for the second target field, since you only have one, just press the enter key. The program will now write all this information to the disk. The program may appear slow in responding to you. Be patient. It has a lot to do at this particular point and will not take more than a few seconds.

So then, what have you done so far? You have told the program what the name of the database is to be, what kind of information will be stored in it, where to put it, what range of data entry will be acceptable, and how much space to take up with it. With this information, the program can now accept data from you, and you can get the information you need.

Entering Data

Let's take a look at how you can get the information you have into the machine in a logical format and how you can get it out again. From the main menu, select **Data Functions**. This will allow you to do one of four things, enter data, change data already in the database, delete unwanted data from the database, and repack the data.

First select the add function. Now the program will ask for the name of the file that you wish to work with. The name assigned earlier was SCORES, so type it in and the program will find the file on the disk and display the date that it was last updated, todays date, and the record number of the next available record. Since this is our first entry into the database, the record number will be one. Enter the following test information when requested by the program. After each record is entered, the program will ask if you wish to enter another record; answer this question with the letter Y until you have entered the last set of data. Figure C-3 shows a sample set of records.

After entering the last record, type N when asked **MORE** and you will then return to the main menu.

Querying the Data Base

From the main menu type 3 to go to the section of the program that will allow you to search the database for any or all. As before, enter the filename SCORES, and the program will respond with:

```
FIELD DESCRIPTOR         : -
OPERAND                  : -
ACTION                   : -
AND/OR                   : -
```

What the program wants is the field descriptor of the field whose value you are going to query. The operand is the value that you will be checking against the value found in this field, the action is the relation of the value within the field to the operand. The **AND/OR** allows you to indicate whether or not more than one selection criteria will be specified for this search.

Let's use the value in the TOTL field as the basis for our query. By entering **TOTL** as the field descriptor, you instruct the program to look in this field for a value. Enter 500 as an operand, this will be what the value within the field is checked against. As an action use the relational operator > so that you have told the program to look into the TOTL fields in all the records and to flag all the records whose value there is greater than 500. Since this is the only check to be made at this point, just enter a return for **AND/OR**. The program will then search the database and tell us how many records that will match our query it has found. In this case it returns with five. It will then ask us to press the P key to print them.

We now enter a P and go to the printing section of the program. You can choose to have the results of the search sent to the printer or the screen, to do

```
RECORD NUMBER 1
        COMP 001
        NAME CHARLTON, J.
        MCH1 296
        MCH2 297
        TOTL 593 - **NOTE** this was automaticaly done
                   for you
RECORD NUMBER 2
        COMP 002
        NAME GREENE, G.
        MCH1 300
        MCH2 298
        TOTL 598

RECORD NUMBER 3
        COMP 003
        NAME GOSLING R.
        MCH1 295
        MCH2 294
        TOTL 589

RECORD NUMBER 4
        COMP 100
        NAME MCKINNON
        MCH1 296
        MCH2 294
        TOTL 590

RECORD NUMBER 5
        COMP 110
        NAME ARDILL, E.
        MCH1 293
        MCH2 297
        TOTL 590
```

Fig. C-3. A sample set of data records.

a sort of the records, or to send the records to a new disk file. If the results are to go to the screen or printer, they can be printed out in a special format of your choosing or in a page format that prints out the entire record. If they are to be sorted, the program will ask which field they are to be sorted on. You can then enter the name of any field in the record and they will be sorted. When the FIELD TO SORT ON prompt appears again, they can be sorted a second time. In this secondary sort, any records that were the same in the first sort will be re-sorted according to the second field value. All records can be sorted in either ascending or descending order. If the records are being sent to a new disk file, they will be copied to a file that you name. The parameters file will be copied over and the entries adjusted to reflect the new number of records. In this way all files can be progressively divided into smaller and more select groups, thus reducing the processing time required for them. No information is ever deleted from the master files, however, so nothing is lost unless you expressly delete individual records.

At this point, press **3** to sort the sports file. When the program asks **FIELD TO SORT ON** enter **TOTL**. Then it will ask if you want to have the sort in ascending or descending order. Since you want the highest score first, indicate that the sort should be in descending order. After the sort is complete, the program will redisplay the **FIELD TO SORT ON** prompt. Since you have no other sorting requirements, just press the enter key and you will have the opportunity to print or display the sorted information. Now the options are for either a formatted or a page report.

The formatted report is one in which you decide what is printed on the line and where. The page report is a complete print-out of the entire record. Select the formatted report, and the following will appear.

REPORT FORMAT TO READ?

At this point the program is asking you to put in the name of a previous report-format file so that it can read it and format the information it has just selected and sorted accordingly. Since we have not yet made up a report, there won't be a format file on the disk. Simply press the enter key. The program will now ask for the report name. Enter whatever name you want; perhaps, **SCORES REPORT FOR MATCH** would be a good one. Now the program will show the following:

FIELD   SUBHEADING   TAB   FORMAT

****

Under the column, FIELD, enter the field descriptors of the data fields that you want to print out in this report. Under the column SUBHEADING, enter the name that you want the field to have for the purposes of this report. You will remember that DBS allows you to substitute a 12 character name for the actual field descriptor so that you can better describe the information in the report. Under the TAB column you can enter the tab stop where you want the information to be printed on the line. If the information is to be printed on the screen, the entire line must not be longer than 64 characters or else the display may become confused. If it is going to be printed on the printer, the program will tab it to the correct spot if the number is not greater than 250. Under the FORMAT column you can specify a particular format for numerical information, such as having it printed with dollar signs and commas and lining up the decimal points. The format described in the BASIC handbook for the print-using statement is used. Look at the chart below and type the values into the chart on the screen.

FIELD	SUBHEADING	TAB	FORMAT
COMP	COMPETITOR #	6**	**********
NAME	NAME********	15*	
TOTL	TOTAL SCORE*	40*	**********

After entering the TOTL line, press the enter key when the cursor is under the FIELD column. You will then be asked **(TOTALS Y/N)**. If you want all the numerical columns totaled columnwise, the program will do so if you answer **Y**. You don't have a need for that feature, so press **N**.

The program will now show the question

FILENAME TO SAVE

You can now save this particular format for use at a later time. If you wish to do so, enter the filename SCORES. This will result in the file SCORES/RPT being saved on disk 0. If you had had a previous file with the same name and extension, it would have been overwritten. This feature allows you to define a particular format that you will use often and to have it available without having to redefine it. Here is what the printout will look like:

```
               SCORES
        COMPET-               TOTAL
REC     ITOR #     NAME       SCORE
 2        2      GREENE, G.    598
 1        1      CHARLTON, J.  593
 4       100     MCKINNON, G.  590
 5       101     ARDILL, E.    590
 3        3      GOSLING, R.   586
```

And this is just the beginning, with this program you can create a database and easily maintain it. If you need a special output routine for mailing labels, form letters, or graphs, these are available in this book. These programs will allow you to use the information from the database to make mailing labels and graphs, and to substitute the information into form letters.

You can now reprint the list, rename it, or re-sort it, all without having to go through the query portion of the program. This will save you time.

Other Features

Page Print. This feature, as mentioned elsewhere, produces a complete printout of the entire file. If you had specified it instead of the formatted printing, it would have looked as shown in Fig. C-4.

Notice how the sorting has reorganized the list.

Change. This section lets you change any value in any field. To change something, enter the Data Functions portion of the program from the main menu and specify change. Enter the filename, and then the record number of the record that you wish to change. The record number is always printed on the left side of the line in any formatted report, and on a separate line in a page report. The program will ask for the field descriptor of the field that you wish to change. Enter it, and the program will display the old information, and you can then enter the new.

Delete. This allows you to flag a record for deletion. The record is not physically deleted until you run the Repack function. You must enter the proper delete code before the program will allow you to delete a record. The code is ERA.

Repack. This section of the program will take a file that has a number of deleted records in it, and pack the file so that the deleted records are removed. The repack function requires a work space on the disk as large as the space for the original file.

Exiting. In order to exit from the program, select the exit function from the main menu. This will ensure that all files are properly closed and all housekeeping chores are done.

Adding Fields. In this version of DBS, fields

```
RECORD NUMBER 2
     COMP 002
     NAME GREENE,G.
     MCH1 300
     MCH2 298
     TOTL 598

RECORD NUMBER 1
     COMP 001
     NAME CHARLTON,J.
     MCH1 296
     MCH2 297
     TOTL 593

RECORD NUMBER 4
     COMP 100
     NAME MCKINNON,G.
     MCH1 296
     MCH2 294
     TOTL 590

RECORD NUMBER 5
     COMP 101
     NAME ARDILL,E.
     MCH1 293
     MCH2 297
     TOTL 590

RECORD NUMBER 3
     COMP 003
     NAME GOSLING,R.
     MCH1 295
     MCH2 291
     TOTL 586
```

Fig. C-4. A sorted set of data records.

can be added. Since HDOS allots each record 255 bytes, you can go back and create a new parameters file and make use of the leftover space. You will have to recreate the original parameters file exactly except for adding the new fields on to the end. In this way, all the original information will be preserved, and you may make use of the new fields. I suggest that you try this out with a few test files until you get the hang of it!

File Structures

DBS will create two separate files, and optionally, a third. The first file is the field parameters file. This is the file that tells the program what goes where, and what data type is being used. This file is always on disk 0. The next file is the actual database itself. It will be on whatever disk drive you specify. The third file which is optional, is the file containing the formatting parameters for output. You may have as many of these as you desire, effectively setting up the system to make a variety of reports.

This then is DBS. Use the file you created and select different records with different criteria. Try to enter new information that is obviously outside the range allowed and see how the error routines prevent this. You will find that the more you use the program, the more things you will think of to use it for. I would be most pleased to hear from anyone who has a suggestion, idea, or question. But please use a self-addressed stamped envelope or I cannot guarantee a reply.

Greg Greene
207-885 Craigflower Rd.
Victoria, B.C. CANADA
V9A 2X4

Appendix D
A TRS-80 Input Routine

This section will look at some practical examples of converting to a very popular computer, the TRS-80 from Radio Shack.

TRS-80 ROUTINES

When translating the routines to the TRS-80, you will find many helpful hints in Chapters 1 through 11. To make things easier, here are some lines of code that demonstrate how to adjust the input and cursor positioning routines for the Radio Shack machines. The routines will place the cursor at the value of X1. Remember that the routines in the main book, use a value for X1 that is based on a 24 row, 80 column screen. These values will have to be adjusted to reflect the smaller size of the TRS-80 screen. Listing 21 presents the code.

The main difference in this routine compared with the one presented in the main text is that the routine at lines 100 to 110 will cause the cursor to flash on the TRS-80. This will help keep the user's attention focused on the line that needs a response. The trade off involved here is that the response of the keyboard which is notably slow in any case, is slowed up even more, and the possibility that the user will type faster than the system can respond is very real. I leave it up to you whether or not to use the following routine, depending on your preference.

I have found that it is necessary to poke the number of the disk drive to the location currently used on the TRS-80 for keeping track of the number of lines per page for the printer. Since the program keeps track of this anyway, it is an unused portion of memory. You must however keep the number above 50. The easiest way to add 55 to the number when you poke it in and subtract 55 when you peek it out.

Doing this will allow you to use the clear command to erase all arrays when you are using the program to work on several different database files that have differing numbers of fields. As the program will attempt to dimension arrays to the exact number of fields in current use, errors relating to attempted redimensioning will result if you don't clear the arrays first. Since this will also result in the loss of all variable values, you are faced with constant questioning of the user as to the data disk number if you don't use this scheme.

You should also change the program to dimension all the variables that make use of the number of fields as soon as the proper parameters file is opened for reading.

LISTING TWENTY ONE
==================

```
 12 CLEAR 8000
 60 DE$="ERA"
 65 DA$=LEFT$(TIME$,8)
 70 DEFDBL M,T,N,O,
        DIM T9(50)
        GOTO 475
 80 PRINT CHR$(28);:PRINT@ X1,"";
        RETURN
 90 XO$=""
 95 X2$=STRING$(255,"*")
100 GOSUB 80
        PRINT LEFT$(X2$,X2);
        GOSUB 80
105 FOR W%=1 TO 5
        X$=INKEY$
        IF X$<>"" THEN 110 ELSE NEXT
        PRINT@ (X1+LEN(XO$))," ";
        FOR W%=1 TO 5
        X$=INKEY$
        IF X$<>"" THEN 110 ELSE NEXT
        PRINT @ X1,XO$;"*";
        GOTO 105
110 IF LEN(XO$)=0 AND X$=CHR$(13) THEN XO#=-1
        PRINT CHR$(28);
        RETURN
115 XO#=0
 (Rest of input code follows here from book)
```

Appendix E
An Alternate Packing Process

The packing routine used in the main book uses a routine to move the valid records to the top of the file. It does not then restructure the file. An alternate method exists whereby the old file is read and all those records that do not have the delete flag set are written to the new file. You can do this in two ways: either use the built in function of the program to break up a large file into smaller ones, or rewrite the code to do it for you. If you use the first method, you will have to give the new file a temporary name and then restore the old name. Otherwise you could be confused as to the current name!!

Index

Index

A
Adding fields, 158
Arrays, erasing, 64, 160

B
BASIC, 4
Byte, 21

C
Changing data, 158
Changing the data, 48
Character, 21
Converting for your computer, 84
Copyright, 80
CPU, 59
Cursor, 9
Cursor addressing, 16, 85

D
Database, 5
Database, hierarchal, 6
Database, relational, 6
Database file, 12
Database Manager program, user's manual for, 150
Database Manager Program flowcharts, 111
Database Manager program listing, 96
Database parameter file, 30

Data dictionary, 30
Data entry, 153, 155
Data storage, 7
Data values, 151
Deleting data, 52, 158
Descriptor, field, 151
Dictionary, data, 10
Disk drives, 1, 160

E
Erasing arrays, 160
Erasing routine, 84
Error trapping, 32
Exiting from program, 158

F
Field, 150
Field descriptor, 151
Fields, adding, 158
Fields, special, 152
Field type, 151
File, 150
Files, subdividing, 65
File structures, 159
File transfer, 152
Flowcharts of the Database Manager program, 111
Format, report, 76
Form letters, 90

G
Graphics, 12, 84
Graphs, 91

I
Input routines for the TRS-80, 160

L
Labels, mailing, 86
Length, field, 151
Length, record, 152
Letters, form, 90

M
Mailing labels, 86
Mathematical capabilities, 35
Memory, 1
Memory map, 23
Menu, 25, 42
Microcomputer system, typical, 1, 2
Minimum data value, 151

O
Organization of data, 9

P
Parameters, reviewing, 77
Parameters file, 154
Parity, 31

165

Printer use, 75
Printing, formatted, 152
Program listing, Database Manager, 96

Q

Queries, 152, 155

R

RAM, 1
Range checking, 16
Record, 150
Record, variable length, 7
Record length, 152

Repacking files, 158
Reports, 68
Retrieving data, 58
Reviewing parameters, 77
Routine, erasing, 84
Routines, sorting, 78

S

Screen mask, 22
Sector, 23
Shell Metzner algorithm, 79
Sorting, 152, 156
Sorting routines, 78
Special function keys, 21

Structures, file, 159
Subdividing files, 65
Symbols, flowchart, 112

T

Transfer, file, 152
TRS-80 routines, 160
Type, field, 151

U

User's manual for the Database Manager program, 150

Database Manager in MICROSOFT® BASIC

If you are intrigued with the possibilities of the programs included in *Database Manager in MICROSOFT® BASIC* (TAB Book No. 1567), you should definitely consider having the ready-to-run disk containing the software applications. This software is guaranteed free of manufacturer's defects. (If you have any problems, return the disk within 30 days and we'll send you a new one.) Not only will you save the time and effort of typing the programs, the disk eliminates the possibility of errors that can prevent the programs from functioning. Interested?

Available on disk for the TRS-80 Models I and III with CONVERT, 48K at $39.95 for each disk plus $1.00 each shipping and handling.

I'm interested. Send me:

_____ disk for *Database Manager in MICROSOFT® BASIC* for TRS-80 (6033S)

_____ Check/Money Order enclosed for $39.95 plus $1.00 shipping and handling for each disk ordered.

_____ VISA _____ MasterCard

Acct. No. _____ Expires _____

Name _____

Address _____

City _____ State _____ Zip _____

Signature _____

Mail To: **TAB BOOKS Inc.**
Blue Ridge Summit, PA 17214

(Pa. add 6% sales tax. Orders outside U.S. must be prepaid with international money orders in U.S. dollars.)

TAB 1567